Not by bread alone

Sjur Bergan

Council of Europe Publishing

Cover design: Documents and Publications Production Department (SPDP), Council of Europe
Layout: Jouve, Paris

Council of Europe Publishing
F-67075 Strasbourg Cedex
http://book.coe.int

ISBN 978-92-871-6971-6
© Council of Europe, April 2011
Printed at the Council of Europe

Contents

IV. Speeches

Preface

What you are about to read is a collection of essays on higher education written over the past decade and published in various contexts. Many have been published in books in the Council of Europe Higher Education Series and, where they have not, permission to include them in this collection has been obtained from the publishers.

While most of the essays are fairly recent some are 8 or 10 years old, which inevitably leaves one with the dilemma of whether to update them for recent developments or not. In most cases, I have chosen not to undertake a full update and wherever modifications have been made, they have been relatively modest. In at least one case, a particular reference to what was a quite intense discussion at the time has been more substantially modified since the issue has long since been resolved. In most articles, key references which appeared after the article was originally published have been added. References to websites were valid at the time of publication but may no longer be so.

More important than the technicalities, however, are the reasons that might justify a collection of essays on higher education. The justification is to be found in a desire to contribute to a public debate that is evolving but which is nevertheless often too narrow. Higher education does have an important economic function but it has equally important functions in terms of democratic citizenship, personal development and the development and maintenance of a broad and advanced knowledge base (Bergan 2005, Council of Europe 2007). For someone responsible for the higher education programme of a values-based organisation like the Council of Europe, contributing a collection of essays that seek to sketch the multiple missions and purposes of higher education seems an important undertaking. The desire to contribute to developing a holistic vision of higher education has also given this book its title. Just as man does not live by bread alone, so too societies do not find their *raison d'être* in the economy alone, however important the economy is.

It is a truism to say that modern societies are complex, that they are characterised by rapid change, and that education is a key factor in the success of modern societies – no society can succeed without well-educated citizens – as well as in success in modern societies – no individual citizen can fully succeed in modern society without education. These truisms are nevertheless a useful starting point for the reflections developed in these essays.

Modern societies are characterised by technological sophistication, by high levels of achievement, by great opportunities for many of their citizens in terms of self-fulfilment, material wealth, mobility and influence over their own lives. One or two generations ago – not to mention a century ago – these opportunities may well have been the aspects that would have been most readily referred to if citizens were asked to describe their societies and not least their expectations of the future.

Today, however, there is an awareness not only of great opportunities, but also of great threats: to the environment, to material well-being, to personal and societal security, to social cohesion, to values, convictions and beliefs and not least to the *status quo*. Few will today think of the development of their societies in terms of uninterrupted, linear improvement, and some will undoubtedly emphasise what they perceive as negative tendencies. Many, however, will have outlooks that may be characterised as "cautiously optimistic" or "cautiously pessimistic". In other words, most people will be aware of opportunities as well as of threats, and even though they may emphasise the former or the latter, they will seek to strike some kind of balance between the two.

The sustainability of our societies is in question. In environmental terms, this has been brought home forcefully by the Intergovernmental Panel on Climate Change[1] as well as, to a larger public, by Al Gore's film *An Inconvenient Truth* (2006). Over the past decade or so, something resembling a consensus has been emerging that climate change is a real threat, that it is at least partially the work of human beings and that there is still time to redress the balance if our societies take decisive action. Taking action requires an ability not only to face painful choices and to consider long-term benefits against short-term sacrifice, but also to analyse highly complex data, to act on complex issues on the basis of expert advice and often also on the basis of incomplete information, and to weigh benefits in one area against disadvantages in another. As regards concrete measures, the consensus has so far been less evident.

Sustainability does not only have an environmental aspect, however. Societies must also be sustainable economically, socially, politically and culturally, and they must be all of these at the same time. A society sustainable environmentally and in terms of overall economic indicators, but not in terms of social cohesion because of gross inequalities in the distribution of opportunities and wealth would probably not be sustainable in the long term. Similarly, a society may be environmentally sustainable without being economically or socially sustainable, or vice versa, or it may be all of these without being politically or culturally sustainable. In each case, the end result is unlikely to be overall sustainability. These diverse aspects of sustainability further underscore the need for societies and their members to be able to deal with highly complex situations and choices. Only exceptionally will the issues that face us be ones of a straightforward relationship between cause and effect.

Whereas previous generations were often faced with technological limitations, present-day limitations are frequently of a different order. Technological develop-ments provide us with possibilities to undertake actions that may be technologi-cally feasible but that raise serious ethical concerns or that would be too costly in economic, environmental or social terms. In this context, it may be worth recalling that deciding whether a given possibility is too costly involves not only

---

1. www.ipcc.ch, accessed on 23 July 2010.

a purely economic consideration – "do we have the funds needed?" – but also issues of priorities and relative merit – "is it more important to invest our funds in this than in other undertakings?" – and of the impact of actions in non-economic terms – "it may be economically profitable to invest in a new factory in city A, but is it defensible in terms of the impact on the environment?". These kinds of considerations require an ability among decision makers, economic actors and voters to assess complex arguments and to make a decision on the basis of an overall assessment of advantages and disadvantages. This again requires decision makers, economic actors and voters who are not only well trained in a specific discipline, but who are also well educated in the true, holistic sense of the term.

As regards social cohesion, there are many more opportunities generally available than at any other time in history. European societies today are incomparably more just and cohesive than those that gave rise to such admired monuments as Versailles, Schönbrunn, Westminster Abbey or the Hermitage. At the same time, however, the gap between those who avail themselves of the opportunities modern democratic societies offer and those who for whatever reason do not or cannot seems destined to grow and threaten the cohesion of our societies unless education on values is given the prominence it requires in our education policy and practice.

Education must play an essential role in developing the ability of our societies to address questions such as these, which concern the very future of our societies. Partly, it may be a question of long-term survival, but it is also a question of setting priorities and deciding on the values by which we wish to be guided. Hughes de Saint-Cher, a 13th-century Dominican, said "First the bow is bent in study and then the arrow is released in preaching" (Radcliffe 2005: 5). While preaching may come easily to academics, the call is for teaching, learning and action, within and outside of universities.

In other words, in seeking to rise to the challenges our societies face, we must include considerations of values and priorities. This will require weighing complex and often difficult priorities in which not all options that would be desirable will necessarily be feasible and in which not all options that may be possible will necessarily be desirable. This also underlines the point that defining the kind of higher education we will need in the future is not simply a matter of identifying the trends and developments to which higher education must respond, but also of identifying how higher education may influence our societies in order to help them develop towards the kind of societies we would want for our children.

The kind of education we will need is not a question of identifying the single most important factor for the development of our societies and then gearing our education system to meet it. It is not a question only of economic performance, only of social cohesion, only of environmentally sound practice or only of democratic participation. The education we need must include and balance all of these as well as many other factors. In short, it must encompass the four major purposes of higher education identified through the Council of Europe's work on the public responsibility for higher education and research, all of which are fundamental:

– preparation for the labour market;

– preparation for life as active citizens in democratic societies;

– personal development;

– the development and maintenance of a broad, advanced knowledge base (Bergan 2005, Council of Europe 2007).

This also implies that the answer to the question "what education do we need?" is not to be found solely in the identification of a set of specialities (such as more information technology specialists, more petroleum engineers, more accountants, more general education teachers or more nurses). It is also not to suggest the opposite: that our societies will not need specialised competence in a wide range of areas. Rather, higher education must provide both specialised and general knowledge, or in more technical terms: subject-specific as well as generic competence. We need subject specialists with the ability to engage with broader issues. In a word, we need intellectuals, even if modern societies often seem to be sceptical of them.

The essays in this collection are organised around three broad themes. The first set of essays address the theme that has just been evoked: the purposes and mission of higher education, and the essays will make it clear that the use of the plural is a conscious choice.

The second broad topic is the public responsibility for higher education. The role of public authorities in financing higher education is strong in Europe, as is the role of public authorities in setting overall priorities for the sector as well as in ensuring its diversity. As society is changing, however, the role of public authorities will also change and public responsibility cannot be exercised in the same way today and tomorrow as it was a generation ago. If we wish to ensure that higher education should remain, as ministers of the European Higher Education Area (EHEA) stated twice, a public good and a public responsibility (Bologna Process 2001 and 2003), we need to take a hard look at how public responsibility may be exercised in modern, complex societies. The second set of essays represent an attempt to stimulate discussion on this crucial issue, the importance of which far exceeds the attention devoted to it in public debate.

The third major topic in this book is competences and qualifications. This is the topic on which I started my career in European higher education policy when I joined the Council of Europe in 1991 and is the subject of a previous monograph in the Council of Europe Higher Education Series (Bergan 2007). It is an area with its share of technical issues, but qualifications and competences are also key to the development of our societies as well as of our own development as an individual. Qualifications may even serve as a small-scale illustration of a proper discussion about education as such: one should master the technical issues but limiting one's attention to these means that one would miss the point. Structures are important but they are important because they serve a set of purposes. If we get the purposes wrong, it is of marginal importance whether we get the technicalities right. The reverse is not true: reaching well-justified goals and fulfilling well-reflected purposes may be made impossible by imperfect implementation. Even if the topic of the third part of the book is narrower than those of the first two parts, the essays in this part, like the others, serve to explore and hopefully help develop our vision of the education our societies need.

The fourth part fits in with the overall concerns of the book but the form is different. This part assembles six speeches I have had the privilege of delivering on significant occasions. Five of them were delivered to ministerial conferences of the European Higher Education Area, while the sixth was held on the seventieth anniversary of International Students' Day. The speeches are shorter than the essays, references are for the most part missing and the form is oral but the concern remains the same: to help develop the kind of society in which we would want to live and in which we want our children and grandchildren to live and to help develop the kind of education that makes this society possible.

The book is a collection of articles written on the same broad topic – the roles and purposes of higher education – over a period of several years. They will hopefully show a certain development in the author's thinking but such a collection also sets an inherent challenge: that of a certain amount of repetition. Readers will find some ideas, turns of phrase and references popping up in several of the essays. It could hardly be otherwise and hopefully a certain degree of consistency of thought will also be seen as a virtue.

My previous monograph includes a long list of heartfelt thanks and dedications. All of them remain valid and they will not be repeated here. However, I am happy to be able to add some new ones. Bastian Baumann, Bruno Carapinha, Vanja Ivošević, Janja Komljenović, Milica Popović and Colin Tück all started contributing to European higher education policies in their days in the European Students' Union (ESU) and continue to contribute from other positions without losing either the enthusiasm or the sense of values that I have come to appreciate so much with the ESU. Andrea Blättler, Olav Øye, Robert Santa, Bert Vandenkendelaere and others continue to remind us all of the importance of student participation.

I have benefited from and greatly enjoyed many stimulating discussions on qualifications and their broader importance with Wilfried Boomgaert, Jeff Bridgford, Mike Coles, Samuel Isaacs, Bryan Maguire, Thomas Mayr, Jim Murray, Eduard Staudecker and Anja Trier-Wang as well as with Gordon Clark, Anita Krémo and Carlo Scatoli of the European Commission, Jens Bjørnåvold and Loukas Zahilas of CEDEFOP and Arjen Deij, Vincent McBride and Madlen Şerban of the European Training Foundation. Agnetha Bladh, Dzulkifli Abdul Razak, Eva Egron-Polak and Juan Ramón de la Fuente of the International Association of Universities (IAU) and Monique Fouilhoux of Education International are all living proof of the crucial importance of higher education institutions and their staff.

The Bologna Follow-up Group (BFUG) and its working groups have benefited from the continued contributions of many of those thanked in the previous monograph as well as of new perspectives conveyed by Peter Baldwinson, Rafael Bonete, Peter Greisler, Toril Johansson, Luka Juroš, Cornelia Racké and many others. All the friends in and around South-East Europe mentioned in the previous monograph continue to provide me with stimulating insights and Edit Dibra and Aleksander Xuvani are added to the list with pleasure and gratitude. Sara Eco Conti, Alessandra Gallerano and Aline Sierp were unusually competent trainees with the Council of Europe's Higher Education and Research Division. So was Kathia Serrano-Velarde, who has also delivered valuable contributions to the European higher education debate through her research and now holds an academic position at the University of Heidelberg.

Two colleagues and friends deserve a particular thank you. Throughout her two terms as President of the European Students' Union, and now as co-ordinator of the Bologna Secretariat, Ligia Deca has demonstrated how an understanding of technical issues can and should go hand in hand with an understanding of the broader issues involved. Hilligje van't Land, Director of Membership and Programme Development of the IAU, has been an exceptional co-editor of a volume on the role of higher education in promoting intercultural dialogue (Bergan and van't Land 2010) with an uncanny ability to spot logical inconsistencies and to open new perspectives. Both are inspiring partners in countless discussions on the past, present and future of education and the purposes of it all.

My hope is that the essays in this volume will illustrate why higher education deserves to be at the top of our agendas as societies and as individuals. Even if some European ministries of education still carry the epithet "national", higher education is international by nature, in practice and by the conviction of most of those who make up the higher education community. The friends and colleagues listed in this preface as well as in the preface to my previous monograph also illustrate that sharing hard work to make one's convictions a reality of policy and practice can also be a true shared joy and the inevitable frustrations along the road are better overcome through international friendships.

References

Bergan S. (2005), "Higher education as a 'public good and a public responsibility' – What does it mean?", in Weber L. and Bergan S. (eds), *The Public Responsibility for Higher Education and Research*, Council of Europe Higher Education Series No. 2, Council of Europe Publishing, Strasbourg; reproduced in this volume.

Bergan S. (2007), *Qualifications: Introduction to a Concept*, Council of Europe Higher Education Series No. 6, Council of Europe Publishing, Strasbourg.

Bergan S. and van't Land H. (eds) (2010), *Speaking Across Borders. The Role of Higher Education in Furthering Intercultural Dialogue*, Council of Europe Higher Education Series No. 16, Council of Europe Publishing, Strasbourg.

Bologna Process (2001), Prague Communiqué.

Bologna Process (2003), Berlin Communiqué, "Realising the European Higher Education Area", adopted by European ministers of education on 19 September 2003.

Council of Europe (2007), Recommendation CM/Rec(2007)6 of the Committee of Ministers to member states on the public responsibility for higher education and research.

Radcliffe T. (2005), *What is the Point of Being a Christian?*, Burns and Oates, London.

I. The missions of higher education

Higher education governance and democratic participation: the university and democratic culture[2]

Background and purpose

As part of the preparation for its follow-up Bologna Seminar on Student Participation in Higher Education Governance (Oslo, 12-14 June 2003), the Norwegian Ministry of Education, Research and Church Affairs commissioned a report from the Council of Europe to survey the state of affairs with regard to formal provision for student participation as well as actual practice. The survey was conducted by Annika Persson, mainly during her period as a trainee at the Council's Higher Education and Research Division in autumn 2002, with some support from Per Nyborg as Chair of the Council's Steering Committee for Higher Education and Research (CDESR) and myself (Persson 2004). The purpose of the present article is to put the findings of this survey in a broader context and draw on other kinds of experience, in particular a pilot project on the University as a Site of Citizenship carried out by the CDESR in co-operation with a consortium of US higher education institutions and NGOs in 2000-01 (Plantan 2004).

Higher education and society

Higher education institutions are an important part of, and play an important role in, society. The institutions are societies unto themselves, but they are also part of broader society. If they remained only societies unto themselves, higher education institutions would be locked up in the proverbial ivory tower and their future would most likely be considerably shorter than their past. On the other hand, higher education institutions, without keeping some distance from society at large, would run a serious risk of losing their capacity to reason in terms of principle, to take a long-term view somewhat detached from the immediate issues of the day and to identify sustainable solutions to the most serious and long-term challenges facing our society.

The pilot project on the University as a Site of Citizenship carried out by the Council of Europe's Steering Committee for Higher Education and Research identified four sets of issues in which higher education institutions have a role to play, as institutions and/or through their individual members, that is, the academic community of scholars and students:

– institutional decision making;

– institutional life in a wider sense, including the study process;

2. This essay was originally published in Sjur Bergan (ed.) (2004): *The University as* Res Publica*: Higher Education Governance, Student Participation and the University as a Site of Citizenship*, Strasbourg: Council of Europe Publishing. Council of Europe Higher Education Series No. 1.

–   higher education institutions as multicultural societies;
–   higher education institutions in their relationship and interaction with the wider society.

While this seminar focused on higher education governance, I will to some extent also draw on the other dimensions identified by the project on the University as a Site of Citizenship where this seems relevant.

Higher education governance

Student participation as defined by the Oslo seminar is an aspect of the broader area of higher education governance, so it may be useful to recall that higher education governance is at the heart of the Bologna Process and will be a key feature of the European Higher Education Area. To an extent, this is taken for granted, and many institutional representatives and higher education policy makers refer to academic freedom and institutional autonomy – or sometimes a mixture of the two – as if these were obvious features of higher education in Europe, freedoms earned at the dawn of time and destined to be with us until some distant academic sunset.

Yet reality, as so often, is slightly more complicated, even if there is general agreement on the need for autonomous institutions. However, once we start asking what this actually means, consensus breaks down as the level of precision increases. Autonomy is often referred to as "institutional", sometimes as "university", but the question of whether there are differences between the two or whether we need to develop a more nuanced view is rarely asked. Similarly, autonomy is often thought of in legal terms, but even where autonomy from ministries is guaranteed by law and honoured in practice, no institution can be an island unto itself. Institutions are influenced by the expectations and financial contributions of other actors, whether these be ministries and other public authorities, private companies or the somewhat imprecise animal normally referred to as public opinion. Institutions not only are influenced by their surroundings, but they should be, at least to an extent. The problem, then, is not one of principle, but of finding the right balance.

Similarly, we tend to take it for granted that universities or higher education institutions – again, there tends to be lack of precision – are headed by an elected official who goes by many different names according to the context but who internationally tends to be referred to as the rector, and governed by a representative body elected by the academic community, typically by various combinations of the words university, academic, senate and council.

Recently, however, a good number of universities have welcomed representatives who are not members of the academic community on their governing bodies – or they have been forced to accept such representatives, as the case may be. These representatives underline the fact that universities are part of broader society, that they have a duty to this society and that they both contribute to and are influenced by it. Nor is this really a new development. It is not the phenomenon of interdependence between higher education and society at large that is new, but rather the form this interdependence may take (see, for example, Hyde 1988, Sanz and Bergan 2007). Some higher education institutions now even have institutional leaders hired on fixed-term contracts and often recruited from the outside rather than rectors elected by the academic community. So far, there has been little debate on the implications of these developments on our concept of higher education governance. The same, albeit to a slightly lesser extent, holds true for the relationship between the higher education institution and its faculties, which is a particularly pertinent issue in several countries emanating from the former Yugoslavia.

Student participation: banging on open doors?

The topic for the Oslo seminar was the specific part of higher education governance that has to do with the participation and contribution of students. This, also, we perhaps tend to take for granted, so it may be useful to remember that times have indeed been changing. This is true for the Bologna Process as well as for higher education governance proper.

Students, represented by the ESU,[3] are now observers on the Bologna Follow-up Group and Board and active contributors to the Bologna Process, so it is easy to forget that student representation was neither foreseen nor much talked about at the 1999 Bologna Conference. Students, in fact, did not move to centre stage until the Prague Conference in 2001, when the President of the ESIB[4] spoke to the ministers and the latter stated that "the involvement of universities and other higher education institutions and of students as competent, active and constructive partners in the establishment and shaping of a European Higher Education Area is needed and welcomed". In the Prague Communiqué, ministers also "affirmed that students should participate in and influence the organisation and content of education at universities and other higher education institutions" and that "students are full members of the higher education community" (Bologna Process 2001). In moving from observers to key actors in the Bologna Process in two years, the students did of course have the support of many ministers of education, some of whom actively pushed for a stronger student participation in the Bologna Process. In this way, the process would be in better conformity with the situation in most of its member countries. Nevertheless, it may be worth noting that at least one respondent to the survey carried out by Annika Persson for the Oslo seminar underlined the need for stronger student participation in the follow-up structures of the Bologna Process.

Also in the governance of higher education institutions, we are used to taking student representation and student participation so much for granted that it is easy to forget that in most European countries, this representation in its current form is little more than a generation old. If the Bologna Process is the most important reform of higher education in Europe since the immediate aftermath of 1968, we should keep in mind that this previous wave of reform was very different. Both

---

3. European Students' Union, see www.esib.org.
4. European Students' Information Bureau, the ESU's name at the time.

reform movements are about adapting higher education to a changing society, but whereas the Bologna Process was started at the initiative of ministers, "1968" was started by students in the street. One of their main demands was the need for stronger student influence not just on higher education governance but on university life in general, with issues ranging from student representation on university senates and improved access for disadvantaged groups to less restrictive rules on gender relations in university dorms (Fischer 2000: 288-290).

Today, there is a feeling that the formal aspect of student representation has largely been settled, but I am not aware of any previous large-scale survey of the facts. Second, there is also a feeling that even if the formal right to representation has been secured, students' actual use of that right is far from satisfactory. To put it crudely, while previous generations of students fought for representation, there is an impression that the current student generation does not make much use of the rights gained. However, it would be helpful to know whether this impression is in fact substantiated by facts and, if so, why present-day students are to a large extent disconnected at least from institutional governance and perhaps even from institutional life. Third, it would be useful to know something about student perceptions of their influence on higher education governance, and this might even offer a clue as to why actual participation is as it is. These, then, are the three topics addressed by the survey.

Formal student representation in higher education governance

What is normally thought of as student participation in higher education governance, namely formal provision for student representation on the governing bodies of higher education institutions, seems to be a general feature of higher education in Europe. Representatives of only two countries indicate that there is no legal provision for student representation on the governing bodies of the institutions. However, legal regulation of such representation at faculty and, even more so, at department level is less common, and at national level provision for student representation is found only in a narrow majority of cases. On closer reflection, however, this may not be surprising. At institutional, faculty and department level, higher education governance takes place within a clearly defined framework of institutional self-governance with clearly defined partners.[5] At national level, the framework is less clear, as both ministries and national assemblies have a general political mandate. It would be interesting to see whether a consultative framework has been developed, to what extent this is formalised and to what extent students have a voice in bodies such as national rectors' conferences.

If we start scratching below the surface to find out what student representation means in somewhat greater detail, we see that in the great majority of cases, regulations stipulate that between one in ten and one in five of all members of higher education governing bodies be students. In no case do students elect a majority of

---

5. Although the newer development with increased external representation has been referred to above.

the representatives on the governing body, and in a number of cases student representation seems to be below 10%.

However, it is not enough to be present, it is also of interest to know what competence – in this case in the legal sense of the term – student representatives actually have. In the vast majority of cases, student representatives are full members of the governing body in the sense that they have the right to speak and vote on all issues that come before the board. However, in eight countries whose representatives replied to the survey, student voting rights were limited to issues that seem to be considered of most immediate concern to the students, while they are not allowed to vote on issues that concern staff appointments, administrative and finance issues, curricula or issues relating to the granting of doctoral degrees. While this relates to only eight countries covered by the survey, it seems worthwhile to dwell on the issue as it raises an important question of principle.

There are two ways of interpreting such differentiated voting rights: they are either differentiated according to the stake students are perceived to have in the issues, or the differentiation is made according to competence – here in the sense of knowledge and understanding of the issues. In both cases, it is difficult to see why students should not vote on financial issues. If real competence is the line of argument, the formal argument for limiting voting rights on the granting of doctoral degrees to staff members who have earned this qualification themselves may seem evident, but it overlooks two factors: first, that the governing bodies tend to act on, and in the great majority of cases follow, the advice of a committee of experts appointed for the occasion, and second, that holding a doctoral qualification in one academic area does not necessarily mean that one is similarly qualified in other areas. A professor of business administration does not necessarily have a comparative advantage in assessing a doctoral thesis in astrophysics.[6]

It therefore seems safe to say that, with the exception of voting rights on some issues that come before the governing bodies, student representation is ensured from a formal point of view. This is particularly true at institutional level, but it also largely holds true at faculty and, to a somewhat lesser extent, at department level. At the national level, however, the representation is less well established in formal terms. These findings coincide with the findings of the pilot project on the University as a Site of Citizenship, with the caveat that, since this project focused on institutional practice, representation at national level was not addressed by the project.

Student politics?

One issue at the crossroads of formal provision and actual practice concerns how student representatives are identified and elected. In fact, elections are almost universal: the survey revealed five countries in which student representatives are appointed rather than elected, and in all but one of these the appointment is made by

---

6. The present author defended this point of view as a student representative on the academic senate of the University of Oslo in 1981-82, in a newspaper debate with a former rector of the Veterinary College.

the student union. In the one case where the university or faculty appoints student representatives, a legal change seems to be on its way. One can of course ask to what extent the student unions making the appointments are representative of the student body at large, but that is a question of practice rather than formal provision.

The most serious question arising in this area is what kind of student organisations are allowed, and in particular whether these may be linked to political parties. These are generally referred to as "political" student organisations, but it may be worth underlining that politics is about organising and governing societies, and that no society can do without politics or a measure of political actors and organisations, even if these are not political parties in the conventional sense of the term. No society can be governed "apolitically", notwithstanding the claims of certain dictators to this effect.

Representatives from 15 of the countries that replied to the questionnaire state that "political student organisations" are illegal in higher education institutions. While the term "political" was not defined in the questionnaire, it was intended to mean "affiliated with a political party", and this is also how the question was understood by the respondents. Of the 15 countries that reported prohibitions of student organisations affiliated with political parties, all but two are to be found in central and eastern Europe. This is consistent with the findings of the pilot project on the University as a Site of Citizenship, which states:

> Another structural characteristic of universities is the legal and administrative prescriptions regarding organised political activity within the university. Many institutions in this study, particularly those in transitional societies or who have recently experienced violent conflict are attempting to respond to new statutory and constitutional arrangements. They are struggling with redefining roles and responsibilities while simultaneously dealing with basic issues of meeting their educational mission within tight fiscal and budgetary constraints (Plantan 2004: 95).

This prohibition may perhaps be understandable in the light of the recent past of most of the countries where the ban is enforced, where political organisations served the needs of the regime, both in controlling academic activity and in recruiting "reliable" future party workers. From a thoroughly "politicised" but tightly controlled system, the temptation to turn to one without both politics and control is great, but the question is still whether this is feasible and desirable.

An additional reason for such a ban is the view that students should "concentrate on their education". This view was expressed to researchers in the pilot project, where:

> [m]ost sites reported that university administrators and many faculty considered many aspects of citizenship and democracy to be entirely a *personal matter* such as decisions to vote, to volunteer in the community, to participate in campus organisations, or to engage in political debate and, therefore, not within their ken nor responsibilities as teachers and scholars (Plantan 2004: 89).

This represents a narrow view of the purpose of higher education that is limited to the role of academic disciplines and that leaves little room for the social function of education, such as developing the ability to live as active citizens in a democratic society.

In a somewhat narrower sense, there is also a desire to keep contentious issues off campus, so as not to make higher education institutions battlefields for groups with sharply divergent views on issues often linked to conflicts that divide the societies concerned, such as ethnic or religious conflicts. In a different context, this view was expressed[7] by the principal of a school in Strasbourg with a high number of foreign students, who publicly made it clear that she would never tolerate students bringing any conflict between their home countries into the school yard or classroom. An example in the opposite sense is, however, provided by Queen's University, Belfast, which has for a long time made consistent efforts to accommodate members of both major religious communities in Northern Ireland and which has pioneered many of the measures that made the Peace Process possible.

While a limitation of the activities of political parties, or organisations linked to these, in higher education institutions may be understandable on the basis of past experience, the limitation may nevertheless be questioned on grounds of principle as well as of efficiency.

The actual practice of student participation

If the survey as well as the pilot project confirm that formal rights to student participation are now almost universal, what use do students make of these rights? Do the formalities work as intended? These questions can be asked from at least two angles: first, is the general student body sufficiently active and interested to give its representatives legitimacy and, second, are student representatives effective once elected, or are they rather helping institutions fulfil the formal requirements of representation without having any real influence on institutional policies? The latter question also concerns how students perceive their influence, to which we will return shortly.

The survey carried out for the Oslo seminar shows that in general it is possible to find motivated candidates to run for office, even if this seems more difficult at department level than at higher levels. It also shows that candidates run either as individuals or on tickets not affiliated with political parties and that the degree of organised politicking increases with the level of representation. In other words, candidates are more likely to run as individuals at department level than at faculty level, and so on. The replies indicate that a plurality of candidates run as individuals at department level, whereas at faculty level a plurality of, and at an institutional level a majority of, candidates run as a representative of an organisation.

This far, the results look good, but this changes when we examine voter turnout in student elections. Although turnout varies considerably, it tends to be low. The overwhelming majority of respondents indicate that voter turnout is in one of the

---

7. At a meeting attended by the author.

three lowest percentage ranges indicated (0-15%, 16-30% or 31-45%). Therefore, most of the time, less than half the student population elects those representing the whole student body, and in most cases voter turnout is actually one in three or less.

These figures indicate that something is wrong, and they are borne out by the pilot project on the University as a Site of Citizenship. This project not only confirms the low voter turnout, indicated as 8-10% at two of the institutions participating in that study, but also indicates some interesting elements of explanation. It is hardly surprising that one important part of the explanation is that students feel under pressure to complete their studies as soon as possible and with as good results as possible, and that they therefore find little time for institutional life. In fact, not finding the time to do something normally indicates giving it a low priority, so participating in and contributing to institutional life in general and institutional governance in particular does not seem to be a priority for many, perhaps most, students.

An interesting observation concerns institutions in countries in which a period of great political conflict and tension has been followed by a period of normalisation. In these cases – exemplified by institutions in Albania and Lithuania, where the most intense period was in the early 1990s, and in Greece, where it occurred around 1974 – student mobilisation was strong in the period of crisis and the immediate aftermath, both in general terms and relating to involvement with institutional governance. However, once the crisis blew over and democratic governance was established, student interest declined considerably. This "democratic fatigue" corresponds to the experience of many institutions in western Europe, where student interest declined once student representation had been secured in the aftermath of 1968. Thus, while it seems possible to mobilise students for a "great cause", it seems much more difficult to maintain a sustained interest in and commitment to institutional life and governance.

A second major point that arises from the survey is that even where formal provision is absent, there may be informal consultations at national level, where in many cases there is no formalised representation. In most countries there seems to be regular contact between the ministry responsible for higher education and student representatives, typically the national student union. This may be unsatisfactory from a formal point of view, but such contacts can nevertheless help students wield considerable influence.

Perceptions of influence

If the formal representation of students in higher education governance is generally provided for but student interest in electing representatives is low, is there a connection with students' perceptions of their influence on university life in general and higher education governance in particular?

The survey did in fact not ask directly whether students feel they can influence university governance, and the selection of respondents was not such that this question would have made much sense. Since the respondents were mostly engaged in university governance, directly or indirectly, as members of student unions, academics or ministry officials, the answers would presumably have been skewed. The survey did, however, ask more nuanced questions about perceived influence, in that it asked respondents to identify the areas and levels where they feel that student influence was the strongest and weakest.

All groups of respondents feel that students have the most influence on what may be seen as "immediate issues", such as social issues, the learning environment and educational content, in addition to the somewhat less decipherable category "institutional level generally". At the other end of the scale we find "hard" issues such as budget issues and criteria for recruiting teaching staff as well as on student admission. Budget policies are clearly a key instrument for implementing institutional policy, and as such they are also of immediate concern to students. In terms of level, most respondents feel that the student voice is more easily heard at institutional and faculty level than at the levels immediately above or below, that is, national and department level.

Another indirect indication of student influence is that a large majority of respondents in all categories feel that student influence should be increased. That 90% of student respondents think so is perhaps no great surprise, but it is interesting to note that 72% of academic and 70% of ministry respondents share this view.

Again, the findings of the survey are borne out by those of the pilot project on the University as a Site of Citizenship, where researchers asked more direct questions about whether or not students felt they had influence on institutional life. The answers are, in fact, not very encouraging, even at institutions that in their own view make substantial efforts at consulting with and involving their students. The summary of the study states this very directly: "Formal and statutory provisions for shared governance, transparency of decision making and protection of faculty and student rights are often at odds with reality and actual practices" (Plantan 2004: 88).

In the body of the study, this is made more explicit. At one university, respondents felt that a few individuals continue to dominate the decision-making process, while at several universities from different parts of Europe the feeling was that students are rarely if ever consulted and that there are no public hearings on university decisions.

These views are clearly linked to the issue of information given to students, which is felt to be insufficient, something that is reflected in the study carried out by Annika Persson for the Oslo seminar as well as in the project on the University as a Site of Citizenship. A dictum has it that "information is power", and information is an important condition for participation as active citizens in a democratic society. At the same time, we know that information is a difficult issue in many areas of modern society. In many contexts, the problem is not lack of information per se, but lack of reliable and targeted information.[8]

---

8. The lack of clear and targeted information was one of the main issues raised at the follow-up Bologna Seminar on Recognition Issues in the Bologna Process, organised by the Council of Europe and the Portuguese authorities in Lisbon on 11 and 12 April 2002. See in particular the articles by Stephen Adam and Chantal Kaufmann in Bergan (2003).

In several countries, there is still a strong tradition that senior faculty "decides every-thing". Where there is student involvement, there is at the same time a feeling that this does not lead to many concrete results, and that student representatives, while part of the process, have little influence on it. There is also a perception that student politics is run by a small elite without much contact with "normal" students. This, perhaps, echoes a frequent complaint about politics in general, but it is a serious challenge to student representatives, politicians in society at large and indeed to all members of society. While it is unfortunately not difficult to find examples of politicians who deserve our scorn, society at whatever level is in serious trouble if it becomes fashionable to despise politics, because it would then be fashionable not to care about how our own societies are run. History has too many examples of what such attitudes of complacence can lead to, from all sides of the political spectrum.[9]

In this project, there even seems to be a consistent difference in the way respondents addressed the issue of perceptions of influence: student respondents tended to emphasise what they perceived as real influence – or lack of it – whereas admin-istrators tended to focus on formal student participation. Therefore, it is possible that the different groups did in fact not answer the same question, even if the same questions were asked of all. It is also interesting to note that students at three universities tended to have a more positive view of their influence. The foremost of these was Queen's University, Belfast, which has not only played a significant role in the Northern Ireland Peace Process – something that could hardly be done without consultation – but where the university leadership at the time the study was carried out was particularly known for collegiate leadership. As the study puts it, "[t]his not only sets a 'tone' for proper democratic demand and problem solving, such leadership typically directs the university mission towards meeting the objectives of civic education and democracy in its education programmes" (Plantan 2004: 98).

Why should students influence institutional governance?

One may perhaps have expected this question to be asked at the outset of this article, but I have preferred to survey facts and perceptions before entering into normative arguments. The survey does, incidentally, provide guidance also on this point, as respondents were asked why they felt – as the majority of them did – that student influence should be strengthened. The replies focused on the role of students as stakeholders in higher education; from many respondents' points of view they are even the main stakeholders.

I will take these arguments one step further and consider the role of students in somewhat more detail. My point of departure is that there is an increasing tendency to think of students as clients. This paradigm does, however, have profound impli-cations for the relationship between students and the institutions at which they

---

9. For an interesting, if depressing, example of the political thought of a right-wing military regime, see Pinochet Ugarte, Augusto (1983): *Política, politiquería, demagogia*, Santiago de Chile: Editorial Renacimiento.

study. Clients essentially expect a number of defined services from a provider, and they would normally take little interest in the provider as long as these services are delivered as expected at an affordable price and acceptable quality, according to the contract, in commercial terms. There may be some exceptions, such as boycotts of companies refusing to hire ethnic or religious minorities, but these remain exceptions. If client expectations are not met, most clients respond by looking for the desired services elsewhere rather than by attempting to take control of the provider to make it deliver the services as stipulated or desired.

Taken to the extreme, the idea of students as clients contradicts the idea of students as members of the academic community (Bologna Process 2001). The idea of community does not exclude the possibility of there being conflicting opinions about the purpose and standard of education, but it sees the students as participants rather than as receivers or buyers of a final product. As members of the academic community, students share a responsibility for their education and for the institution that provides the framework for this education. If the education is unsatisfactory, the response would be to try to improve the institution and the education it provides rather than to go elsewhere.

In real life, none of these extremes will be readily found. Students do legitimately have specific expectations for their education (in terms of quality, profile, price, conditions of study, etc.) and few students can afford to spend years of their life trying to improve an institution if what it gives them does not come reasonably close to their expectations, especially if other institutions – or alternative experiences outside higher education – can better meet their expectations and needs. Most students embark on higher education because the qualifications they earn will help them reach their goals later in life. Academic mobility, that is, getting students to move between higher education institutions, is of course also an important policy goal for higher education institutions as well as governments and international organisations.

However, students also see themselves as members of a community, as participants. While most students have utilitarian reasons for taking higher education, few would think that higher education does not also have an intrinsic value. I think it is worth emphasising that while much of the current discussion on higher education, inside as well as outside the Bologna Process, focuses on its role in relation to the labour market, we should take into account the full range of purposes of higher education. In my view, these are at least four:

- preparation for the labour market;
- preparation for life as active citizens in a democratic society;
- personal development;
- development and maintenance of an advanced knowledge base (Bergan 2005, Council of Europe 2007).

Students should have clear expectations of higher education institutions – expectations that are not always met – but they should also see themselves as a part of the

103378713   25

institution. That may not always mean they identify very strongly with the institution as such[10] but they do at least identify with groups within the institution, such as the student body as a whole, a specific department or students in a specific department. This identification is not and should not be uncritical, and students should make demands on their institutions and teachers, but if they no longer consider themselves as a part of the institution and the academic community, I believe higher education in Europe will have a very serious problem. In a sense, students must be members of an "imagined community"[11] that crosses national and institutional borders.

If we believe that higher education has a role in developing the democratic culture without which democratic institutions cannot function and democratic societies cannot exist, it is, as the pilot project on the University as a Site of Citizenship points out, important to realise that these attitudes cannot be developed simply by seeing and learning. Doing is of the essence. Therefore, students must be encouraged to participate, and they must feel that their participation has an impact.

At least two caveats may be in order, and they both have to do with the democratic character of higher education institutions. The first is whether higher education institutions and their staff and students are necessarily democratic, and it is, unfortunately, not difficult for any of us to think of examples to the contrary. Here, I will therefore only point to a few examples. Many of the Council of Europe's member states – and current or future participants in the Bologna Process – in their recent higher education history have no shortage of examples of how communist regimes used higher education institutions for their own purposes and how many staff members and students played along. The judges at show trials (Mählert 1999: especially, 62-65) were graduates of law faculties, and party membership was no disadvantage in securing staff appointments or places of study, provided the membership was in the "right" party. In the Germany of the 1920s and 1930s, most university teachers were nostalgic for pre-First World War elitist society and lukewarm to the Weimar Republic and even if the majority of them were not Nazi supporters, it was only a minority that fought actively against the Nazi regime (Hammerstein 1991). Even as anti-intellectual a movement as the Nazi Party had its student organisations and student supporters. In Portugal, the main leaders of the Salazar regime had their roots at the University of Coimbra (Torgal 1999). In Chile, the Pinochet regime received strong support from a group of economists at the Universidad Católica who had some of their formative experience at the University of Chicago and who were therefore known as the Chicago boys. They were the moving force behind the economic liberalism of the Pinochet regime and they were largely unconcerned by its human rights abuses (Huneeus 2001). Nor is this a prerogative of the undemocratic

---

10. It may even be that some models of higher education tend to encourage a stronger institutional identification than others. It is at least a superficial impression that US students identify more closely with their institutions than many continental European students do.
11. The term "imagined community" is normally used in discussions of nationalism and was coined by the political scientist Benedict Anderson (Anderson 1983) but, if used with care, the term may be fitting also for other kinds of communities.

right. On the undemocratic left, we find students and staff in Maoist movements in Europe, and a little further afield, the leader and ideologue of the Peruvian terrorist movement Sendero Luminoso (Shining Path), Abimael Guzmán, was a philosophy lecturer at the University of Ayacucho.[12]

The point is of course not that universities, scholars or students are inherently undemocratic. For each of the examples mentioned, counter examples can be found. In central and eastern Europe, the movements that ultimately brought down the communist regimes were also often led by academics, and immediately after the political changes in the early 1990s, some university departments were decimated because many of their members had been democratically elected to parliament. Germany not only had Nazi students, but also student and staff members of the resistance who paid with their lives, such as the Scholl siblings and other members of the Weisse Rose. Academics played an important role in the opposition to the Salazar regime, especially from the 1960s onwards; voices such as José Afonso gave artistic expression to this through the *fado de Coimbra* (Silva 2007).[13] Chilean academics played an important part in the opposition to the Pinochet regime and Maoist student movements were not unopposed even in the immediate aftermath of 1968. Under the Milošević regime, which in 1998 passed a particularly repressive higher education law that was implemented by government-appointed rectors and deans, academic and democratic values were upheld by members of the academic community who often lost their jobs and who were in many cases members of the Alternative Academic Education Network.

The point is, rather, that politically, higher education institutions and their members are not much better or worse than society at large, and while they may tend to phrase their arguments in more theoretical terms, democracy must be maintained through both reflection and practice, on campus as elsewhere in society.

The second caveat is whether universities should be democratic and, if they should, in what way.

University governance – how democratic is it?

A universal feature of the legal regulations is that students hold a substantial yet minority number of seats on the governing bodies. In other words, seats on the governing bodies are not distributed according to numerical strength. The democratic principle of one person, one vote is, then, not the norm in higher education institutions, where the votes (or number of representatives) of three groups are weighted according to their perceived roles in institutional life. Academic staff, perceived as having the main responsibility for the key missions of the university – teaching and research – in general elect a majority of the members of the decision-making

---

12. An enjoyable fictional account probably modelled on the Sendero Luminoso is Mario Vargas Llosa: *Historia de Mayta* (1984).
13. Afonso's "Grândola, Vila Morena" became the emblematic song of the revolution that overthrew the military regime in 1974.

bodies, whereas students often elect a larger number of representatives than the administrative and technical staff (although students are not better represented if, rather than the total number of representatives, one measures the number of voters per representative).

Votes, then, are weighted according to competence or function in relation to the missions of the university. Is this in contradiction to democratic principles, or is it simply that it is possible to define competence or function in the context of the university but not in that of civil society, in which all members have an equal stake? It may be noted that such weighting of votes is not unique to universities. It is found in a variety of contexts ranging from commercial companies (voting in relation to the number of shares owned) to diocesan councils (with separate representation of clergy and laity)[14] and international organisations.[15] It may also be noted that attempts at introducing competence tests, such as literacy tests, into general elections are generally seen as undemocratic and even as attempts to keep less favoured groups from voting.[16] Weighted representation of specific groups is generally regarded as undemocratic but is none the less seen as acceptable in certain circumstances, generally in terms of geography[17] or to increase the representation of an under-represented group (such as specific quotas for women), to ensure representation of a group whose voice may otherwise not be heard[18] or to ensure a *modus vivendi* in a highly conflictual society.[19]

It should also be noted that academic staff, students and administrative and technical staff are not necessarily homogenous groups given to bloc voting. Members of each of these groups may influence members of other groups by their arguments, and a majority may consist of some academic staff, students and administrative and technical staff. It is even conceivable that a majority of academic staff may be voted down by a coalition of students and administrative and technical staff with

---

14. It should be noted that neither commercial companies nor diocesan councils, while concerned with a measure of representativity, necessarily aim or claim to be democratic.

15. In the United Nations, five countries are permanent members of the Security Council and may veto decisions of this body. In most other contexts, including the General Assembly of the United Nations, international organisations are generally run on the principle that each country has one vote, regardless of the size of its population, so that the basic unit of representation is the country or government rather than the individual.

16. One example among many is the literacy tests used in the US Deep South in parts of the 20th century.

17. In many countries, there are fewer votes behind each representative elected from rural than from urban districts. In Switzerland, the provision that a proposal put to a national referendum must win a majority not only in the referendum at large but also in a specified number of cantons tends to weight voting in favour of the less populous cantons.

18. The institutionalised representation of the Māori population in the New Zealand Parliament, the quota of representatives of the Serb population and other minorities in the Kosovo legislative assembly or the existence of the Sámi Parliament, an advisory body, in Norway are three examples. (Reference to Kosovo shall be understood in full compliance with United Nations Security Council Resolution 1244 and without prejudice to the status of Kosovo.)

19. Examples include the presidency of Bosnia and Herzegovina, with one representative of each major ethnic community, and the increasingly contested provisions made in the Lebanese Constitution, with a Maronite president, a Sunni prime minister and a Shiite speaker of parliament.

a minority of academic staff representatives. Incidentally, the survey indirectly underlined this point in that respondents from the same country did not always agree on their interpretation of the facts, or even on what the facts are.

The way ahead

At least as a preliminary conclusion to our consideration of the formal provision for student representation, it seems reasonable to say that the issue is largely settled, perhaps with the exception of representation at national level in a good number of countries and in more limited cases of the right of student representatives to vote on all issues that come before the governing body. While students have fewer representatives than academic staff, this is justifiable on theoretical grounds, and from a practical point of view, a student representation of 10-30% does not seem to be widely contested.

It is also comforting to see that those who provided input to the Council of Europe study seem to agree on a wide range of issues, including the need for improved information and the desirability of improving student representation in higher education governance. The starting point for our discussion of further action – or for the road map for our way ahead, to use the most recent policy-speak – is therefore a reasonably high level of consensus, at least on the main principles.

If the formalities are settled, what are the issues on which the Bologna Process should focus if student representation is still to be on its agenda?

First, there seems to be an issue concerning the level of representation, which particularly concerns student participation at national level and seems to be an issue of both formal provisions and practice. How can the further development of national higher education systems – and the European Higher Education Area itself – best benefit from the contribution of students, and how can these important stakeholders gain the same influence they now have at institutional level?

Second, even if student representation is almost universal, we have seen that, in some countries, student representatives cannot vote on all issues. Is this really reasonable? Even if we accept that academic staff may have a stronger representation than students for reasons of competence in the core areas of higher education (teaching, learning and research), is it reasonable that, once the student representation on governing bodies has been determined, students should not speak or vote on all issues brought before these bodies?

A greater challenge is linked to real influence rather than formal representation. These issues may be linked in a vicious circle: if students believe they have little or no interest, why should they participate in governance or even vote? However, if students do not vote, why should they have a greater influence? Here we touch on institutional culture, on the way in which institutions are governed and decisions made, and this is an issue that goes beyond student representation. To what extent should decisions be consensual, and to what extent do institutions need strong leadership?

The answer to this question is not as straightforward as it would seem, and I believe the issue should be considered within the Bologna Process. On the one hand, institutions where staff and students are committed to common goals and common reforms have a considerable advantage over those where no such consensus emerges, and institutional leadership should not be too aloof from the average staff member. The same could of course be said of the relationship between student representatives and the average student. In the project on the University as a Site of Citizenship, Queen's University Belfast was identified as an institution with an inspirational leadership that achieved considerable results through persuasion. On the other hand, a consensus-oriented governance model can also be a recipe for stalemate under which small groups or certain parts of the university can block any attempt at reform. The situation in many countries of the former Yugoslavia, where faculties have an independent legal personality and a correspondingly weak institutional leadership (rectorate), is perhaps an extreme example, but the dilemma is real at many institutions in all parts of Europe.

The question of the relative weight of institutional self-governance and external influence is linked to this. It indirectly concerns student participation but is really an essential aspect of overall institutional governance. The issue is that of defining the stakeholders in higher education and their relative role as well as the relationship between stakeholder interest and their actual higher education competence. To what extent should society at large, which contributes substantially to financing higher education, have a direct say in institutional governance, and who should represent this society at large which strongly resembles the proverbial duck: we recognise it when we see it but it is difficult to define and, I would add, to operationalise. The social partners (employers and trade unions) are important partners also for higher education institutions, but can they alone represent society at large? In most democracies, society is represented by politicians, but is the participation of political parties in higher education governance the right way to go? The material presented here at the very least indicates that views on the role – if any – of party politics at higher education institutions are highly diverse.

This leads me to what is perhaps the greatest challenge of all, namely the low interest that students show in the governance of their higher education institutions and systems. Again, as important as this is for the issue of student representation, I would tend to see this in the context of disenchantment with the political process in society at large as well as the problem of providing clear and targeted information in a society where most people receive far more information than they can possibly absorb, and I have already underlined the seriousness of the issue. Therefore, an important part of the discussion should focus on how we can stimulate students as well as staff to take an active interest not only in their own teaching, learning and research but in the life and governance of their institution and the society of which it is a part. In the classical French tragedies, the ideal was to be loved, but it was better to be hated than to be ignored, and I sometimes wonder if this is not true for higher education governance as well.

I would therefore point to two overall conclusions that, in addition to the questions just raised, should guide the further work within the European Higher Education Area. First, we need to stimulate interest in and commitment to higher education among those most directly involved: students and staff. Second, however important student participation, it is a part of the overall issue of higher education governance and should, in my view, be considered within this framework.

Last, but not least: governance issues are not a luxury or a concern of the few while the majority of staff and students get on with their work. Rather, they are part and parcel of the contribution of higher education to developing and maintaining the democratic culture without which democratic institutions cannot function, and they are crucial to ensuring that the academic community of scholars and students be not only an imagined community but also a real and healthy one.

References

Anderson B. (1983), *Imagined Communities: Reflections on the Origin and Spread of Nationalism*, Verso, London.

Bergan S. (ed.) (2003), *Recognition Issues in the Bologna Process,* Council of Europe Publishing, Strasbourg.

Bergan S. (2005), "Higher education as a 'public good and a public responsibility' – What does it mean?", in Luc W. and Sjur B. (eds), *The Public Responsibility for Higher Education and Research*, Council of Europe Higher Education Series No. 2, Council of Europe Publishing, Strasbourg.

Bologna Process (2001), Prague Communiqué.

Council of Europe (2007), Recommendation CM/Rec(2007)6 of the Committee of Ministers to member states on the public responsibility for higher education and research.

Fischer D. (2000), *L'histoire des étudiants en France de 1945 à nos jours*, Flammarion, Paris.

Hammerstein N. (1991), "Universities and democratisation: an historical perspective. The case of Germany" (paper written for the Council of Europe Conference on Universities and Democratisation, reference DECS-HE 91/97).

Huneeus C. (2001), *El régimen de Pinochet,* Editorial Sudamericana, Santiago de Chile.

Hyde J. K. (1988), "Universities and cities in medieval Italy" in Thomas Bender (ed.), *The University and the City. From Medieval Origins to the Present*, Oxford University Press, New York.

Mählert U. (1999), *Kleine Geschichte der DDR,* Verlag C. H. Beck, Munich.

Persson A. (2004), "Student participation in the governance of higher education in Europe: results of a survey", in Sjur B. (ed.) (2006), *The University as*

Res Publica: *Higher Education Governance, Student Participation and the University as a Site of Citizenship,* Council of Europe Higher Education Series No. 1, Council of Europe Publishing, Strasbourg, pp. 31-82.

Plantan F. (2004), "The university as a site of citizenship", in Sjur B. (ed.) (2006), *The University as* Res Publica: *Higher Education Governance, Student Participation and the University as a Site of Citizenship*, Council of Europe Higher Education Series No. 1, Council of Europe Publishing, Strasbourg, pp. 83-128.

Sanz N. and Bergan S. (eds) (2007), *The Heritage of European Universities*, Council of Europe Higher Education Series No. 7, second edition, Council of Europe Publishing, Strasbourg.

Silva M. (2007), "The University of Coimbra and its traditions at the beginning of a new millennium", in Nuria S. and Sjur B. (eds) (2007), *The Heritage of European Universities*.

Torgal L. R. (1999), *A Universidade e o Estado Novo*, Livreria Minerva Editora, Coimbra.

Democracy: institutions, laws, culture and the role of higher education[20]

Let us think back to our school textbooks in civics and related courses. What image did they give of democracy? Certainly, like publicity for universities all over the world, they gave an impression of smiling people living in an eternally sunny climate. Yet, beyond that, chances are that they presented democracy as a set of institutions. As long as we had the mechanisms of democracy and the constitution of democracy, we had democracy. People should vote, of course, but otherwise get on with their lives.

Maybe I am exaggerating, but alas not as much as I probably should to make the point that democracy, to be sustainable, in addition to sound institutions and sound laws, needs to be rooted in a vibrant, living culture. Institutions are important, but they will only work if they are rooted in a democratic culture in the same way that a guitar needs strings of the right dimensions, but it will also greatly benefit from a motivated and skilled guitarist.

The Council of Europe, I think we have to admit, is among those who have learned something about democratic culture over the past couple of decades. We are dedicated to democracy – it is our *raison d'être*. Yet, our concept of democracy has evolved since the Council of Europe was established in 1949 – when women did not yet have the right to vote in all European countries – and not least since the Berlin Wall came tumbling down in 1989.

Many Europeans were euphoric when it did, and we had the right to be. Yet, we were also somewhat naive when we seemed to think that democracy would come overnight. It did not take long to set up democratic institutions and hold elections; indeed, technical expertise accomplished a lot in a short time. Looking back, I think we also have to say that, for the most part, things went remarkably well.

Even so, it became clear by the mid-1990s, at the latest, that developing a sustainable democratic culture was the most difficult challenge. This requires developing attitudes, and, like Rome, democracy was not built in one day.

We should be very clear, however, in reminding ourselves that democratic culture is not something that only needs to be developed in new democracies. Democratic culture needs to be built anew in each successive generation as well as at different stages of the life of a person. It is not like riding a bike – once you have learned it, you have it – but like a language: if you do not practise it, you may lose it. The challenge to education is obvious, and we are reminded of it weekly through the news.

---

20. This essay was originally published in Huber, Josef and Harkavy, Ira (eds) (2007): *Higher Education and Democratic Culture: Citizenship, Human Rights and Civic Responsibility*, Strasbourg: Council of Europe Publishing. Council of Europe Higher Education Series No. 8.

Democracy and diversity

Democratic culture has many ingredients, and a willingness to consider other views is key among them. It is not only a question of letting others speak, but of listening to what they have to say. It is also about the possibility of admitting that we may be wrong ourselves. Personally, I find that a reasonable amount of doubt is an important ingredient of a keen mind.

Democratic culture is also about accepting diversity. There are of course situations in which it is important that we all speak with one voice, but very often those who say we need to speak with one voice really mean to say we need to speak with their voice.

Diversity is mostly a strength, not a problem. One of the joys of learning a new language is to see that a concept can be expressed very differently in another language. In Germanic languages, we are or have right, in Romance languages we have reason. If we had all thought in the same way and described the world around us in the same way, little intellectual or practical development would have taken place.

I think our US friends have given excellent expression to the balance of diversity and unity that I think is also one of the hallmarks of Europe, and I am pleased to note that they have done so in an old European language: *e pluribus unum*. Out of many, one.

Sustainable democratic culture

Intellectual debate is one of the great joys of life, and it is a defining feature of the human condition. Life without intellectual debate and stimulus would hardly be worth living. The point was made succinctly by Descartes in his famous *cogito ergo sum*: I think, therefore I am. Yet, precisely for this reason, we must not only debate, but also act on our convictions. Only then will we be able to shape a society in which free and open debate is the key tool for reaching decisions. Only then will we shape a society in which all – or at least most – members feel they have a stake in the decisions made and want to contribute to implementing them. Only then, in fact, will we have sustainable, democratic societies.

Concern for sustainability is, of course, not limited to concern for democracy, but democratic culture and democratic practice are keys to enabling societies to reach and implement the difficult decisions that will make them sustainable environmentally, economically, socially and culturally. This requires considerable sophistication in citizens as well as in leaders. It requires analytical capability; it requires the will to make difficult choices and the will, understanding and foresight to make sacrifices now in exchange for later gains. It would be difficult to claim that these are areas in which contemporary societies excel. It is equally difficult to believe that we will be led there by a coalition of the *carpe diemists* and the Immediate Gratification Party, or by those who believe that all values are expressed in euros or dollars.

So debate must be followed by action. Democratic culture is about debate, but also about the ability to make decisions. As Clement Attlee said: "Democracy means government by discussion but it is only efficient if you can stop people talking".[21]

Competences for democratic culture

In Europe, we are engaged in a quite intensive discussion about what constitutes a qualification (Bergan 2007), and there is agreement that a qualification is made up of both subject-specific and transversal competences and skills (González and Wagenaar 2005). Both are – or at least should be – developed through higher education.

Democratic culture, to be sustainable, depends on well-developed transversal skills, such as:

–   analytical ability;
–   the ability to present an issue clearly;
–   the ability to identify alternatives;
–   the ability to see an issue from different angles;
–   the ability to step outside one's own frame of reference;
–   the ability to solve and preferably to prevent conflicts;
–   the ability to debate, but also to draw conclusions and put them into practice;
–   maybe even the ability to read between the lines – to read the unstated as well as the stated.

One important transversal skill is the ability to identify and then resolve paradoxes; but, as societies, we are not particularly good at it. How else would we explain our attempt to become ever more attractive, yet be very upset when we are sufficiently attractive for people not just to want to visit, but also to stay to live and work with us, in our countries? Why else would we be upset when people from other parts of the world do what many Europeans did from the 17th to the early 20th century? Why else would we celebrate European migrants to North and South America while reviling African and Asian migrants to Europe?

I am particularly concerned about the seeming inability of political debate in many of our societies to look beyond the immediate issues. What is expedient in the short run may not be right in the long run. If you are on a diet, it is normally not for the pleasure of starving, but because you think you will be better off in the long run. Yet, while diets are "in", transferring the same kind of reasoning to political debate seems decidedly "out".

The role of higher education

There is no single role for higher education; there are several roles, and the term "higher education" should be seen as covering not just higher education institutions,

---

21. In a speech in Oxford in June 1957.

but also the individuals working at these institutions as academic and non-academic staff or as students. Perhaps the main issue has best been summed up by Walter Lippmann: "No amount of charters, direct primaries, or short ballots will make a democracy out of an illiterate people" (Lippmann 1914).

The same point is made by Goolam Mohamedbhai (Mohamedbhai 2008). First of all, higher education must continue the work of primary and secondary education, as well as of informal education, in developing the transversal skills and competences that are essential to democracy. We live in increasingly complex societies in which understanding the key issues is increasingly demanding. Complex democracies need sophisticated citizens who are able to cope with the nuances of an issue and do not believe that all questions can be answered either by yes or no, or by dollars and euros.

The details of climate change are understood only by specialists, and they are mostly to be found in higher education and research. They have a duty to explain the issues in comprehensible terms and to spell out the alternatives. But higher education has a duty not only to develop the specialists, but also to convey the skills and competences that enable higher education graduates to analyse and act on the information given by specialists, and to understand why it is important to do so.

This, however, can only work if higher education not only trains technical competences, but also educates for reflection and values. We need not only *homo sapiens* – the knowledgeable human – but also the thinking human, the human who is capable of understanding complex realities and, not least, who has convictions and values and is ready to stand up for them, as Tatsiana Khoma[22] and her fellow students are doing in Belarus, as many people in France did in the Dreyfus case 100 years ago, or as many Americans did in the civil rights struggle in the 1950s and 1960s.

Secondly, higher education must also encourage participation, not only in higher education governance, but in all sorts of activities related to the life of higher education. Theoretical studies are important, but it is also important to engage in the life of our society. Also, for their own credibility, higher education institutions should practise what they teach. One cannot support participation in theory, but not in practice, and remain credible.

Thirdly, higher education must encourage the feeling of community, and of the individual mattering to the community. Here, I think we have a lot to learn from our US friends, in the same way that US higher education has something to learn from Europe when it comes to involving students in institutional policy making. Building a community makes people feel they are a part of something important, and that they have a stake in trying to improve the community. If students feel a part of the higher education community, they will work to improve it, and a positive experience of community at a decisive stage of their lives will encourage them to engage with the communities they find themselves in later.

---

22. Tatsiana Khoma was expelled from her university in Belarus in late 2005 because of her activities in the European student movement – although her university used a technicality as justification for its decision.

In Belarus, students and other academics play an important role in the democracy movement, and they have done so in many other parts of the world. Yet, we cannot afford to be complacent and to believe that higher education automatically leads to democratic culture. For every example of academics that have shown commitments to the values, principles and practice of democracy and have made sacrifices, there are, alas, counter examples of academics who – out of conviction or by taking the road of least resistance – have defended and collaborated with dictatorships. For Dietrich Bonhoeffer, Father Alfred Delp SJ, the Scholl siblings and others who resisted the Nazis, there were academics like Mengele and far too many others who collaborated and led. For Andrei Sakharov and others who opposed communist regimes, there were academics who collaborated and led, including the judges of show trials. For the many Latin American academics who opposed dictatorship of various political colours, there were the Sendero Luminoso, Chilean economists of the Pinochet era, academics defending Castro and others who offered theoretical and practical support for models of society that showed scant regard for essential democratic values.

Developing and maintaining democratic culture is therefore a double task for the higher education community. It must do so for itself and it must do so for the benefit of others.

For itself, the higher education community must pursue its research and teaching in all areas of importance to sustaining our societies. That includes the ethics, values and principles on which we found our societies as well as the mechanisms that make them work. That includes research in and teaching of human rights, which is a rich interdisciplinary field for philosophers, political scientists and others as well as for lawyers. It includes the natural and life sciences that make our environment sustainable – or that can help wreck it – as well as economics and business studies that can help make the difference between sustainable development on the one hand or, on the other, extreme development toward an environmental and social abyss: lack of sustainability for lack of development. That includes the humanities and social sciences, including history, sociology and languages that encourage us to reflect on who we are, where we come from, and how we communicate with others. Not least, it includes bringing all of the different academic disciplines together for the benefit of all, rather than developing a world of compartmentalised research and battles for academic turf.

But for itself, the world of higher education must not only pursue teaching and research. It must also live by the principles it proclaims. *Orthodoxia* – correct teaching – must be complemented by *orthopraxis* – sound practice.

Higher education institutions cannot credibly proclaim the virtues of participation and democratic culture if they themselves run on models of marginalisation and decision making by small groups in closed fora. Institutional governance, as well as the broader area of institutional life, must give all members of the academic community a reasonable stake in the development of the institution and of the higher education system. The European experience shows that this is entirely possible while also making allowance for the different roles of students and various categories of staff.

Indeed, it is not only possible: the student contribution is vital to the development and well-being of institutions and higher education systems. Students as members of the academic community have a stake in the development of their institutions and are encouraged to contribute to its well-being. Students as clients have no commitment to their *alma mater* – which they would hardly call by this name – and if not satisfied, they will shop for education elsewhere. In Europe, the Bologna Process has fully shown the great contribution students and their organisations can make to the development of higher education, as well as what we would miss by not encouraging their participation.

With the larger society, the higher education community must engage. The image of the ivory tower is, I believe, a considerably exaggerated image. If it were correct, universities would not be a part of contemporary societies, but would have expired as viable models for the development and transmission of knowledge many genera- tions ago. Yet, we often talk about the "society surrounding higher education" and forget that this is not an ocean surrounding an island. It is the very society of which higher education is a part. Members of the academic community must engage with and function in society as citizens, and universities must do so institutionally. Higher education and research have a lot to contribute, and we should not wait to be asked. We live in an age where the claims for public funding and public attention increase, as do the demands for performance. As higher education leaders, we must admit that contributing to the economy is important, but we must define a playing field that is much broader than that. Higher education must contribute to society and not just the part of it that can be counted in dollars and euros.

Higher education must engage with local society, to improve the opportunity for those living in its immediate neighbourhood as well as further afield to share the benefits of higher education. It must engage with local society to improve that society and to make it sustainable – by helping develop its economy, by helping make its physical and social environment sustainable, by encouraging local citizens to participate in the life and politics of the community and take responsibility for the future of their own community, by transmitting the necessary competences and by regaining the credibility of research-based science. In short, higher education must make every effort to give the local community hope. Without hope, no society is sustainable.

Many higher education institutions do what I have just described, and I would like to mention just three examples. The University of Pennsylvania is engaged in community projects in west Philadelphia, where students and faculty work in one of the most disadvantaged parts of the community – precisely to make that part of town feel included in the larger community and to provide opportunities and hope. The University of Cérgy-Pontoise, on the outskirts of Paris, is located in an area whose residents come from some forty different ethnic groups, many of whom have had little or no previous contact with higher education. Again, this university plays a significant role in the development of its local community and in bringing hope and a sense of purpose to vulnerable groups. Nobody who lived through the events of November 2005 in France will underestimate the importance of that contribution. Queen's University Belfast has made consistent efforts in making both Catholics and Protestants feel welcome on campus and feel that the university is their common home. Queen's has in fact pioneered many of the policies and developments that later made the Peace Process possible. Ultimate success will still take hard work, but without the contribution of Queen's, the danger of failure would have been much greater.

At national and global level, academics – as individuals, as a community and insti-tutionally – must engage in public debate and public service, including by seeking political office. In so doing, they should defend key values of higher education: free debate, a scrutiny of the facts and making decisions based on solid evidence. They should also make full use of the transversal academic competences like the ability to reason in abstract terms, analytical ability and the ability to explain complex realities in terms understandable to non-specialists. Not least, they should fight hard to extend the time perspective of public policies.

Conclusion

I hope the Higher Education Forum that gave rise to this book[23] was an important step towards a stronger contribution by higher education to developing and maintaining democratic culture. I believe the declaration the forum adopted and, in particular, the mechanism we are putting in place for following it up will be important.

There is a public responsibility for higher education (Weber and Bergan 2005), but there is also the public responsibility of higher education, and contributing to building a sustainable democratic culture is at the heart of this responsibility.

With only modest exaggeration, the importance of education – including higher education – to sustainable democratic culture can be summed up by two Greek letters, alpha and omega, or by a Latin term: *sine qua non.*

Ambrose Bierce was an American journalist who rode into the sunset some time during the Mexican revolution and was not heard from again. What he left behind, however, was a wonderful collection of humorous – if often cynical – definitions known as *The Devil's Dictionary.* Beneath it all, they have more than a grain of truth, and what he has to say about education may also guide us in our discussions of the role of higher education in developing sustainable democratic culture:

> *Education, n.* That which discloses to the wise and disguises from the foolish their lack of understanding (Bierce 1983: 105).

---

23. www.coe.int/t/dg4/highereducation/DemocraticCulture/Default_EN.asp#TopOfPage.

Our role, as higher education policy makers, then, is to help make our societies wise, and then to help us improve. It may be a proposition that is both challenging and expensive, but I would hate to contemplate – and even more to experience – the alternatives. Education may be expensive, but ignorance is definitely not cheap.

References

Bergan S. (2007), *Qualifications: Introduction to a Concept*, Council of Europe Higher Education Series No. 6, Council of Europe Publishing, Strasbourg.

Bierce A. (1983), *The Enlarged Devil's Dictionary* (ed. by Hopkins E. J.), Penguin, Harmondsworth (first published in 1911, then as *The Devil's Dictionary*).

González J. and Wagenaar R. (eds) (2005), *TUNING Educational Structures in Europe: Universities' Contribution to the Bologna Process. Final Report Pilot Project Phase 2*, Publicaciones de la Universidad de Deusto, Bilbao and Groningen.

Lippmann W. (1914), "Revolution and culture", in *A Preface to Politics*.

Mohamedbhai G. (2008), "Creating the right environment for sustainable democracy in developing countries", in Josef H. and Ira H. (eds) *Higher Education and Democratic Culture: Citizenship, Human Rights and Civic Responsibility*, Council of Europe Higher Education Series No. 8, Council of Europe Publishing, Strasbourg.

Weber L. and Bergan S. (eds) (2005), *The Public Responsibility for Higher Education and Research*, Council of Europe Higher Education Series No. 2, Council of Europe Publishing, Strasbourg.

Higher education between market and values[24]

The Council of Europe headquarters are the House of Europe – in the true sense of the word. As of June 2010, the Council of Europe had 47 member states, and 50 countries were party to the European Cultural Convention, which is the framework for our activities in culture and education. Kazakhstan is the latest country to adhere to the European Cultural Convention, in March 2010. With the sad exception of Belarus, no European country is now outside of the European political family. In the space of half a generation, since the changes symbolised by the fall of the Berlin Wall, this Organisation has developed from being the Council of half of Europe to being the Council of all of Europe.

The fact that the overarching goals of the Council of Europe – democracy, human rights and the rule of law – have not changed even as its membership has soared testifies to the great changes Europe has experienced and ultimately to the success and attractiveness of the values on which this Organisation is founded.

Europe today is certainly no image of perfection, but it is doing well. Democracy, human rights and the rule of law are more firmly rooted throughout our continent than they have ever been. Few political movements and even fewer countries oppose these values in principle, and we are also making considerable progress in putting them into practice. Most European countries have a reasonably well functioning economy, or at least they did until the financial crisis hit in autumn 2008. Europeans are fairly well aware of the challenges of climate change, even if that awareness has so far not translated into as much action as it should. Europe, which has in recent centuries been a continent of emigration, now attracts large numbers of immigrants. While many Europeans see this as a challenge, we should not forget that immigrants would not come here if Europe were not attractive and we should not forget that new arrivals bring new ideas and new impulses. As US higher education researcher Cliff Adelman has put it: "those who learn from others thrive; those who don't, don't".[25]

This is of course a very incomplete sketch of where Europe stands today, but my purpose in this article is not to give a political, social or economic overview of Europe. Rather, my purpose may be summarised as trying to answer a seemingly simple question: what does education have to do with it?

---

24. This article is based on an address given at the opening of the International Week of the Strasbourg Management School of the University of Strasbourg (then Université Robert Schumann – Strasbourg II) on 12 November 2008.
25. In his presentation to the Conference on National Qualifications Frameworks and the European Overarching Frameworks: Supporting Lifelong Learning in European Education and Training, in Dublin on 15 April 2010.

A quick glance at public debate in Europe today might lead one to conclude that education serves one overriding purpose: to prepare young people for the labour market.

This is an important purpose of higher education and it would be unwise to deny that higher education does have an important economic function or to try to belittle that function. It would indeed not only be unwise, but counterfactual. My problem with the tone of our current debate is not that it emphasises the role of higher education in preparing learners for the labour market, but that it emphasises this role alone. Higher education is multidimensional, even if one would not necessarily get that impression from observing the current European public debate.

The Council of Europe takes a broader view of higher education. In our view, higher education must fulfil four key purposes:

–   preparation for the labour market;
–   preparation for life as active citizens in democratic society;
–   personal development;
–   the development and maintenance of a broad and advanced knowledge base (Bergan 2005, Council of Europe 2007).

These four purposes are equally important, and they are not contradictory. Rather, they complement and support each other. Many of the qualities one needs to be an active citizen also make one attractive on the labour market and contribute to one's personal development.

Our tendency to compartmentalise illustrates one of the key challenges of education today. We are very good at educating highly qualified specialists in a range of disciplines. We are, however, much less good at educating intellectuals, by which I mean people who can put their advanced knowledge and understanding of a specific field into its proper context and ask fundamental questions about the purposes of our existence.

We do need people who are highly specialised in a specific field, but we also need people who can ask critical questions about where we should go as societies and about which values should guide us on our way. Not least, we need people who are subject specialists and intellectuals at the same time.

One of my home country's most distinguished writers – Henrik Ibsen – famously declared "Jeg spørger kun, mitt kall er ei at svare".[26] Translated from 19th-century literary Norwegian to 21st-century international English, what he said was: "I only ask the questions; my calling does not lie in providing answers". This is not quite good enough. It is important to ask critical questions, but it is equally important to provide constructive and innovative answers.

---

26. Ibsen, Henrik: *Et rimbrev* [A Letter of Rhymes], written to Georg Brandes.

It may be useful to contemplate a seemingly simple question: would we have been in our current financial crisis if the financial industry had been somewhat better endowed with the ability to ask critical questions? Would we have been in this crisis if banks had been less eager to lend money and more concerned with whether their actions were sustainable in the longer run? Would we have been quite as badly off if business leaders had been as concerned with whether their actions are ethical as they are with whether their actions are profitable?

In a word, would we not have been better off if all our higher education had been aimed at fulfilling all of the major purposes of higher education? At the risk of being repetitive, would we not have been better served if more highly specialised people had also been intellectuals? The fact that many readers are likely to perceive these questions as rhetorical underscores their importance and makes it difficult to understand why they do not seem to have been asked where it mattered most.

We read almost every day that we live in a "global world". Personally, I do not care much for this expression, which bears a striking resemblance to an oxymoron. However, it is undisputed that we live in a world where international contacts are ever closer. We live in a global age. That raises the question not only of global markets, but also of global dialogue and global understanding.

The three are not unrelated. Just as democracy will not function without the democratic culture that makes our democratic institutions work in practice, global markets will not function without intercultural dialogue.

For the Council of Europe, intercultural dialogue is at the very heart of our concerns and our activities. Everything the Council of Europe is doing and has done since its creation in 1949 is directly or indirectly related to managing and protecting cultural diversity and intercultural dialogue. The Council's core mandate is to defend and extend human rights, democracy and the rule of law. Most of the Council's activities aim at protecting these rights and values, which are at the heart of our European identity. The respect for and the observation of these rights and values are vital preconditions for a thriving, culturally diverse society. Our work has always aimed at creating societies in which people live with each other, not against each other and European history underscores why this is a crucial endeavour.

These concerns led to the development of the White Paper on Intercultural Dialogue (Council of Europe 2008). The White Paper, entitled "Living Together as Equals in Dignity", was adopted by the Committee of Ministers in May 2008. It covers almost all aspects of the Council's activities but I will focus on how education contributes to intercultural dialogue.

The starting point is very simple. Put bluntly, intercultural dialogue is impossible without education. We cannot expect people to be born with the knowledge, understanding and skills they need to live together in harmony. These qualities must be transmitted, taught and nurtured through life.

Ultimately we need a new culture of respect for diversity, shared by all or at least by the vast majority of our citizens, which promotes intercultural dialogue and supports open-mindedness and co-operation. Cultural diversity must come to be considered as a source of mutual enrichment rather than as a threat of invasion by the unknown into our narrow comfort zone.

Higher education is an obvious partner in intercultural dialogue, even if it must also be admitted that the world of higher education has not always been articulate about its responsibilities in this area. There are academic heroes who have dedicated their lives and careers to furthering democracy and intercultural understanding but there are also those who have done the exact opposite. They range from those who devised the Holocaust through those who deny it today to those on the opposite extreme of the political spectrum – which is perhaps not all that opposite after all. A more appropriate way of defining the political spectrum may be to distinguish those who do not believe in democracy and dialogue from those who do and who further these values with dignity and respect. Alas, academics may be found on both sides of this divide.

Historically, higher education is one of the most international endeavours the world has known. That gives higher education great possibilities and great responsibilities. Higher education has been international in its culture and essence since the founding of the first universities in the 11th and 12th centuries (Sanz and Bergan 2007). I cannot resist the temptation of noting that the longest lived institutions in European societies – the church, parliament and the university – are all international in scope. It is very tempting to draw the conclusion that whoever wants to ensure long-term survival must be international.

Being international in the sense of transborder is not enough, however. Open borders are to little avail if minds are closed. Neither the borders of a country nor the borders of the mind are conducive to intellectual development, nor to political, social or economic development. Rather, progress in research and teaching requires open minds, a spirit of enquiry, readiness to co-operate across borders and a willingness to learn by exploring the unknown.

There is a popular stereotype of universities as ivory towers, but like so many stereotypes, it is a false one. Had it been true, universities would not have survived for centuries. To paraphrase John Donne: no university is an island unto itself. What higher education does today has a direct impact on our societies, both today and tomorrow. If not, higher education would be failing to do an important part of its job.

In training future teachers and other professionals in a whole range of academic disciplines as well as in forming public opinion, the attitudes and values conveyed through higher education will be transmitted in very varied contexts and in all walks of life. Through their research, universities open minds and identify possible solutions to the challenges we face as societies. Who, today, can seriously maintain that learning how to live together as equals in dignity in a culturally diverse world is not one of the main challenges we face?

In training our youth as well as in training those who will in their turn train the youth of tomorrow, education will decide the future of our societies. If our schools look inward, our societies will too. If our schools are open to the world, our societies have a good chance of coming to value more highly the diversity that is a reality of our existence across oceans and time zones. Education is not only about learning "facts and skills"; it is at least as much about conveying the attitudes and abilities to put their knowledge and understanding into practice in a responsible way.

Higher education must be founded on a firm and well-reflected set of values as well as on a willingness to consider the values of others and to reassess one's own convictions in the light of new and convincing evidence. Dialogue presupposes openness of mind in all partners, including the capacity to look at their own values and frame of reference with critical distance.

Dialogue, though, does not mean that all views are equally valid. Some values are non-negotiable, and many of them are found in the European Convention on Human Rights. As higher educationalists, we are used to submitting arguments to the test of evidence. Intercultural dialogue faces some of the same dilemmas as our democracies: what are the rights of those who seek to avail themselves of the liberties of democracy and dialogue to destroy the very foundation on which these values are built? Not all views and values are of equal worth, and there are views that are unacceptable in modern democratic societies, notably those that deny the human dignity of others. However, while there are unacceptable views and positions, this is no excuse for not trying to understand how and why those views and positions were developed. Seeking to understand the world is not the same as saying "everything goes". Trying to understand why and how the Holocaust happened in no way reduces or denies its character as a crime against humanity.

The role of higher education in promoting intercultural dialogue therefore extends well beyond the number of staff and students engaged in higher education at any one time. It extends to all those who graduate from universities to work in the broader society of which higher education is an essential part. It extends to all those who will learn from and work with university graduates.

What will the attitude of future leaders be, all the more so as in highly complex modern societies, most leaders will have taken at least some higher education? Will the attitude of political, societal and business leaders be one of seeking short-term gain at any price, or will it be one of seeking sustainable well-being on a basis of ethical reflection and social conscience as well as high technical competence?

Will future leaders, in short, aspire to be educated leaders in the modern world? Educated persons of today must understand their own history and cultural background but must also know and understand the histories and backgrounds of others (Council of Europe 2001, Stradling 2001). Citizens as well as leaders can be neither monolingual nor computer illiterate, and they must be able to understand subtle cultural signals as well as they are able to read a balance sheet. Not least, they must be able to transcend the categories of "us" and "them".

European higher education is based on the conviction that each human being has intrinsic value as an individual and also that each human being is inherently responsible for the development and well-being of other human beings, of human society as a whole and of the environment on which we depend for our survival.

To be consistent with its own values and heritage, higher education must commit to the Council of Europe's key values: human rights, democracy and the rule of law. This must be a commitment not only in words but in deeds. In this context, one of the main contributions of higher education – as well as of other areas of education – is helping develop, maintain and transmit to new generations the democratic culture which is indispensable to making democratic institutions and democratic laws work and to make democratic societies sustainable. Democracy and intercultural dialogue are not one and the same, but many of the values and attitudes that make democracy function in practice are also required for intercultural dialogue.

Higher education is committed to dialogue with those whose convictions differ from our own, as a means of improved understanding and of resolving conflicts by peaceful means. These fundamental values underlie the international co-operation – throughout Europe as well as with other parts of the world – that is part and parcel of the heritage of higher education. They underlie the European Higher Education Area as well as the relationship and co-operation between the European Higher Education Area and other regions. They must, I believe, also underlie the business culture of tomorrow. Business cannot thrive if it is locked in by narrow borders, but it also cannot thrive if it is locked in by narrow minds.

The European Higher Education Area[27] is, in my view, one of the most important efforts at European integration apart from the setting up and development of the European Union and the Council of Europe. The Council of Europe is an important contributor to the European Higher Education Area, which has, in its first decade, in particular focused on structural reform: the three-tier system of qualifications (often referred to as "bachelor – master – doctorate"), qualifications frameworks, quality assurance and recognition. As we move beyond 2010, when the Bologna Process became the European Higher Education Area, two of the main challenges will be, on the one hand, to implement these structural reforms throughout European higher education and, on the other hand, to link the structural reform of European higher education to a broader consideration of the purposes of higher education as well as of the roles of its different actors. In particular, there is need for sustained reflection on the public responsibility for higher education and research (Bergan 2005, Council of Europe 2007). A third challenge will be to see how the European Higher Education Area interlinks and co-operates with the rest of the world.

Higher education plays a key role in ensuring this richness of diversity at a time when many developments pull towards greater harmonisation rather than greater

---

27. www.ond.vlaanderen.be/hogeronderwijs/bologna as well as www.coe.int/t/dg4/highereducation/ EHEA2010/Default_en.asp.

appreciation of diversity. Is it not a paradox that we value a diversity in the choice of the products we want to buy, but seem much less appreciative of the diversity of backgrounds in the people with whom we interact? If research-based knowledge and understanding of diversity is lost and is no longer transmitted, cultural diversity will ultimately be lost.

That brings us back to the need to address all major purposes of higher education, and it takes us to the question of why we have higher education in the first place. I referred to Ibsen. I will end by drawing on a different part of my own background and go to the shores of the Pacific rather than those of the North Atlantic. One of my favourite quotes on education comes from the Chilean sociologist Eugenio Tironi, who says that the answer to the question: "what kind of education do we need?" is to be found in the answer to another question: "what kind of society do we want?" (Tironi 2005).

Whether we are in business studies or in political science, whether we are in physics or in linguistics, whether we are in law or history, as members of the academic community of students and scholars we have a duty not only to observe that society from a distance but to engage in developing it.

References

Bergan S. (2005), "Higher education as a 'public good and a public responsibility' – What does it mean?", in Weber L. and Bergan S. (eds), *The Public Responsibility for Higher Education and Research*, Council of Europe Higher Education Series No. 2, Council of Europe Publishing, Strasbourg.

Council of Europe (2001), Recommendation Rec(2001)15 of the Committee of Ministers to member states on history teaching in twenty-first-century Europe.

Council of Europe (2007), Recommendation CM/Rec(2007)6 of the Committee of Ministers to member states on the public responsibility for higher education and research.

Council of Europe (2008), "White Paper on Intercultural Dialogue – 'Living Together as Equals in Dignity'".

Sanz N. and Bergan, S. (eds) (2007), *The Cultural Heritage of European Universities*, second edition, Council of Europe Higher Education Series No. 6, Council of Europe Publishing, Strasbourg.

Stradling R. (2001), *Teaching 20th-Century European History*, Council of Europe Publishing, Strasbourg.

Tironi E. (2005), *El sueño chileno: comunidad, familia y nación en el Bicentenario* [The Chilean Dream: Community, Family and Nation at the Bicentenary], Taurus, Santiago de Chile.

The European Higher Education Area: challenges for the next decade[28]

A reminder at New Year

The final days of 2007 saw two highly disturbing developments. In Pakistan, the main leader of the opposition, Benazir Bhutto, was assassinated in a suicide attack that also killed many bystanders, which led to further violence in reaction to the killing and which cast further doubt on the immediate prospects of elections as well as the longer term developments of the country. In Kenya, a hotly contested presidential election gave rise to accusations of electoral fraud and violence that within a few days left more than 300 people dead – some of them killed inside a church where they had sought sanctuary – tens of thousands homeless and the future of the country in doubt as both voting patterns and the violence seemed to follow ethnic lines. In Pakistan, as well as in Kenya, civic dialogue suffered a dramatic breakdown.

The disturbing developments in Pakistan and Kenya were accompanied by two events that gave rise to great hope. On 1 January, Slovenia took over the European Union presidency from Portugal. The rotation of EU presidencies on a 6-month basis has become so commonplace that we may easily lose sight of the importance of this particular rotation. Slovenia was the first of the 10 countries that joined the EU in 2004 to hold the rotating presidency, and it was hence the first country from central and eastern Europe to do so. Slovenia was, however, not the first country with a relatively recent non-democratic past to hold the presidency. Portugal, which has by now been a member of the EU for two decades and of the Council of Europe for three, is itself an example of a highly successful democratic transition. The handover of the EU presidency from Portugal to Slovenia represented far more than changing the "chair of the board": it symbolised the democratic transformation of Europe that has taken place within the lifetime of many of its citizens.

The second event that gave rise to hope took place in Oslo on 10 December 2007, even if the basis for it was laid well before. On that day, former US Vice President Al Gore and the International Panel on Climate Change jointly received the Nobel Peace Prize, whose recipients are selected by a committee appointed by the Norwegian Parliament which includes representatives of the major political parties in the country. In one way, the Nobel Peace Prize is an indication of trouble: there would be no prize for those who seek to raise consciousness of climate change if climate change were not a serious challenge in the first place. At the same time,

28. This article was written in early 2008 as an invited contribution for a publication on the European Higher Education Area beyond 2010. However, the publication could in the end not be issued as planned and this is the first publication of the article. The author is grateful to Stephen Adam, Kathia Serrano-Velarde, Athanassia Spyropoulou and Pavel Zgaga for comments to a draft of this article.

however, the 2007 Nobel Peace Prize illustrates that concern for climate change has now become a mainstream concern that may come to impact on the political agenda worldwide, as it already does in a number of countries.

Higher education – For what?

At first glance, all four events may seem to be at a safe distance from the concerns of the European Higher Education Area. However, first glances are often superficial. All four events, in fact, point directly to one of the crucial debates that European higher education as well as European society at large will need to face in the next phase of the European Higher Education Area: that of the purposes of higher education and its link to the society of which it is a part.

This relationship is already a part of public debate and it was present in the Bologna Process from the very beginning. However, the public debate on education and higher education is highly focused on the economic importance of higher education. This was also reflected in the earliest phase of the Bologna Process, with its emphasis on the international competitiveness of the European higher education system. While this term does not need to have a purely economic connotation, this was how it was widely read and, most likely, also intended.

If we look at the four cases, however, they illustrate the fact that there is more to society than its economic well-being, and that economic well-being depends on far more than a classic analysis with costs and benefits expressed neatly in euros and cents. While it may be argued that Pakistan has over the past couple of decades been fairly far removed from a model of economic success (Cohen 2004), Kenya as well as Portugal and Slovenia have all been considered economic success stories. Yet, Kenya, which was widely considered as a model for Africa, seemed on the verge of disaster as we entered 2008,[29] whereas Portugal and Slovenia seemed to justify their good reputation even if recession seemed to lurk around the corner not only in these two countries, but across the world. Little more than half a year later, of course, the world found itself in a financial crisis. In public debate, environmental concerns have often been dismissed as being at odds with the need for economic growth and sometimes even as a luxury for richer countries. Yet, the 2007 Nobel Peace Prize signals that reality is more complex than public debate sometimes leads us to believe.

That is also one of my main points about education policies. My point is emphatically not that economic performance is unimportant, that education is not a key factor in economic success, or that economic well-being is a luxury for the rich and an obsession of the poor. Denying the importance of economic performance is as unwise as treating the economy as the only game in town. Denying the importance of education to developing and maintaining economic performance is every bit

---

29. On the effects on the Kenyan tourist industry, see for example the *International Herald Tribune* of 29 February 2008: www.iht.com/articles/2008/02/29/africa/kenya.php.

as blind eyed as treating preparation for the labour market as the only purpose of education. To paraphrase a famous slogan, it may well be the economy, stupid, but it is not just the economy.[30]

Kenya at the beginning of 2008 and the issue of climate change illustrate the broader point that economic performance alone does not guarantee a healthy society (Diamond 2006), while Portugal and Slovenia both illustrate the benefits of a strong civic culture. An important part of my argument here is that good education policies based on a broad view of the purposes of education – in our context, specifically of higher education – are vital to the success of our societies. To stay with the terminology of the European Higher Education Area, as it has developed since 1999, education is vital to making our societies not only competitive but attractive in a broader sense – as well as able to survive.

Towards a balanced view of education

Education, then, is about the economy as well as about society and the individual. The Council of Europe has identified four major purposes of higher education:

- preparation for sustainable employment;
- preparation for life as active citizens in democratic societies;
- personal development;
- the development and maintenance, through teaching, learning and research, of a broad, advanced knowledge base (Bergan 2005, Council of Europe 2007).

These four purposes should not be seen as mutually exclusive but rather as complementary. As major employers have underlined,[31] qualities needed for democratic citizenship are also of great use in the labour market. Personal development is not a side issue to be left for idle off hours. It is at the heart of education even if public debate tends to treat it with deafening silence, perhaps because personal development is not seen as tangible and immediately useful. It is, however, as fundamental to the labour market competences of an individual as basic mathematics is to bookkeeping or the running of computer programmes.

The discussion of skills and competences is key in this respect. One key aspect of the development of the European Higher Education Area is the emphasis on learning outcomes – what an individual knows, understands and is able to do on the basis of a qualification – rather than on the formal process that leads to the qualification (Bergan 2007). While the discussion of qualifications is rich in technical elements, it is the policy thrust of this debate that is of interest to us here.

---

30. A slogan posted in Bill Clinton's headquarters in 1992 reminded the campaign staff that "It's the economy, stupid".
31. See for example the conference report from the Bologna Seminar on Qualifications Structures in Higher Education, København, 27-28 March 2003: www.bologna-bergen2005.no/EN/Bol_sem/Old/030327-28Copenhagen/030327-28Report_General_Rapporteur.pdf.

Competences for and of the future

Mention of qualifications tends to bring forth images of what in technical language is called subject-specific competences: what a chemist knows about chemistry on the basis of a first degree or what a second-degree holder in history knows about history. However, there is a second component of qualifications: the transversal or generic competences (González and Wagenaar 2005). These are competences that all holders of a higher education degree at a given level (for example, a first degree or a doctorate) may be expected to have. Generic competences cover a broad field, but typical examples include analytical skills, communication skills and the ability to reason at a level of abstraction. Generic competences also have to do with developing attitudes. As paradoxical as it may sound, the ability to question received truths and to doubt requires a certain level of sophistication as well as self-assurance – as does the ability to keep one's doubts within reasonable limits and avoid shattering self-doubt. Hamlet's question of "to be or not to be" is worth asking but it is important to find an answer reasonably quickly so as not to be paralysed by the question.

In the same way, the ability to accept that the views of others may have the same value as the views one holds oneself, as well as to admit that others may be right and we ourselves may be wrong, are crucial generic competences in democratic societies, as is the ability to maintain certain key values that prevent a sound openness of mind from being converted into the kind of relativism that holds no truth to be self-evident.

As with the purposes of higher education, the issue of competences is not a question of either/or: higher education graduates need both subject-specific and generic skills, and so do societies. Those possessing mainly narrowly defined subject-specific competences are sometimes characterised by the savoury German term *Fachidioten*, for which an adequate English term seems to be lacking – the literal translation "subject idiot" does not have quite the same flavour – while a fair share of those who believe one can get by on generic competences alone seem to be making careers as management consultants.

Democratic societies are based on the assumption that their citizens possess a high degree of generic competences. This should not be read as saying that subject-specific competences are unimportant: the ability to avoid looking at the world through Manichean lenses marked "either/or" is one of the important generic competences required in democratic societies. Democratic societies rely on a combination of subject-specific and generic competences, and they are based on the principle that the major decisions of our societies are made by applying the generic competences of all its adult citizens, which all carry equal weight. This is the deeper foundation of the democratic principle "one person, one vote", in which democratic societies differ from the recommendation of John Stuart Mill that the number of votes citizens may cast be linked to their educational qualifications[32] or indeed the more classical

---

32. I am indebted to Stephen Adam for the reference to Mills.

notion that voters needed a minimum threshold of wealth. Whether a dam should be constructed in River A to increase the supply of electricity, or whether it is more important to conserve the natural environment of that river is a decision made on the basis of the generic competence of citizens – in their role as voters in a specific referendum on the issue or as voters in a general election. If the decision is made to build the dam, the specificities of the construction are left to specialists, but issues may arise in the course of construction that may need to be decided on the basis of the generic competences of citizens. Whether a country should join the European Union is a decision to be made on the basis of generic competences, whereas the details of the long and technical negotiations that will follow a positive decision of principle is a matter for highly trained specialists. The end results of the negotiations may nevertheless be the subject of a second decision made on the basis of generic competences.

Genuinely democratic societies, then, require committed and preferably relatively sophisticated citizens. This is an issue not only of competence in the narrower sense of the term but also of commitment to and identification of individual citizens with society. Social cohesion is only possible where citizens feel they have a stake in society, and where they can be reasonably confident they have a chance to be heard. Disenchantment with the political process, widespread voter apathy and citizens focusing on their own private spheres are in the long run as grave threats to democratic societies as organised groups actively trying to undermine democracy.

Therefore, democratic societies require citizens that have not only received highly specialised training but also a solid education, in the true sense of the word – one that develops character and generic competences in addition to subject-specific skills and that also develops attitudes. Democracy does not work well in societies where a high proportion of citizens suffer from severe educational deficiencies, but it also does not work well in societies where citizens are unable to see beyond their immediate concerns, their narrow personal interests and their own occupational specialisation.

It is a truism that modern societies become ever more complex technically and socially, and this represents a formidable challenge for our education systems. As citizens, we all need good knowledge and understanding of natural sciences as well as of history; of foreign languages as well as of ethics. The perhaps most important challenge our societies face – climate change – requires competences in all of these domains as well as in many others. Today, people without education qualifications beyond those of compulsory education – and perhaps with poor results, namely insufficient learning outcomes at this level, to boot – face severe problems in their professional lives as well as in their lives as citizens and as individuals. Whereas a couple of generations ago, people with only basic education qualifications could still find meaningful and reasonably well-considered occupations and roles in society, today this is exceedingly difficult. For our societies, the challenge is one of social cohesion and individual justice as well as one of using the resources of our societies in the best possible way.

Higher education in Europe faces a double challenge in this respect. On the one hand, since individuals need to master an ever greater and more complex body of knowledge, understanding and abilities to thrive in contemporary society, this would indicate that most individuals need to spend a longer time in education programmes. This is indeed what has happened over the past few decades. The number of students in higher education has increased dramatically, and most European countries have moved from elite to mass higher education within the past four or five decades, some countries even later (Nyborg 2007: 5-40). Instead of leaving school after primary and secondary education, namely after seven to 12 years of schooling, in most countries an increasing proportion of learners stay in education for at least 15 years, often longer.

Longer studies for a better education?

Among those who do not enter higher education, more learners seem to be taking some kind of specialised vocational education at secondary level or beyond, as an alternative to leaving school after primary education or even after general secondary education. This also implies that many of those who a generation ago would have left school with a bare minimum of general competences now stay on for some kind of specialised education and hence remain in school for at least one additional year, often longer. Secondly, many of those who do enter higher education obtain more than a first degree. Therefore, not only do more learners enter higher education, a considerable number of learners also remain in higher education beyond the first "exit opportunity". Thirdly, more learners alternate between education and work and come back to education to obtain further qualifications under lifelong learning arrangements, even if it must be admitted that the higher education sector has, with some honourable exceptions, hardly been a model of good practice in this respect.

This means that the time the average person spends in education programmes is already quite long. At the same time, our societies are ageing, so that those of working age constitute a smaller proportion of the overall population, and they have to support a higher proportion of citizens at the two extremes of life: those who are not yet of working age, and those who are beyond working age. Therefore, there are good reasons to doubt whether the average time of study can reasonably be extended further, at least as a general measure for those in classical, "first time" education. There is concern not only about the qualifications needed in modern society but also about what learners do with these qualifications once they have been obtained, since retirement age in most countries seems to have been reduced rather than increased.

In other words, increased time spent in education programmes tends to have as a direct corollary that the active working lives, at least of many people, are shorter. This leads to a concern about the balance between the working and the non-working population (here defined as those earning a salary or self-employed; this should not be taken to imply that students, those working at home and others who may work hard without earning a salary do not "work") as well as concern about the longer term viability of our social security systems. These concerns are reinforced by demographic trends: on average, we enjoy longer lives and hence longer retire-ments and more of us live to an age where, again on average, our need for medical care increases significantly. In many countries, birth rates are also insufficient to maintain, much less increase, the population. Many governments have now launched discussions about increasing retirement age and ending or at least modifying arrangements under which those in certain occupations may retire at an earlier age. The issue of immigration, which is currently highly contentious in most European countries, may come to be reconsidered in the light of demographic developments.

These are important issues for our societies but in our context here, the most important implication may be that it is difficult to imagine that the need for learners to master an increased body of knowledge may be met by a further increase in the average time our citizens devote to initial formal education programmes. This has already appeared as a concern in the European Higher Education Area, not least in the insistence by ministers that the first degree should be of value to the labour market as well as for further study (Bologna Process 2001). Those with a well-developed sense of history may object that long studies followed by a relatively brief professional life is nothing new. In 13th-century France, a doctorate in theology was rarely obtained before the age of 35, and doctoral candidates in medicine and law were seldom less than 28 years old (Rouche 2003: 378-383). First and second degrees also required longer studies than today. However, those with higher education degrees constituted a minimal proportion of the total labour force, so the impact of long studies on the overall economy cannot be compared with today's situation, where our societies to a large extent depend on those with advanced qualifications.

Liberal education

This is linked to another important challenge, which is the changing nature of knowledge, understanding and ability to do (the classical definition of learning outcomes) that citizens will need to have. Here, we return to the need for a proper balance between subject-specific and generic competences. While the exact balance may vary over time and between societies as well as between occupations, all will need a reasonable balance between the two. This, in a word, raises the question of whether European higher education should look to the US model of liberal education for inspiration (AAC&U 2007).

Liberal education is hardly an easy model to sell in Europe, where the tradition of most countries is that a diversity of subjects is covered in primary and secondary education, whereas higher education is for specialisation in a limited number of disciplines, sometimes in only one, such as in the classical professional studies like law or medicine. The traditional European response to the US liberal education model is that the standards of US secondary education are such that American students need two years of college to catch up with what European students learn in secondary education. There is no denying the problematic aspects of US secondary education. Many US high schools are indeed of questionable quality, but there is also no denying that many are of good quality. Like US higher education, US secondary education shows great variety and includes very high as well as very low quality programmes and institutions. At the same time, we should not forget that not all European secondary schools and programmes are of excellent quality. There may be a problem with US secondary education, but that is not to say there is no problem with its European counterpart.

The argument is not that the US liberal education model should be copied blindly in European higher education but rather that it is worth considering whether there are not important elements of the liberal education model that are worth examining. In fact, some such developments have taken place already. The credit system opens opportunities for including elements of subjects that are not directly within the main fields of concentration in a degree, for example, by allowing engineering students to include a number of credits in a foreign language or students of history to include statistics or economics in their qualifications. The credit system is also a tool to promote more student-centred learning, since it offers learners more choice and flexibility, including better possibilities to take courses across the boundaries of academic disciplines.

Europe therefore faces a formidable challenge over the coming years: to fundamentally change our thinking about education and higher education to develop a holistic view of the roles, functions and justification of higher education in our societies. Our collective challenge is nothing less than to broaden our minds, which is a traditional challenge of education but also a very demanding one. There will certainly be those who will continue to argue in favour of the primacy of the economy. They would do well to reflect on whether the goal set up by the European Union under the Lisbon Strategy – to become the most competitive economy in the world by 2010 – has been reached and whether our approach to education might have something to do with the degree of attainment of that particular goal. Whoever sees a church or a concert hall and can only think of a building contract has undoubtedly missed some essential points along the way.

Beyond parochialism

Parochialism comes in many shapes but essentially entails a limitation of vision and frame of mind. It may be imposed by a particular context or by a lack of broader experience. An important function of education is to extend the limits of our experience and to enable learners to combine different elements of their experience and learning into a coherent whole. In the first decade of the 21st century, education can no longer be only local or only national.[33] Higher education must be imbued with a spirit of multiperspectivity, a concept developed by the Council of Europe in the context of history teaching (Council of Europe 2001, Stradling 2001), which means that issues are not looked at merely from one's own perspective but also from the perspective of one's neighbours and of those further afield. Higher education must, in the spirit of liberal education, open the minds of learners, and two distinct but linked elements seem particularly important to do so.

---

33. Even if some European countries still have ministries of *national* education (emphasis added).

Firstly, European students must be proficient in foreign languages – and the plural is intentional. English is an instrument of international communication in a way the world has hardly seen before. Comparison with the position of Latin in the classical and medieval world is illustrating but also halting. Latin was an unusual medium of international communication but it was also limited to an educated elite as well as to a smaller geographical area in which communication was far more difficult than in today's "globalised world". English is spoken much more widely as a foreign language than Latin ever was, in terms of both the number of speakers, their social and educational background and the geographical area covered.

Yet, fluency in English is not universal and English, like all languages, carries values and ways of thinking. Whoever speaks only his or her mother tongue is limited to his or her mother's world. Foreign language proficiency is essential to understanding other cultures, and while nobody can speak all foreign languages, most higher education graduates should have the capacity to be acquainted with two or three. Fluency in English is vital but it cannot replace knowledge of the language(s) spoken in a country in which one is interested. It is essential for a country that its citizens have good knowledge not only of the main language of international communication – English – but also of a wide variety of other languages. For Europe, it is essential that our citizens have good knowledge not only of each others' languages but also of languages spoken outside of Europe. Stimulating foreign language learning must therefore be a vital goal of education and higher education in Europe and we must fully use the possibilities of the credit system to encourage those specialising in other fields to improve their language learning. A knowledge of more than one foreign language must come to be seen as an essential generic competence.

Secondly, horizons cannot be broadened by staying put. Mobility is a key goal of the European Higher Education Area but it is a goal which we still find difficult to reach. Like learning, mobility has a specific and a generic aspect. Spending a period of study abroad will give learners direct experience of another country and another culture, or ideally of several cultures since mobile learners will hopefully meet not only students from the host country but also other foreign students. The experience of another culture should also have a more generic effect in opening learners' minds to the value and opportunity of diversity. It should help make learners more proficient not only in a given foreign language but also in dialogue between people from different cultural backgrounds. Mobility is an essential experience in educating the whole person. This is hardly a new idea: it is the assumption behind the classical European idea of the "Grand Tour" which, however, stems from an age in which education was thought of as a concern only of the elite and the range of cultures considered worthy of study was very limited.

Improving academic mobility within as well as beyond the European Higher Education Area must remain one of the key goals of the EHEA beyond 2010. It is an extraordinarily complex goal because it involves a whole set of technical and political measures. Learners must be well informed about possibilities, they must be well received by hosting institutions, and they must receive fair recognition of their qualifications. Many learners are not classical students without family or work obligations and they may not be able to participate in traditional student mobility programmes that require students to be aboard for a semester or a year. Mobility is expensive and even if considerable financial aid is available, it is insufficient and it is unevenly distributed.

Academic mobility faces particular challenges at a time when many governments seek to limit migration and make no exceptions for academic mobility. In spite of attempts by some members and consultative members of the Bologna Process to put the issues of immigration rules, work permits and social security on the table, the European Higher Education Area has so far largely skirted around the issue,[34] since these measures do not depend on the public authorities responsible for higher education. However, they depend on the governments of which ministers for education are members and the ambitious goals for academic mobility cannot be reached unless governments make the link between higher education policies and other areas of public policy.

Actors and responsibilities

Fundamental changes normally do not happen by themselves – they are driven by actors. Incidentally, the *status quo* is also not maintained all by itself, but by actors who are unable or unwilling to change. A multiplicity of actors is one of the characteristics of modern societies and indeed one of the hallmarks of democracy. In complex societies, no person or institution can lay claim to all the insights required to make the decisions needed to make society work, nor can a narrow set of actors make such decisions and be seen as legitimate. Decisions need to be made, but they also need to be accepted. A fast decision is not always the best decision since it may be perceived as illegitimate and hence be resisted. This is not to say that decision making should not be efficient, but simply to say that legitimacy must be counted among the criteria for efficiency. Decisions need to be legitimate and to be made in reasonable time – just one of the two will not suffice.

The complexity of actors is found at all levels and in all areas. In political science, even governments – which have traditionally been perceived as unitary actors – are increasingly seen as complex coalitions of forces with different interests, and not only those that arise from different ideologies or world views. Even within a government where all ministers come from the same party, the minister for education does not necessarily have the same interests as the minister for foreign trade, who again may not agree with the minister for agriculture or of the interior.

Within higher education, with ministries, autonomous institutions, articulate students and staff and a wide range of agencies and organisations, the number of real and potential actors is very high. So far, the vast majority of them has supported the

---

34. The issue is mentioned in the Bergen and London communiqués (Bologna Process 2005 and 2007a) but in relatively weak terms.

Bologna Process and worked hard to establish the European Higher Education Area. It will be important to keep alive the energy mobilised. That can only be done if the members of the academic community, the institutions and other actors are convinced they have real influence on policies and that higher education is seen as a significant and respected actor in broader society. This brings us to the role of public authorities, not because public authorities are the most significant actors but because they may well have the most complex role.

The key role of public authorities was made explicit by ministers in Prague and Berlin (Bologna Process 2001 and 2003), when they twice stated that higher education is a "public good and a public responsibility". The operational part of that statement is the part about public responsibility, and the fact that it was repeated at two ministerial meetings can either be seen as ministers stating the obvious or expressing a concern that what had been a key characteristic of European higher education could not be taken for granted in the future.

In my view, ministers were not stating the obvious. However, the main reason for concern about the statements is not that ministers expressed a strong concern but rather that they said so little about how their concern may be met. What do we need to do if public responsibility is to remain a key feature of European higher education? We cannot shy away from this issue in the development of the European Higher Education Area beyond 2010.

To defend and develop the principle of public responsibility for higher education, we need to look more closely at what this principle means in modern, complex societies. The Council of Europe did so in 2004 and 2005 through a project on the public responsibility for higher education and research, the highlights of which were a conference in September 2005 followed by a publication and a policy recommendation (Weber and Bergan 2005, Council of Europe 2007). We need to develop a more nuanced view of the public responsibility for different aspects of higher education policy. The political recommendation adopted by the Council's Committee of Ministers as a result of the project suggests that the responsibility of public authorities for higher education and research should be nuanced and defined relative to specific areas. The text broadly recommends that public authorities have:

–   exclusive responsibility for the framework within which higher education and research is conducted;

–   leading responsibility for ensuring effective equal opportunities to higher education for all citizens, as well as ensuring that basic research remains a public good;

–   substantial responsibility for financing higher education and research, the provision of higher education and research, as well as for stimulating and facilitating financing and provision by other sources within the framework developed by public authorities.

This recommendation is a good basis on which to build. It points clearly to different roles public authorities can play as well as to the fact that public authorities may have an important role in some areas without claiming a monopoly. In other areas, the role of public authorities cannot be shared with other actors. For example, public authorities lay down the framework within which higher education is provided. This includes legislation, establishing the qualifications framework of a given education system or ensuring that there is provision for quality assurance. The latter point is particularly illustrative because while it is the responsibility of public authorities to lay down the framework for quality assurance, public authorities should not be the executive agency. Quality assurance should be carried out under a mandate from the competent public authorities – who may revoke the mandate – but the ministry or other competent public authority should not double as a quality assurance agency.

The implications are important also for funding. Public authorities have an important responsibility for funding a country's higher education system. However, few higher education institutions can fulfil their ambitions through public funding alone. Therefore, the responsibility of public authorities is not limited to providing direct funding. It includes laying down the rules under which alternative funding may be sought and provided.[35] To put it simply, private funding of higher education must be provided under rules established by public authorities and, at the same time, public authorities should not use the existence of private funding as an excuse to cut direct public funding of higher education.

These are important examples, but examples all the same. The Council of Europe recommendation is a good start but not the final word. In developing the European Higher Education Area beyond 2010 we must give closer consideration to the proper role of public authorities. The European Higher Education Area is in fact an excellent context for this reflection, as it provides a framework within which there should be agreement on overarching principles but also an awareness of the need to take account of local circumstances and traditions in applying these principles. This issue also shows the strong connection between higher education and the broader society, as I am convinced that defining the role of public authorities in general will be one of Europe's main political challenges in the years ahead, when we will need to navigate between the Scylla of stifling over-regulation and the Charybdis of laissez-faire.

Autonomy and governance

Discussing the role of public authorities leads to a consideration of the role of higher education institutions, which are the main building blocks of the European Higher Education Area. How should institutions and systems be governed in the EHEA? Again, there is no question of providing a single model to fit all but rather of raising some issues that concern all.

The most important issue is the relationship between higher education institutions and the society of which they are a part. University autonomy is a key element of the

---

35. For the experience of a system with an exceptionally high proportion of private higher education institutions – Chile – see Mönckeberg (2005).

foundation on which the European Higher Education Area is built,[36] and universities have traditionally enjoyed internal self-government under which, in most countries, the rector is elected among professors of the university and the governing body is made up entirely or overwhelmingly by representatives elected by and among faculty, students and technical and administrative staff.

Autonomy has traditionally been understood as the independence of universities from public state authorities (for which the most common term has been "the state") as enshrined by law. Yet, a university can perfectly well enjoy legal autonomy without enjoying de facto autonomy. It may even be worth asking whether the traditional model of university funding in Europe, with an overwhelming proportion of university budgets being provided through annual budgets voted by political authorities, is necessarily conducive to autonomy. Even if public authorities have generally not given detailed instructions about how universities are to be run, funding by a single source does potentially give the funder a significant role in setting the priorities of those who receive the funding. If public authorities provide earmarked funding for study programmes in petroleum engineering and information technology, few universities will refrain from competing for these funds and instead spend funds of their own on strengthening study programmes in dentistry or constitutional law. Reliance on a single funder, whether public or private, does not reduce dependence, yet in the European context it is difficult to envisage an alternative to very substantial public funding of higher education and research.

It is of course entirely legitimate for public authorities to have goals for their funding of higher education. It would even be verging on the irresponsible for them not to have such goals. It is legitimate for public authorities to consider some academic disciplines as particularly important to achieving these goals. Apart from the important point that public authorities should be responsible for funding programmes in a wide range of academic disciplines, including those that have little opportunity to obtain funds from other sources,[37] the argument is therefore not that it is wrong for public authorities to provide funding according to their policy priorities, but rather that we need to develop a more nuanced view of autonomy, as we do of public responsibility.

University autonomy is an important foundation of higher education in Europe, and we need to acquire a better understanding of what this means in modern societies

---

36. There are two references to university autonomy in the Bologna Declaration (Bologna Process 1999), and a secretariat document on requirements and procedures for joining the Bologna Process includes university autonomy as one of five underlying principles of the Bologna Process to which new applicants must adhere. Significantly, this document was published in 2004, at a time when several further applications for membership were expected. See www.bologna-bergen2005.no/Docs/01BFUG/040614-B/BFUGB3_7_Accessions.pdf.

37. One interesting example of work done to foster teaching and research in subjects with a low number of students is the initiative of the German Rectors' Conference (HRK) on so-called "small subjects"; see "Im Brennpunkt: kleine Fächer" [In Focus: Small Subjects], www.hrk.de/de/brennpunkte/4013.php, which also provides links to further documentation.

characterised by a multitude of actors. Autonomy is not only a question of the legal relationship of universities to public authorities. It is ultimately about the relationship between universities and other actors – be they public authorities, private or public business companies, political parties, organised interest groups or other actors in society – in a wide variety of dimensions, of which funding is at least as important as legislation. It is also about degrees of independence or dependence. It may be worth recalling that even legal autonomy from public authorities does not exempt universities from abiding by the law of the land. To take just a few examples, universities are bound by public accounting regulations, by safety regulations for laboratories, by labour legislation (which may or may not contain specific provisions on faculty) and by immigration legislation as concerns foreign faculty and students. This is generally not seen as infringing on university autonomy, which implies that we have already accepted that autonomy is not absolute.

Discussions about autonomy tend to focus on "university autonomy" rather than "institutional autonomy". Yet, not all higher education institutions are universities. Should the autonomy be the same for an institution that has at its main purpose to offer professionally oriented first degree programmes as for universities that aim to train future researchers and to carry out research in a wide range of disciplines?

An important argument in favour of autonomy is that higher education institutions must be free to criticise the existing order and to question accepted dogmas (Sanz and Bergan 2007). This is an essential mission of universities, and even from a purely pragmatic point of view, it is difficult to see how universities can train future researchers if they cannot encourage critical thinking. It may be worth considering whether the concerns of institutional autonomy are equally strong for all kinds of higher education institutions or whether the degree of autonomy should be related to the profile and missions of the institutions. The answer may well be that the same degree of autonomy should be enjoyed by all higher education institutions, regardless of their profile, but the case needs to be considered and the argument needs to be made, since the current arguments for autonomy tend to focus on the research aspect: the right and need to develop and transmit new knowledge without fear of being bound by received truths, political considerations or corporate interests.

Ultimately, the main argument in favour of institutional autonomy is, in my view, the need for critical distance. Higher education should be both of the broader society and in the broader society, but higher education also needs to have sufficient distance from the immediate concerns of the broader society to take a longer term and more principled view. In the age of the sound bite, the need for institutions that by definition take the longer view is stronger than ever before. This partly has to do with the relationship between higher education and other major actors in our societies. Higher education cannot allow itself to be directed only by the short-term concerns of other actors, yet it also cannot be blind and deaf to those concerns. In part, it concerns having the time and resources to address the fundamental issues of our existence. This requires that faculty as well as students have the time to think and that demands for productivity be cast as producing substantial contributions to society in the longer and medium term rather than devising quick fixes in time for the next election, the next budget year or the next quarterly report.

Incidentally, the position of public authorities with regard to institutional autonomy is paradoxical: only public authorities can guarantee institutional autonomy, but an important part of that guarantee is to leave institutions free to act on their own. That, at least, is the more classical definition of institutional autonomy. In modern society, it is less straightforward. Public authorities are still the main actors in guaranteeing autonomy, but the guarantee is far from absolute – "guarantee" may not even be the most appropriate term – and other actors also play an important role. The complexity of university autonomy reflects the complexity of modern societies.

Our views on autonomy impact on our views on university governance. The model of academic self-governance alluded to in an earlier paragraph ultimately arises from a view of university autonomy, along with the view that those holding the highest degree of academic competence – full professors – should also have the strongest voice in institutional governance. This is why the traditional European governance model is one of rectors elected by the academic community among the institution's professors and of governing boards composed of members of the academic community, elected by their peers, and represented according to their function in the academic community: a majority of tenured faculty, more students than administrative and technical staff and also representation by non-tenured faculty (Bergan 2004, Persson 2004).

This traditional model is not a model of the past but it is a model challenged by another in which the rector is hired from outside or the governing body includes a significant number of representatives of the broader society, or both. This model emphasises the need to strengthen the link between higher education and broader society, and – where the rector is hired from the outside – also emphasises managerial experience over competence in the primary tasks of higher education: research and teaching. The two models also implicitly express different views on the constituency of the institutional leadership. In the classical European model of the elected rector, the rector's constituency is to be found within the institution, whereas in the newer model of the appointed rectors, the constituency is to be found primarily outside of the institution, even if that broader society is often not clearly defined.

The reasons for including outside representations are easy to see, and few would argue that strengthening the relationship to broader society is harmful. Two arguments need to be considered, however, and they are rarely stated. The first concerns the kind of competence needed to govern. As in the case of the rector contracted from outside, the inclusion of a significant number of external representatives implies that competence in the core business of higher education is downplayed in favour of competence rooted in the broader society, since this model normally implies that faculty no longer has a majority of the representatives in the senate or the board. No group does. The other issue is what parts of the broader society the new members of the governing bodies represent. Without having anything like a complete overview, my impression is that they tend to represent the economy and much less civil society at large. Seen in the context of the discussion of what higher education is about, this is a worrying development. The principle of outside representation is sound, but outside representation should not be reduced to employers and trade unions alone. They have an important role to play but so do other sectors of society. Ultimately, such broad representation may even help garner much needed society support for the roles and importance of higher education.

The priorities of the European Higher Education Area beyond 2010 should comprise a thorough discussion of how higher education should be governed as well as a renewed consideration of institutional autonomy, and this discussion should be linked to the discussion of the roles and purposes of higher education. Not making the link would be tantamount to writing a law without giving thought to why we need it in the first place.

Ethics and transparency: making the EHEA credible

Transparency is an important concept in the Bologna Process, and there is much talk about the need for transparent and easily understandable degree systems. However, transparency is an issue also in another sense of the word. Are all institutions and degrees in all parts of the European Higher Education Area sound, or is there an issue of transparency in the sense of unfair and obtuse procedures tainted by corruption (Heyneman 2009)?

Corruption may be understood as providing a public service in return for private gain. In higher education, the classical example is a professor allowing a student to pass an exam for which the student is unqualified – or in which the student obtains a better grade than warranted by his or her real achievements – against payment. However, corruption can take many forms. The private reward need not be financial – allowing students to pass in exchange for what is inappropriately called "sexual favours" is another form of corruption – and it may take more subtle forms than trading better grades for direct cash payment. For example, in some countries, professors may sell their own textbooks directly to students, and there may be a spoken or unspoken assumption that students who do not buy the books but consult them in the library, or who use textbooks owned by friends, will find it difficult to pass the exam. Nor is corruption limited to exams: access to student housing, to specific courses with limited access or exchange of favours – such as a professor giving a colleague a lenient assessment in the expectation that the favour will be returned at the next crossroad – are other examples. Corruption may be individual, but it may also be institutionalised, formally or – more often – informally. There may be an institutional culture of corruption or, in a broader sense, of academic malpractice (Barblan, Daxner and Ivošević 2007). The issue is serious enough to be addressed with increasing urgency explicitly both by some governments and at international level. Academic malpractice is a more urgent problem in some countries than in others and the issue may take different forms in different countries, but it is found to some degree in most countries. Contrary to popular perceptions, it is not a problem limited to countries of central and eastern Europe (Ivošević 2007), even if it seems particularly urgent in some of them and some governments are taking steps to address the issue.

Corruption and malpractice in education are serious for a number of reasons, not the least of which is that such practices give students the impression that being dishonest is the best way to succeed. The consequences of institutions failing in their mission of educating the whole person and not only transmitting subject-specific knowledge are serious and long term. They may shed new and not entirely welcome light on the relationship between higher education and broader society. A number of cases in recent years, from a falsified cloning experiment in South Korea to a case in Norway in which a medical researcher had falsified data from a public register which had come into existence only after the time at which he claimed to have received the data, have also showed that ethics in research is a serious concern and that some researchers are not above falsifying research results. This is of course an issue that concerns a minority of researchers, but it is an issue nonetheless.

In the shorter term, the most urgent issue is perhaps whether the existence or perception of corruption will threaten the credibility of the European Higher Education Area. Will the inclusion of education systems that are – or that are perceived as being – corrupt, or in which academic malpractice is seen as wide-spread, reflect on the European Higher Education Area as a whole and make it difficult to establish the EHEA as an attractive "brand name" for European higher education (Heyneman, Anderson and Nuraliyeva 2008)? Is there a danger that we may have a European Higher Education Area that is circumferentially enhanced but credibility challenged?

The danger should not be discounted but it is also not inevitable. The question, in fact, has two parts. Firstly, will the European Higher Education Area become a brand name and, secondly, if it does, will it be an attractive one? The first part of the question may in fact be the steeper challenge. The Bologna Process is above all a framework for agreeing on overall policies that are implemented nationally. There is a degree of convergence among national policies, exemplified by the reform of the degree structure and the development of national qualifications frameworks compatible with the overarching framework of qualifications of the European Higher Education Area. Countries are reluctant to transfer authority over their education system, which also testifies to the importance of education. This has not least been visible in the discussions around the Strategy for the Global Dimension of the European Higher Education Area, which was adopted at the ministerial conference in London in May 2007 (Bologna Process 2007b, Zgaga 2007), and in the subsequent discussions on the implementation of the strategy. While many smaller countries feel they have much to gain, in a global context, from being identified as a part of the European Higher Education Area, some of the larger countries with a high number of fee-paying foreign students show little inclination to market themselves as a part of the EHEA and prefer to market their own national higher education brand. The first part of the challenge is therefore to establish the European Higher Education Area as a brand name.

That challenge could, however, meet with less difficulty if there were no issues of corruption and academic malpractice. This is an area in which the dishonest few can destroy the reputation of the honest majority, and where reputations are much more easily destroyed than made. Corruption and malpractice must be dealt with at national, institutional and department level, but action at these levels could be made less difficult if there were European guidelines and not least European recognition that this is an issue that needs to be dealt with, to different degrees and in different ways in each country, perhaps, but in each country all the same. There is no pressure like peer pressure. Corruption and malpractice are not a pleasant issue to raise and some institutions and countries may feel their reputation is at stake. However, their reputation is likely to gain in the long run if they have the ability and the courage to tackle this painful issue, and the credibility of the European Higher Education Area would gain from making this a political issue. The European Higher Education Area beyond 2010 will need to ask whether it has room for higher education systems in which corruption and malpractice are widespread and which may hurt the reputation of the whole EHEA.

Remaining issues and organising the EHEA

Basing a discussion of the future of the European Higher Education Area on the assumption that the goals stipulated for 2010 will all have been reached is optimistic, to say the least. The stocktaking exercises for 2005, 2007 and 2009[38] show that good progress is being made, but they also show that in some policy areas many countries have still to reach the goals, and it shows that some countries need to make significant progress in a good number of policy areas. Hence, as the European Higher Education Area is established in 2010 there are policy areas in which we are unable to claim that the Bologna Process has succeeded fully and there are some countries that, in an honest assessment, can hardly be said to be on the doorstep of the European Higher Education Area as it has been defined through successive ministerial declarations and communiqués. The challenging question for 2010, of course, is how to deal with this.

One option would have been for ministers to close their eyes and declare the Bologna Process a complete success, on the basis of which they could have declared the European Higher Education Area a reality, let the past be the past and set further goals for the future. A more credible option was for ministers to declare the Bologna Process a success but at the same time to recognise that in some areas more work needs to be done. Luckily, this was the option chosen (Bologna Process 2010) and this does not mean the European Higher Education Area was not credibly launched at the Budapest-Vienna ministerial conference in March 2010. On the contrary, even if some problems remained, the success of the Bologna Process is real and it fully warrants establishing the EHEA. Ministers and all others involved in the Bologna Process can still look to the future with confidence and they can still define goals

---

38. All available through the main website for the European Higher Education Area: http://www.ehea.info

for the next five or ten years. The point is that they can do so with greater credibility since they also acknowledge the unfinished business that will need to be a part of the agenda beyond 2010.

The fact that there are policy areas where significant progress still needs to be made is not necessarily problematic because these issues will concern most members of the Bologna Process and they do not change the fact that the Bologna Process has been successful. Acknowledging that some work remains on the 2010 goals enhances rather than reduces the credibility of the process and it shows that the stocktaking exercise as well as the independent assessment of the Bologna Process (Westerheijden et al. 2010) are taken seriously. One area of concern is the development of national qualifications frameworks, where ministers in 2009 recognised that the original deadline was unrealistic and set a new one (Bologna Process 2009). This is an area that became a part of the Bologna Process relatively late, through the Bergen Communiqué in 2005 (Bologna Process 2005). It is also important that the national frameworks be developed well rather than that they be developed fast. For the credibility of the Bologna Process, it is more important to have credible national frameworks within the next five years or so than to have formal frameworks within the next two years if these do not work in practice, even if the ideal situation would of course have been to have fully functional frameworks very soon. Also, qualifications frameworks are not an isolated reform: they are a part of the overall emphasis on qualifications, where all countries have already introduced a three-tier structure.

The politically more difficult question is what to do if some countries will remain far from reaching the goals of the European Higher Education Area in a number of policy areas. On the one hand, it is not easy for ministers to tell one, two, five or ten of their colleagues that they cannot remain in the European Higher Education Area unless they put their house in order and this has so far not been done. On the other hand, it will not strengthen the credibility of the European Higher Education Area if its own stocktaking exercise – in which the ministers' representatives in the BFUG have approved the methodology and to some extent the questions asked – were to have no consequences for those who come up short and if progress were not to be assessed after the formal launch of the EHEA in 2010.

These consequences do not have to be the exclusion of the countries concerned. On the contrary, the Bologna Process is built not only on the principle of national implementation of policies agreed at European level, but also on that of mutual support and assistance. Our first impulse should not be to exclude countries – and thereby cut them off from support – but rather to see how the European Higher Education Area can most effectively assist those of its members who experience difficulties in specific areas. This, of course, also presupposes that the countries concerned recognise their difficulties and the need for assistance.

Also in this respect, the ministers set the tone by the approach they take to the achievements of the Bologna Process overall. Saying that the Bologna Process has been a success even if some work remains to be done sent a very different signal from the one ministers would have sent had they said that we have achieved all goals. It may well be wise, when considering the EHEA, to foresee the possibility that a country may be suspended or excluded or may withdraw from the European Higher Education Area, but these safety valves should be used only in extreme cases, where a country manifestly violates the basic principles and values of the EHEA (for example, through massive violations of institutional autonomy and academic freedom or pervasive occurrence of academic malpractice), makes no attempt to implement the policies commonly agreed on or does not even recognise that a serious problem exists.

The EHEA beyond 2010

One of the reasons the Bologna Process was successful is that it managed to define a limited number of important goals for European higher education which could be achieved within roughly a decade. This article is an attempt to look at some of the elements that are likely to determine the further development of higher education in Europe and to put the European Higher Education Area into a proper context. This is a much needed exercise but it should end with a limited number of goals for the next decade. These may not be as concrete and as easily verifiable as the structural reform that has been a hallmark of the Bologna Process but they should give clear guidance to the European Higher Education Area as it grows from puberty to maturity.

It is on this background that I end by putting forward some points for the European Higher Education Area 2010-20:

1. **Wrap up unfinished business**. When formally establishing the European Higher Education Area, ministers should be explicit about the success of the Bologna Process but also be frank about areas in which the original goals have not been met and either stipulate how the goals will be met and by when or otherwise explain why it is no longer important to reach the goals.

2. **Support those who need assistance in reaching the goals, but also be clear about the consequences of continued non-compliance**. The EHEA is, among other things, a mutual assistance community, and there is no shame in making use of the experience and expertise of one's peers in order to overcome one's own difficulties. The main purpose of the European Higher Education Area is to advance and not to exclude. Nevertheless, it should also be made clear that the EHEA is not a club and that if there is to be a way, there must be a will.

3. **Spell out the non-negotiable values of the European Higher Education Area**. The Bologna Declaration and the subsequent communiqués refer to the fundamental importance of university autonomy, academic freedom and student participation, but 2010 will be a golden opportunity to adopt something like a basic charter of the European Higher Education Area and to make it clear that the EHEA only has meaning as a fundamental part of a democratic Europe. This should include a commitment to avoid making students and educational staff the victims of conflicts between governments.

4. **Make the European Higher Education Area be about the kind of societies in which we want to live**. The link to point 3 is obvious, but this point is wider. Ministers should make explicit that higher education is an important part of modern societies because higher education helps make our societies European. Our societies cannot exist without a sound economic basis, but Europe does not live from the economy alone. Ministers should be explicit that the European Higher Education Area will play a key role in fulfilling all major purposes of higher education. This is what justifies continued substantial public investment in higher education, and this is what makes the promise of further investment credible. The often difficult discussions of the social dimension of higher education should be a part of these considerations.

5. **Acknowledge the link between higher education and other areas of public policy.** The European Higher Education Area cannot be built in a vacuum, and many of its key goals do not depend exclusively on the public authorities responsible for higher education.

6. **Develop coherent policies for mobility**. The link between higher education policies and other public policies is particularly important, since increased academic mobility will not come about unless all countries of the EHEA institute rules for immigration, social security and work permits that value academic mobility and distinguish it from classical labour migration. Mobility policies must bring together political initiatives of this kind with a range of practical measures running from recognition through financing to receiving students at host institutions. Mobility policies also must devise and offer different formulas for mobility to seek to include students who have family and work obligations. Reaching the ambitious goal of 20% mobility by 2020 (Bologna Process 2009) will require serious effort along these lines.

7. **Clarify the role and responsibility of public authorities**. If the public responsibility for higher education is to be a reality in 2010, it must be defined in a realistic way and take account of the roles and responsibilities of other actors. The responsibility of public authorities must be defined in relation to various policy areas.

8. **Go beyond structures to actual practice.** Structural reform is not easy, but it is easier to devise structures than to put them into practice. However, aspects of structural reform such as an emphasis on learning outcomes and on quality education will only work if actual practice is developed along with the structures. The European Higher Education Area needs to become an area of compatible structures but also of good practice that stimulates key skills such as analytical ability, communication and constructive criticism. Good practice in these areas, which are ultimately the hallmarks of quality education, must be one of the strengths of the European Higher Education Area. Qualifications frameworks must describe the reality of our qualifications, quality assurance must certify quality education and our recognition practice must promote

mobility through fair assessment. The EHEA cannot afford to be seen as a group of countries characterised by strong declarations of intent but lacking the will or ability to implement them.

9.   **Deal with academic malpractice.** This should be done by providing guidelines at European level and by committing to dealing with persistent malpractice within a given system through a two-pronged approach: assistance from EHEA partners in overcoming the problem combined with action in cases where the problem persists at a significant level or is not addressed by the country concerned.

References

AAC&U (2007), "College Learning for the New Global Century", Washington, DC: Association of American Colleges and Universities, available at www.aacu.org/advocacy/leap/documents/GlobalCentury_final.pdf.

Barblan, Andris, Daxner, Michael and Ivošević, Vanja (2007), *Academic Malpractice: Threats and Temptations*, Bononia University Press/Observatory for Fundamental University Values and Rights, Bologna.

Bergan S. (2004), "Higher education governance and democratic participation: the university and democratic culture", in Bergan S. (ed.), *The University as* Res Publica*: Higher Education Governance, Student Participation and the University as a Site of Citizenship*, Council of Europe Higher Education Series No. 1, Council of Europe Publishing, Strasbourg, pp. 13-30, reproduced in the present volume.

Bergan S. (2005), "Higher education as a 'public good and public responsibility' – What does it mean?" in Weber L. and Bergan S. (eds), *The Public Responsibility for Higher Education and Research*, Council of Europe Higher Education Series No. 2, Council of Europe Publishing, Strasbourg, pp. 13-28.

Bergan S. (2007), *Qualifications: Introduction to a Concept*, Council of Europe Higher Education Series No. 6, Council of Europe Publishing, Strasbourg.

Bologna Process (1999), "The European Higher Education Area: the Bologna Declaration of 19 June 1999", joint declaration of the European ministers of education.

Bologna Process (2001), "Towards the European Higher Education Area", communiqué of the meeting of European ministers in charge of higher education in Prague on 19 May 2001.

Bologna Process (2003), Berlin Communiqué, "Realising the European Higher Education Area", adopted by European ministers of education on 19 September 2003.

Bologna Process (2005), "The European Higher Education Area – Achieving the Goals", communiqué of the Conference of European Ministers Responsible for Higher Education, Bergen, 19-20 May 2005.

Bologna Process (2007a), London Communiqué, "Towards the European Higher Education Area: Responding to Challenges in a Globalised World".

Bologna Process (2007b), "Strategy for the Global Dimension of the European Higher Education Area". Also available at www.dfes.gov.uk/londonbologna/ uploads/documents/ExternalDimension-finalforconference.doc.

Bologna Process (2009), "The Bologna Process 2020 – The European Higher Education Area in the New Decade", communiqué of the Conference of European Ministers Responsible for Higher Education, Leuven and Louvain-la-Neuve, 28-29 April 2009.

Bologna Process (2010), "Budapest-Vienna Declaration on the European Higher Education Area".

Cohen, Stephen Philip (2004), *The Idea of Pakistan*, Brookings Institution Press, Washington, DC.

Council of Europe (2001), Recommendation Rec(2001)15 of the Committee of Ministers to member states on history teaching in twenty-first-century Europe.

Council of Europe (2007), Recommendation Rec(2006)7 of the Committee of Ministers to member states on the public responsibility for higher education and research.

Diamond, Jared (2006), *Collapse: How Societies Choose to Fail or Survive*, Penguin, London.

González, Julia and Robert Wagenaar (eds) (2005), *TUNING Educational Structures in Europe: Universities' Contribution to the Bologna Process. Final Report Pilot Project Phase 2*, Publicaciones de la Universidad de Deusto, Bilbao and Groningen.

Heyneman, Stephen P. (ed.) (2009), *Buying Your Way into Heaven: Education and Corruption in International Perspective*, Sense Publishers. Global Perspectives on Higher Education, Rotterdam/Taipei, Volume 15.

Heyneman, Stephen P., Anderson, Kathryn H. and Nuraliyeva, Nazym (2008), "The cost of corruption in higher education", *Comparative Education Review*, Volume 52, Number 1, pp. 1-25.

Ivošević, Vanja (2007), "Academic alienation and exploitation", in Andris Barblan, Michael Daxner and Vanja Ivošević, *Academic Malpractice: Threats and Temptations,* Bologna: Bononia University Press/Observatory for Fundamental University Values and Rights, pp. 66-93.

Mönckeberg, María Olivia (2005), *La privatización de las universidades* [The Privatisation of Universities], Copa Rota, Santiago de Chile.

Nyborg, Per (2007), *Universitets- og Høgskolesamarbeid i en brytningstid. Femti års utvikling* [University and Polytechnics Co-operation in a Time of Transition. Fifty Years of Development], Unipub, Oslo.

Persson, Annika (2004), "Student participation in the governance of higher education in Europe: results of a survey", in Bergan S. (ed.), *The University as* Res Publica*: Higher Education Governance, Student Participation and the University as a Site of Citizenship*, Council of Europe Higher Education Series No. 1, Council of Europe Publishing, Strasbourg, pp. 31-82.

Rouche, Michel (2003, 1981), *Histoire de l'enseignement et de l'éducation I: V^e av. J.-C. – XVe siècle* [History of Teaching and Education I: 5th Century BC to 15th Century], Edition Perrin, Paris.

Sanz N. and Bergan S. (eds) (2007), *The Heritage of European Universities*, second edition, Council of Europe Higher Education Series No. 7, Council of Europe Publishing, Strasbourg.

Stradling, Robert (2001), *Teaching 20th-Century European History*, Council of Europe Publishing, Strasbourg.

Weber, Luc and Bergan S. (eds) (2005), *The Public Responsibility for Higher Education and Research*, Council of Europe Higher Education Series No. 2, Council of Europe Publishing, Strasbourg.

Westerheijden, Don et al. (2010), *The Bologna Process Independent Assessment. The First Decade of Working on the European Higher Education Area*, Twente and Kassel.

Zgaga, Pavel (2007), "Looking Out: the Bologna Process in a Global Setting", Norwegian Ministry of Higher Education and Research, Oslo. Also available at www.dfes.gov.uk/londonbologna/uploads/documents/0612_Bologna_Global_final_report.pdf.

Developing attitudes to intercultural dialogue: the role of higher education[39]

Introduction

For dialogue to be possible there must be two parties, but two parties do not guarantee dialogue. If one party does all the talking, as in a classical auditorium lecture or a televised speech, there may be tens, hundreds or thousands of participants but communication is one way. Monologue has its rightful place in many situations. If a fire breaks out, shouting "get out" is better justified than engaging in a dialogue about the potential harm of overly high temperatures. One-way communication can also bring forth positive or negative reactions that circumstances may not allow to be expressed immediately but that may give rise to intense communication later. Few who heard President Obama's acceptance speech at the Nobel Peace Prize ceremony (Obama 2009) will have been unmoved and the speech may have given rise to numerous conversations and it will certainly be studied in classrooms and seminars in many countries.

Dialogue, then, requires the ability of two or more participants to speak and to listen in real time. Both acts are equally important: someone who leaves time for his or her interlocutors to speak but who spends this time preparing the next set of arguments rather than listening to those of the interlocutors will not contribute to dialogue. In this case, we will have serial monologues rather than dialogue.

Intercultural dialogue requires not only several participants but also that they come from different cultural backgrounds. For a large part of human history, most people would have had problems finding interlocutors with whom to hone their skills in intercultural dialogue and many would even have been unaware that other cultures existed. This does not mean that interaction between cultures is a modern phenomenon, however. Cultures have interacted for as long as human beings became numerous enough, or lived closely enough together, to come across beings of a similar nature but raised in different circumstances learning different languages, different customs and different sets of behaviour and values. Cultures learned from each other and adapted values, beliefs and words that at first seemed foreign to fit their own frames of reference.

What is modern is not the phenomenon of dialogue across cultures but the extent to which most members of society are faced with the phenomenon. It is this urgency that led the Council of Europe to develop a White Paper on Intercultural Dialogue,

39. This article was first published in Bergan, Sjur and van't Land, Hilligje (eds) (2010): *Speaking Across Borders: the Role of Higher Education in Furthering Intercultural Dialogue*, Strasbourg: Council of Europe Publishing. Council of Europe Higher Education Series No. 16. The author would like to thank Hilligje van't Land for valuable comments on the first draft of the article.

which is significantly called "Living Together as Equals in Dignity". The White Paper defines intercultural dialogues as:

> … a process that comprises an open and respectful exchange of views between individuals and groups with different ethnic, cultural, religious and linguistic backgrounds and heritage, on the basis of mutual understanding and respect. It requires the freedom and ability to express oneself, as well as the willingness and capacity to listen to the views of others. Intercultural dialogue contributes to political, social, cultural and economic integration and the cohesion of culturally diverse societies. It fosters equality, human dignity and a sense of common purpose. It aims to develop a deeper understanding of diverse world views and practices, to increase co-operation and participation (or the freedom to make choices), to allow personal growth and transformation, and to promote tolerance and respect for the other (Council of Europe 2008, section 3.1).

Frames of mind

For intercultural dialogue to take place, then, not only must the potential interlocutors have the physical or technological means to communicate, they must also have a frame of mind that will make dialogue possible. On this score, many individuals and many cultures have a long history of closed minds. Europe is not alone in this but it offers ample examples and since my own background is European, these are the ones that most easily come to mind.

For a long time, the Middle Ages were referred to as the Dark Ages because since we knew less about this period than about the glories of ancient Greece and Rome, it was supposed that people of the Middle Ages had contributed little to cultural development. Even as our knowledge and understanding of this period of our history has improved and our understanding of culture has deepened so that we no longer look for a single "gold standard" from the distant past, the expression has somehow seemed to stick. Ignorance is also betrayed by our persistent belief that the history of the Americas began with the arrival of the first Europeans to settle permanently. Even if attitudes and awareness are changing also in this respect, the belief is sufficiently persistent to have guaranteed the success of a book on the Americas before Columbus[40] (Mann 2006).

Language reveals our frames of mind. English is not alone in making an etymological connection between what is "strange" and the "stranger" (cf. French *étrange* and *étranger* or Spanish *extraño* and *extranjero*). In Europe's often heated debate on immigration and identity, some political movements try to make a point of distinguishing between foreigners who are closer to them in culture and those who are less close and consequently are presumed to be more "strange". For this, several Germanic languages have coined precise terms, exemplified by the German *Fernkulturellen*, literally "those who are culturally distant".

Education is about changing attitudes and helping develop our frames of mind. In an age in which contact with individuals with very different cultural backgrounds

---

40. A name that is itself a Latinised form of the original Italian Colombo and the Spanish Colón.

is not an option but an everyday reality, education cannot remain indifferent to this basic fact of human existence. Even if the majority of people live in or close to their place of origin and even if many will continue to work mainly in local or national contexts, they will at various times in their private and professional lives come into contact with people of different backgrounds. One important task for our schools and universities is to prepare our citizens for these encounters, to recognise cultural diversity as an intrinsic value and an opportunity for cultural enrichment rather than as a danger. Historically, it is not the cultures that have learned from others that have perished but those that have tried to isolate themselves or that have stubbornly stuck to their own ways even in an unfamiliar environment, such as the Norse colonies in Greenland (Diamond 2006).

The ideals of higher education

Few endeavours should be better suited to promoting an understanding of the need for and value of intercultural dialogue than higher education, and few endeavours should be better suited to developing and transmitting the competences needed. The origins of universities are international and even if most early universities were concentrated in south and central Europe, their students came from much further afield. It may be said that even if medieval students and teachers varied in their national origins, they shared an academic language and culture. This is undoubtedly true, but it is equally true that this was the native culture of few of them and the native language of none.

The medieval academic community displayed exactly the kind of mix of what its members had in common and what was particular to each or some of its members that characterises our broader society today. After all, intercultural dialogue requires not only open minds but also a common language, and increasingly this dialogue is carried out in a language that is native to few or even none of the interlocutors. The spread of the most frequently used language of international communication, English, is often compared to the extended use of Latin in the Middle Ages but the comparison is halting for at least two reasons. Firstly, by the Middle Ages no native speakers of Latin remained whereas the different varieties of English have several hundred million native speakers. Secondly, the use of Latin was restricted to a social and intellectual elite in Europe. Even if a working knowledge of English is far from universal, it is not restricted to a single segment of the population or to a single continent.

Higher education is committed to assessing ideas not on the basis of their origin but on the basis of their intrinsic merit. Like the Ten Commandments, this commitment is often honoured in the breaching of it, but it nevertheless represents an ideal against which our actual performance – our openness of mind – is measured. It is an ideal that sets a powerful standard for intercultural dialogue, which cannot take place unless each participant admits the possibility of good ideas originating with others from very different backgrounds. If one enters into verbal exchange with the purpose of demonstrating the superiority of one's own views and refuting the views of others, the result may be entertaining but it will hardly qualify as dialogue – at most as what French refers to as *un dialogue de sourds*: a dialogue of the deaf.

Linked to this is another basic characteristic of higher education and research, namely the assumption that progress is made by challenging received ideas. Had it not been, we would still have sought to explain mental illness as a lack of balance among four basic body fluids and the movement of stellar constellations in relation to Earth as the fixed point at the centre of the universe. Yet, it takes courage to challenge received wisdom, also at universities. Research aims to develop new knowledge and European higher education underlines the link between teaching and research but, at times, university teachers have been obliged to teach in accordance with established dogma whereas they expressed very different ideas in their published works (de Ridder-Symoens 2007).

The history as well as the ideology of higher education should therefore grant it a particularly important place in furthering intercultural dialogue, and we would seem to be justified in expecting higher education institutions and graduates to be particularly open-minded and fluent in intercultural dialogue. Alas, this cannot be taken for granted. The horizon of many staff and students is restricted to the limits of their own discipline and they often see little reason to engage in broader issues (Plantan 2004). It is not difficult to think of academics who have done much to further dialogue and democratic culture and who stood up for democracy at great personal risk. These examples include the Weisse Rose, the student group around Hans and Sophie Scholl, as well as the theologians Dietrich Bonhoeffer (Protestant) and Fr Alfred Delp, SJ (Catholic) in Nazi Germany (Gotto and Repgen 1990); Portuguese students under Salazar, especially from the 1960s onward; Chilean students under the Pinochet regime; Greek students under the regime of the Colonels; Academician Andrei Sakharov in the Soviet Union or the Alternative Academic Education Network under the Milošević regime, and the list could be made much, much longer.

Unfortunately, it is also easy to think of a list of counter examples of academics who have led and assisted oppressive and dictatorial regimes closed to dialogue and looking askance at the concept that valid ideas may originate outside of the regime's culture or ideology. This list includes many right-wing German academics and students in the 1930s (Hammerstein 1991); the leaders of the Salazar regime, who had their roots at the University of Coimbra (Torgal 1999); the "Chicago boys" – the economists that hailed from the University of Chicago and the Universidad Católica de Chile and who played an important role in the Pinochet regime (Huneeus 2001); academically trained judges in the GDR and other communist states (Mählert 1999); the leaders of far too many universities and academies of science who served the same regimes; the teachers and students at the University of Ayacucho who founded the Peruvian left-wing terrorist movement Sendero Luminoso and those involved with European left-wing terrorist groups like the Rote Armee Fraktion (Baader-Meinhof) in Germany or the Brigate Rosse in Italy. Alas, this list, too, can be made much longer.

The image of the ivory tower is, I believe, a considerable exaggeration. Had it been exact, it is difficult to believe that universities would have survived for several centuries. Yet, we often talk about the "society surrounding higher education" and forget that this is not an ocean surrounding an island. It is the very society of which higher education is a part. The examples mentioned also show that it cannot be taken for granted that the ideals underlying higher education describe actual practice. Higher education needs to disengage sufficiently from everyday issues to be able to consider the fundamental questions of our societies and to take a longer term view but it does need to engage on these fundamental issues as well. Even a perfunctory look at modern societies would make it difficult to argue that developing our ability to conduct intercultural dialogue is not among them.

The purposes of higher education

Not least, higher education must engage in a thorough reflection on its purposes in modern, complex societies. While Europe has been successful in reforming its higher education structures and to a considerable extent also its practices through the Bologna Process, we have been less successful in considering the purposes for which we reform our structures (Bergan 2009).

An outsider following the public debate on higher education in Europe could easily be led to believe it has one purpose and one purpose only: to prepare learners for a productive life as future economic actors, mostly as employees although entrepreneurship is increasingly on the higher education as well as the political agenda. This is a reductionist view of education, not because preparation for employment is not an important purpose but because it is not the only important purpose. We do not need to look far to see why preparation for employment is important and if a reminder were needed, autumn 2008 served it with the most serious financial crisis in decades. At the same time, the financial crisis also reminded us that the competences needed for a prosperous economy span considerably wider than those most frequently associated with business studies. Had the main economic actors, most of whom are higher education graduates, had a somewhat sounder and more holistic view of their activities and their obligations to broader society and had they had a better education in the true sense of the word, the economic crisis might have been less serious.

Without downplaying the obvious role of higher education in preparing for the labour market, then, we need to take a more coherent view of its multiple purposes. While the details of these may be debated, we suggest that higher education has four broad purposes (Bergan 2005, Council of Europe 2007):

- preparation for the labour market;

- preparation for life as active citizens in democratic societies;

- personal development;

- the development and maintenance of a broad, advanced knowledge base.

These purposes are equally important and they are not mutually exclusive. Rather, they should reinforce each other: the qualities and competences that make learners well suited for employment, such as analytical ability, communication skills and proficiency in foreign languages, may also help make them active citizens in democratic societies and further their personal development.

A major challenge in European policies is to explicitly recognise the multiple purposes of higher education, not least the fact that the education of the whole person is not something that can safely be concluded at the latest by the end of secondary education. In this sense, European higher education leaders and policy makers have much to learn from the US concept of liberal education, which takes a much broader view of what is "useful" (AAC&U 2007, Zernike 2009). That leads us to consider the purposes of higher education from a slightly different angle, namely that of the kind of competences with which it should provide its learners.

Competences for intercultural dialogue

The issue of competences permeates the discussion of what higher education could and should contribute to modern societies. While the contribution of higher education cannot be reduced to the development of competences in learners, this aspect is particularly important for the purpose of this article, which will address the issue from three angles: competences for intercultural dialogue, competences for dialogue and, more generally, higher education competences, focusing in particular on the distinction between generic and subject-specific competences.

One way of seeing education is as a process of developing a set of competences in individuals. This is admittedly a somewhat reductionist view of education but it may nevertheless be useful to adopt it at least temporarily. It immediately leads to the question of what we mean by competences. The classical definition of learning outcomes contains three elements (Bergan 2007):

– knowledge;
– understanding;
– ability to act.

This is at variance with the most traditional view of education, which emphasises its role in developing and transmitting knowledge. Most likely, this would also be the view of education expressed most frequently if we were to question the proverbial "man in the street".

Knowledge is important and encyclopedic knowledge is often admired. However, knowledge alone is insufficient. To revert to the example of language learning, it is not easy for someone with a different linguistic background to master the intricacies of the case declensions of Slavic languages like Russian or Serbian, or Baltic languages like Lithuanian. Learning the different case declensions according to gender and classes of nouns and adjectives requires patience and persistence. It is, however, only useful if one also develops an understanding of when the different forms should be used and what connotations the different cases convey, for example, that the accusative may convey sense of movement and the locative a fixed position, that the accusative may also signal a direct object and the dative an indirect one.

Nevertheless, operational language learning has been accomplished only when knowledge of the case declensions and understanding of their function and connotations have been supplemented by the ability to use them correctly in practice.

Competence, then, is made up of knowledge, understanding and an ability to act, and this author has increasingly come to ask whether attitudes should not be included in the definition. This is hardly a revolutionary thought, since one of the traditional aims of education has been to socialise young people into the societies of which they form a part by developing identification with that society's values, as exemplified by the current Norwegian education legislation, which says that:

> The pupils and apprentices shall develop knowledge, skills and attitudes allowing them to master their lives and in order to participate in work and community. They shall be allowed to develop the joy of creativity, engagement and the need to investigate.
>
> The pupils and apprentices shall learn to think critically and to act ethically and to be conscious of the environment. They shall share in responsibility and have the right of participation.[41]

At the same time, the traditional goal of instilling these values in a way that leaves them unquestioned cannot be an educational goal in today's world. That would prevent dialogue, since we would all then limit our discussions with those from other backgrounds to defending the position of our own societies. These may be deeply held values but they may equally well be unquestioned habits. Our definition of competences should include attitudes and one of the attitudes it should develop is the willingness to question and reassess one's own values and habits. The goal is not to throw all the values of one's own culture and society overboard but rather to reassess them critically as our societies evolve. This will ultimately strengthen our fundamental values and also help us find ways in which these values may be made a living reality in evolving societies.

This view of competences must mean that education is about much more than developing "knowledge of facts". Again, Europe will find much of interest in the concept of liberal education. As defined by the Association of American Colleges and Universities, liberal education is:

> ... an approach to learning that empowers individuals and prepares them to deal with complexity, diversity, and change. It provides students with broad knowledge of the wider world (e.g., science, culture, and society) as well as in-depth study in a specific area of interest. A liberal education helps students develop a sense of social responsibility, as well as strong and transferable intellectual and practical skills such as communication, analytical and problem-solving skills, and a demonstrated ability to apply knowledge and skills in real-world settings.[42]

The ability to deal with complexity, diversity and change will be required in almost every nook and cranny of the workplace but it will equally be required

---

41. www.stortinget.no/no/Saker-og-publikasjoner/Vedtak/Beslutninger/Odelstinget/2008-2009/ beso-200809-042/, accessed on 27 December 2009, author's translation.
42. www.aacu.org/leap/What_is_liberal_education.cfm, accessed on 27 December 2009.

when we act as citizens in democratic societies and when we interact with people from other societies and backgrounds – as neighbours or as colleagues, as casual visitors or as friends.

Education at all levels, including higher education, must have a strong responsibility for developing the competences that will allow learners to participate in all aspects of the lives of their societies as well as internationally and, again, it would be difficult to argue that these competences should not be defined with a view to intercultural dialogue. Education must be seen as more than the sum of the knowledge an individual will gain in the course of a programme of study, in the same way that universities must be more than the sum of their individual academic disciplines.

A practice of dialogue

Higher education, then, must seek to convey competences that make their students and graduates fit and willing to engage in intercultural dialogue. Before turning to consider the kind of competences needed, it is important to underline that these competences cannot be developed through classical study programmes alone. Intercultural dialogue must also be practised on campus and beyond. One can no more learn dialogue by listening to lectures than one can learn how to swim without getting into the water.

Many higher education institutions aspire to attract foreign students and many already have a high number of students from outside of the country in which they are located. A large foreign student population as well as a large body of national students from various cultural backgrounds should provide an excellent opportunity to put the principles of intercultural dialogue into practice on campus, yet many institutions do not seem to seize the opportunity. In many cases, staff and students focus on their own academic discipline and do not consider the broader goals of higher education to be their concerns. Undoubtedly, what a previous project found to be widespread rejection among staff and students of a role of the university as a site of democratic citizenship (Plantan 2004) is equally true for the role of the higher education institution as a site of intercultural dialogue. It is also a measure of what remains to be done that many institutions seem to consider this an issue to be left to the personal choice of individual staff and students. Few institutions seem to have policies that aim to create a climate of intercultural dialogue on campus and often foreign students spend their spare time with other students from the same linguistic and cultural background instead of developing friendships with other foreign students as well as students from the host country.

There are nonetheless examples of good practice. The policies that Queen's University Belfast instituted to make members of both major communities in Northern Ireland feel welcome on campus (Plantan 2004) can also be adapted to making foreign and minority students and staff an integrated part of the local academic community. A number of European universities have developed institutional policies to value the cultures and specificities of foreign and minority students while also making them well acquainted with the language and culture of the host institution (Bergan and Restoueix 2009).

A practice of intercultural dialogue on campus must take as its point of departure that higher education is a learning process and not just a matter of teaching. It must see the institution as a holistic learning environment that spans across disciplines and extends beyond the lecture hall and the library. It must provide space and opportunities for students and staff from different backgrounds and different disciplines to interact and to learn from each other. It must encourage extra-curricular activities that offer foreign and minority students opportunities to share their own cultures with fellow students and staff as well as to get acquainted with the culture(s) of the host country. These opportunities must extend beyond folklore to explore fundamental values and cultural patterns and they must be open to respectful debate based on the basic principles of intercultural dialogue as outlined in the Council of Europe White Paper.

Higher education competences

If we go back to the "man in the street" and ask what kind of competences higher education should develop, chances are that the answer would emphasise knowledge of specific disciplines, like physics, history or law. This is, of course, an important aspect of higher education: we do expect a history graduate to be knowledgeable about history, if we go to a medical doctor, we expect him or her to have a solid understanding of medicine and we would not be happy with a dentist whose competences were limited to pulling teeth.

These are referred to as subject-specific competences and designate what higher education graduates know, understand and are able to do in a specific discipline. Subject-specific competences are complemented by generic or transversal competences, which describe what every higher education graduate may be expected to acquire (Bergan 2009: 45-67). They include analytical ability, communication skills, the ability to work individually as well as part of a team and the ability to make decisions on the basis of incomplete evidence and under pressure of time.

The list of possible generic competences is quite long, but the project TUNING Educational Structures in Europe (González and Wagenaar 2005), which brought the distinction between subject-specific and generic competences fully into European higher education debate, points to three main categories. Instrumental competences are those that serve as instruments in applying subject-specific competences or in putting one's whole range of competences to use, such as the ability to communicate, to use technical aids (such as information technology), organise ourselves or make decisions. For the latter, think of a competence that is too often lacking: the ability to bring a discussion to a structured conclusion. Interpersonal competences enable us to relate to others and to function in a social environment, whether that environment is our own or that of another culture. They include what we are able to do as individuals, such as expressing our own ideas clearly as well as understanding the ideas of others (provided they are in their turn expressed understandably), as well as what we are able to do together with others, such as develop a project as a member of a team. System-specific competences enable us to understand how elements fit into a whole – a system – and to understand how changes in individual elements may change the system.

I have devoted more space to describing generic than subject-specific competences not because they are more important but because they are less easy to grasp intuitively. An education that provided only one set of competences without the other would be incomplete. It may be true that the academic world provides examples of those who focus only on subject-specific competences and the attitudes to activities that fall outside of the academic discipline described in the survey by Plantan referred to above reinforce this impression. On the other hand, both the "new public management" and parts of the business community overemphasise generic at the expense of subject-specific competences, as demonstrated by the belief that once someone has been recruited to a company or an organisation, the person is qualified for most jobs within the organisation at a given level. German has a fitting term for those who possess mainly subject-specific competences: *Fachidiot*, literally "subject idiot". On the other hand, English may have the best term for those who believe one can get along in life with only generic competences: management consultant.

In defining the competences it wishes to give its graduates, higher education needs to find a reasonable balance between subject-specific competences and avoid the Scylla of *Fachidioten* and the Charybdis of management consultants. Finding the proper balance requires continuous reflection. I believe our higher education institutions are excellent at training highly competent subject specialists with a detailed understanding of specific academic fields. I am less sure we are equally good at educating intellectuals, by which I mean graduates with a good general culture and the ability to put their own academic discipline into a broader context, assess advantages and disadvantages not only in terms of their own disciplines but also in terms of their effects on broader societal goals as well as in a longer term perspective and who are able to take account of knowledge and understanding from several academic fields. Nevertheless, it is essential that our higher education institutions provide us with intellectuals as well as subject specialists. Higher education graduates need to be both, and it is essential that our broader society is able to value intellectuals. As the Canadian philosopher John Ralston Saul puts it:

> Of course, separating out elements in a complicated world is a valid intellectual activity. It must be done. But the capacity to see how the elements fit together is a completely different form of intelligence and is of equal if not greater importance (Saul 2009: 37).

I would add that higher education must aim to enable its graduates to combine these two kinds of intelligence. It is on the ability to understand the elements and then put them together into a coherent whole that the survival of our societies will depend. How else will we be able to meet the challenge of climate change or of the need not only to live peacefully but to co-operate and interact constructively with our neighbours?

Another essential competence that higher education should convey is the awareness of the limits of our knowledge and understanding. It is this awareness that drives research since if we were omniscient, there would be no reason to explore further. On the other hand, if we believe we know and understand everything, there is no reason to enter into dialogue with others in order to benefit from their wisdom. In this case, our purpose in talking to others would be limited to conveying our wisdom to them, and then we would engage in monologue rather than dialogue. As Ambrose Bierce reminds us in his usual laconic style, education is: "that which discloses to the wise and disguises from the foolish their lack of understanding" (Bierce 1983: 105).

Competences for dialogue

The competences needed for dialogue are a mix of the subject specific and the generic. Language proficiency is an obvious competence, since – as we have already mentioned – dialogue is impossible without a common language. It is equally important to be aware of the potential pitfalls of a common language, especially one that is spoken in several varieties, like English and Spanish, or is frequently used by non-native speakers who may transfer expressions and habits from their native languages to the languages used for international communication. To take a banal example, a Dutch, German or Scandinavian who asks you to come at "half ten" will expect you at 9.30 whereas a Scot or an Irish using the same expression will intend that you come at 10.30. An awareness of potential linguistic and cultural pitfalls in intercultural communication is important for all higher education graduates.

Beyond the ability to communicate, knowledge of foreign languages also serves to make us aware that ideas can be expressed in several different ways and that translations can sometimes be misleading. Translations are of course indispensable since nobody can know all languages, but there is a grain of truth to the Italian expression *traduttore – traditore*: translator – traitor. Germanic languages use varieties of "I am right" or "I have right" (*jeg har rett*), whereas Romance languages prefer to say that "I have reason" (*tengo razón* or *j'ai raison*). Several Slavic languages have masculine and feminine forms not only of common nouns but also of proper names, including family names, and Lithuanian – a Baltic rather than a Slavic language – even distinguishes between separate forms denoting married or unmarried women. These forms arise from an age when divorce was unthinkable and linguistic convention is challenged by modern society, also by making the distinction between unmarried and married for feminine forms only. The importance of distinguishing gender in Indo-European languages contrasts with Turkic languages, where grammatical gender is unknown for nouns and adjectives and even for personal pronouns. The point is not that certain choices are better than others, so that a language that marks gender is more or less sophisticated than one which does not, but rather that getting acquainted with a language that makes choices different from the ones we have come to take for granted helps us see issues from different angles and question some of our own basic assumptions.

The Association of American Colleges and Universities provides an interesting summary not only of what the competences required for a "global world" may be but also of how the concepts have evolved, under the headline "remapping liberal education" (AAC&U 2007: 18):

	Liberal education in the 20th century	Liberal education in the 21st century
What	– an elite curriculum – non-vocational – an option for the fortunate	– a necessity for all students – essential for success in a global economy and for informed citizenship
Where	– liberal arts colleges or colleges of arts and sciences in larger institutions	– all schools, community colleges, colleges, and universities; across all fields of study (recommended)
How	– through studies in arts and sciences fields ("the major") and/or through general education in the initial years of college	– through studies across the entire educational continuum: school through college (recommended)

One of the key competences that higher education should provide may be summarised as multiperspectivity. This concept was developed by the Council of Europe in its programme on history teaching (Council of Europe 2001, Stradling 2001) but its validity is not restricted to history. All higher education graduates need the ability to analyse issues from different points of view. In history teaching, the point that no country or culture has developed in isolation from its neighbours and that others – neighbours and those further away – may legitimately hold dissenting views of the history of one's own country has been accepted in principle. Accepting this in practice has sometimes proven difficult when the principle is applied to the more painful part of history of which no country is entirely devoid. It is much easier to flag one's heroes than one's villains. To take an example from this author's country of origin, it is much easier for a Norwegian to refer to Fridtjof Nansen, who was not only a natural scientist and Arctic explorer but also a diplomat and prominent in the efforts by the League of Nations to help refugees in the aftermath of the First World War, than to Vidkun Quisling, who was one of Nansen's assistants in the League of Nations' efforts but who then went on to become the archetypical traitor during the Second World War by collaborating with the Nazi occupation, to the extent that his name has become a common noun for traitor in several languages.[43] That Norwegians are after all relatively open in discussing Quisling is possibly due to the fact that he is seen as a representative of an alien regime with little local support rather than as a home-grown phenomenon. Had he been a civil war leader in a divided nation, open discussion would have been much more painful.

---

43. One resistance joke during the Second World War had Quisling arriving to visit Hitler and announcing himself to the guards by saying "I am Quisling", to which the guard replied: "Yes, I know, but what is your name?"

What is true for history is equally true for other areas of education and research. Literature, arts, social conditions and habits, values and religious views have benefited from external influences over centuries, and it is difficult to think of a single thriving culture that has not received strong impulses from outside. It is equally difficult to think of a thriving culture that has not to some extent been selective about what it has adopted from the outside and that has not adapted outside impulses to its own circumstances. As has been said about the 17th century, during which European interaction with other parts of the world changed:

> With second contacts, the dynamic of encounter changes. Interaction becomes more sustained and likelier to be repeated. The effects they produce, however, are not simple to predict or understand. At times they induce a thorough transformation of everyday practices, an effect that Cuban writer Fernando Ortiz has called "transculturation". At other times they provoke resistance, violence, and a loss of identity. In the seventeenth century, most contacts generated effects that fall between these two extremes: selective adjustment, made through a process of mutual influence. Rather than complete transformation or deadly conflict, there was negotiation and borrowing; rather than triumph and loss, give and take; rather than the transformation of cultures, their interaction. It was a time when people had to adjust how they acted and thought in order to negotiate the cultural differences they encountered, to deflect unanticipated threats and respond cautiously to equally unexpected opportunities (Brook 2009: 21).

Intercultural dialogue requires the ability to look at issues from several angles and to understand the reasons that may lead others to conclusions and values very different from our own. Understanding, however, does not necessarily mean acceptance, and intercultural dialogue is not a prescription for moral relativism.

The US journalist and author Sandra Mackey, who is intimately familiar with the Arab world, claims:

> "Understanding" is perhaps the most used and abused word in the realm of human relationships. Nevertheless, comprehending the experiences, values, psychological anchors, broken moorings, soaring pride, and debilitating fears of the "other" is where accommodation begins (Mackey 2008: 255).

Saying that others may be right is not the same as saying all views are equally valid. There are such things as good and evil, and examples of both can be found in all cultures. Some values are absolute, and the Council of Europe points in particular to those enshrined in the European Convention on Human Rights. Competences for intercultural dialogue must therefore also include a thorough consideration of values. In this context, it may be useful to point out that while the forms and manifestations of democracy evolve the basic value of democracy remains. As underlined by the Council of Europe's Steering Committee on Higher Education and Research (CDESR 2006):

> Intercultural dialogue must be founded on a firm and well-reflected set of values as well as on a willingness to consider the values of others and to reassess one's own convictions in the light of new and convincing evidence. Dialogue presupposes openness of mind in all partners, including the capacity to look at their own values and frame of

reference with critical distance. These are also essential values and characteristics of higher education.

European higher education is based on the conviction that each human being has intrinsic value as an individual, and also that each human being is inherently responsible for the development and well-being of other human beings, of human society as a whole and of the environment on which we depend for our survival.

The CDESR is committed to the Council of Europe's key values human rights, democracy and the rule of law. In this context, the CDESR sees the main contribution of higher education – as well as the main contribution of other areas of education – as helping develop, maintain and transmit to new generations the democratic culture which is indispensable to making democratic institutions and democratic laws work and to make democratic societies sustainable.

Commitment to intercultural dialogue should start at home but it should not end there. We should express concern when European countries attempt to ban minarets but we should also express concern when non-European countries ban churches or synagogues. We should protest when societies oblige their members to profess certain beliefs as well as when they prevent them from doing so.

The rationale for education

As someone who has spent decades in education, first as a student and then as a policy maker, I will be among the last people to deny the intrinsic merit of education. Yet intrinsic merit is insufficient justification in an age where competition for public attention and public funding is fierce. Education is important because it provides our societies with the competences we need to survive and because it provides individuals with the competences they need to thrive.

Education is important because it opens minds, because it develops awareness of values as well as of different approaches to life, because it teaches us not to take things for granted or accept them at face value and because it teaches us the importance of time: what may be beneficial in the short run may be disastrous in the long run. Higher education, in particular, must develop knowledge, understanding, attitudes and the ability to act, all at the same time. Higher education must educate the whole person – and in our age and time, this cannot be done without opening the horizon of each individual to the world that lies beyond our immediate neighbourhood.

We still have some way to go before our higher education institutions fulfil this role and we may have even further to go before our political decision makers and our societies at large accept this as the true role of education. As John Ralston Saul says:

> … I find our education is increasingly one aimed at training loyal employees, even though the state and the corporations are increasingly disloyal. What we should be doing is quite different. It turns on our ability to rethink our education and our public expectations so that we create a non-employee, non-loyal space for citizenship. After all, a citizen is by definition loyal to the state because it belongs to her or him. That is what frees the citizen to be boisterous, outspoken, cantankerous and, all in all, by corporatist standards, disloyal. This is the key to the success of our democracy (Saul 2009: 318).

Higher education must aim to develop the competences that will help make Earth – and not only our own country – the kind of place in which we would like our children and grandchildren to live (Tironi 2005). It must engage in the debate on what the kind of society in which we would like to live should look like and how we can make it a reality. We need societies that are sustainable environmentally and politically, socially and ethically, economically and culturally. Higher education must provide a workable and inspiring vision of the contribution of higher education to a society based on democracy, human rights and the rule of law and proficient in intercultural dialogue; a society coherent enough to be strong and diverse enough to be interesting; a society unafraid to engage with the broader world. Neither our curiosity nor our responsibility stops at our national borders, and even if we were tempted to withdraw and leave "the rest of the world" to others, we would not live long in the illusion that what happens elsewhere is not important to us.

Ultimately, higher education must inspire and prepare us to do well, but also to do good. We cannot do that unless we are able and willing to engage in intercultural dialogue.

References

AAC&U (2007), "College Learning for the New Global Century", Association of American Colleges and Universities, Washington DC.

Bergan S. (2005), "Higher education as a 'public good and a public responsibility' – What does it mean?", in Weber L. and Bergan S. (eds), *The Public Responsibility for Higher Education and Research,* Council of Europe Higher Education Series No. 2, Council of Europe Publishing, Strasbourg, pp. 13-28.

Bergan S. (2007), *Qualifications. Introduction to a Concept,* Council of Europe Higher Education Series No. 6, Council of Europe Publishing, Strasbourg.

Bergan S. (2009), "Introductory statement at the ministerial meeting of the Bologna Process, Leuven/Louvain-la-Neuve, April 28-29, 2009", available at www.ond.vlaanderen.be/hogeronderwijs/bologna/conference/documents/CoE_ address_Leuven_280409.pdf, accessed on 26 December 2009.

Bergan S. and Restoueix J.-P. (eds) (2009), *Intercultural Dialogue on Campus,* Council of Europe Higher Education Series No. 11, Council of Europe Publishing, Strasbourg.

Bierce A. (1983, 1911), *The Enlarged Devil's Dictionary,* edited by Hopkins E. J., Penguin American Library, London.

Brook T. (2009), *Vermeer's Hat. The Seventeenth Century and the Dawn of the Global World,* Profile Books, London.

CDESR (Council of Europe's Steering Committee on Higher Education and Research) (2006), "Statement on the Contribution of Higher Education to Intercultural Dialogue".

Council of Europe (2001), Recommendation Rec(2001)15 of the Committee of Ministers to member states on history teaching in twenty-first-century Europe.

Council of Europe (2007), Recommendation CM/Rec(2007)6 of the Committee of Ministers to member states on the public responsibility for higher education and research.

Council of Europe (2008), "White Paper on Intercultural Dialogue – 'Living Together as Equals in Dignity'", Council of Europe Publishing, Strasbourg.

Diamond J. (2006), *Collapse. How Societies Choose to Fail or Survive*, Penguin, London.

Gotto K. and Repgen K. (eds) (1990), *Die Katholiken und das Dritte Reich*, Matthias-Grünewald-Verlag, Mainz.

González J. and Wagenaar R. (eds) (2005), *TUNING Educational Structures in Europe. Universities' Contribution to the Bologna Process. Final Report of Pilot Project Phase 2*, Publicaciones de la Universidad de Deusto, Bilbao and Groningen.

Hammerstein N. (1991), "Universities and Democratisation: an Historical Perspective. The Case of Germany" (paper written for the Council of Europe Conference on Universities and Democratisation, Warsaw, 29-31 January 1992, reference DECS-HE 91/97).

Huneeus C. (2001), *El régimen de Pinochet*, Editorial Sudamericana, Santiago de Chile.

Mackey S. (2008), *Mirror of the Arab World. Lebanon in Conflict*, W. W. Norton, New York.

Mählert U. (1999), *Kleine Geschichte der DDR*, Verlag C. H. Beck, Munich.

Mann C. C. (2006), *1491. The Americas Before Columbus*, Granta Books, London.

Obama B. (2009), speech in acceptance of the Nobel Peace Prize, available at www.nytimes.com/2009/12/11/world/europe/11prexy.text.html, accessed on 26 December 2009.

Plantan F. (2004), "The university as site of citizenship", in Bergan S. (ed.), *The University as* Res Publica, Council of Europe Higher Education Series No. 1, Council of Europe Publishing, Strasbourg, pp. 83-128.

de Ridder-Symoens H. (2007), "The intellectual heritage of ancient universities in Europe", in Sanz N. and Bergan S. (eds), *The Heritage of European Universities*, second edition, Council of Europe Higher Education Series No. 7, Council of Europe Publishing, Strasbourg.

Saul J. R. (2009), *A Fair Country. Telling Truths about Canada*, Penguin Canada, Toronto.

Stradling R. (2001), *Teaching 20th-Century European History*, Council of Europe Publishing, Strasbourg.

Tironi E. (2005), *El sueño chileno. Comunidad, familia y nación en el bicentenario*, Taurus, Santiago de Chile.

Torgal L. R. (1999), *A universidade e o estado novo*, Livreria Minerva Editorial, Coimbra.

Zernike K. (2009), "Making college 'relevant'", online version of the *International Herald Tribune*, published 29 December 2009, www.nytimes.com/2010/01/03/education/edlife/03careerism-t.html?pagewanted=1&em, accessed 4 January 2010.

Safeguarding ethics and values in higher education: a shared responsibility[44]

Common challenges

Higher education, whether provided by classical universities or professional higher education institutions and regardless of academic discipline, is faced with a number of common challenges. Some are particular to higher education whereas others are shared by other parts of society. Some of them may even arise from that untranslatable and perhaps indefinable concept: *Zeitgeist*. "The spirit of the times" may give an approximate indication of what is meant but without the evocative force of the original.

The sum of available knowledge has virtually exploded over the past generation or two. True, some knowledge has been lost. Languages change and so do occupations, leisure activities and technology. Modern readers may enjoy Balzac's novels but they find numerous terms that need explanation since Balzac provided vivid descriptions of 19th-century society with trades that have long since disappeared. In many cultures, indigenous knowledge of nature is lost when the habitat changes – yet another challenge of climate change – or when lifestyles change with increasing sedentariness and urbanisation. Contemporary English and their ancestors may speak different versions of the same language but the language has evolved in ways which makes it difficult for English of today to read Old or even Middle English texts without specialised training. A very vivid example of how the relevance of specific competences changes may be found at the Technical Museum in Berlin, which displays a correspondence course in the Morse code, complete with cassettes. Luckily, the exhibit does not oblige visitors to listen to the endless repetition of dots and strokes but it does bring home the point that what was once a cutting edge competence that required quite some effort to acquire is now little more than a curiosity, quite literally a museum piece.

Nevertheless, much more knowledge is newly developed than recently forgotten and it is impossible for any single individual to be at the forefront of knowledge development in anything but a narrow field. Many universities may originally have had a single chair for a broad discipline but research competence is now developed in highly specialised sub-fields. The increasing diversification and specialisation of knowledge is an inevitable consequence of our success in developing new knowledge and is in this sense to be welcomed rather than regretted

44. This article is based on a presentation to the 2010 international conference of the International Association of Universities, IAU, held on the topic "Ethics and values in higher education in the era of globalization: What role for the disciplines?" in Vilnius on 24-26 June, see www.iau-aiu.net, accessed on 21 July 2010. The author would like to thank Hilligje van't Land for comments to a first draft of this article.

but it does present a challenge in terms of maintaining an academic community with shared values, common concerns and a shared understanding of its roles and responsibilities.

This understanding is under pressure not only from the development of new knowledge, which is an important function of the academic community even if it is certainly not an academic monopoly, but also from developments in society at large. One of the most important elements is the increasing demand for accountability. At one level, this demand is easy to understand and to justify. Higher education and research receive substantial public funds and have an obligation to use them responsibly. At the same time, the demands on public funding increase and far exceed the available funds – or at least the public funds our societies are willing to raise. It is perhaps one of the paradoxes of modern societies that while the demand for public funding increases and extends to new areas, our collective willingness to provide funding decreases or at least does not increase. As an unnamed official in the Obama administration recently put it: "The tension is that the public still wants big things to happen on the economy, but they have big-number fatigue."[45] The classic method of raising general public funds – taxation – is in many countries an important element of political discourse, in which case the issue is how to reduce taxes. Demands for public funding for specific sectors, on which there is little consensus, is therefore matched by demands for reduced overall availability of public funds, at least through taxation. Fairly broad political agreement on the need to reduce public expenditure is unmatched by agreement on where cuts should be made.

At another level, however, the increased demand for accountability is disturbing. This is less because of the emphasis on the need for accountability than of how this demand is operationalised. What has come to be called the "audit society" or the "evaluation society" emphasises detailed technical compliance with quite elaborate criteria through resource intensive procedures that nevertheless seem strangely unconcerned with some of the more fundamental questions. A given activity may well comply with technical evaluation criteria yet contribute very little to the overall well-being of our societies. The "audit society" is above all characterised by an abundance of technical requirements, forms and reports combined with a shortage of concern for the broader purposes of the activities under assessment. The technical reporting requirements are also so time and labour intensive that one suspects they diminish the time and mental agility required to address the broader issues. Perhaps the early 18th-century author and playwright Ludvig Holberg unwittingly provided an apt description of the "audit society" with his ironic statement "he died, it is true, but the fever left him".[46]

At the same time, our time perspective is pronouncedly short term. Whereas those who set out to build the cathedrals of medieval Europe knew they would never see

---

45. Quoted in *Time Magazine*, 26 July 2010, p. 20.
46. The phrase, or variations thereof, appears in several of Holberg's works; the earliest occurrence appears to be in *Peder Paars* (1719-20).

the final results of their labour, current society finds it difficult to look beyond the immediate future, defined by the next reporting deadline, the next budget year or the next election. Neither time frame is inherently good or unworthy: seeing everything in the perspective of eternity can easily be made an excuse for doing nothing today, whereas expecting everything for tomorrow makes it difficult to undertake sustained longer term efforts or to reflect on the purpose of what one is doing. The point is that our societies need to combine a sense of urgency with the ability to think in a medium- and long-term perspective. Not least, our societies need the ability to weigh immediate against long-term consequences and higher education should play a crucial role in developing this ability in its learners as well as in its own policies and practice.

An imagined community

Internal and external developments combine to challenge the notion of an academic community with shared responsibilities. Benedict Anderson coined the term "imagined communities" (Anderson 1983) and his point was not that imagined communities are somehow artificial but rather that all communities are imagined: without a shared consciousness and a shared set of values, convictions and practice, there can be no community. While Anderson's work is a contribution to the theory of nationalism, the concept of "imagined communities" may be useful to communities other than national, all the more so as identities are not one dimensional: one can identify with one's country of birth or residence – or both – and at the same time have a professional identity, identify with an interest group or a group that shares one's convictions (for example, religious or political), with a sports team, with a given city or with a whole continent. These different identities are not necessarily of the same importance, and the intensity with which one identifies with them may change with circumstances. The part of our identity foremost in our mind is likely to be different in church, mosque or synagogue than during our city's jubilee celebrations, a sports event or an election campaign.

The academic community is very much an international one, bound together by similar circumstances, interests, concerns and values. The academic community is made up of scholars and students, and in a European context, the inclusion of students as part of the academic community developed in the aftermath of the student unrest of 1968 and has been made explicit by a group that strictly speaking does not belong to the community. In 2001, the European ministers responsible for higher education referred to "students as competent, active and constructive partners in the establishment and shaping of a European Higher Education Area" (Bologna Process 2001), and in 2010 they defined the academic community as "institutional leaders, teachers, researchers, administrative staff and students" (Bologna Process 2010). The academic community also shares a heritage (Sanz and Bergan 2006) and also some myths, the most persistent of which may be that of the ivory tower. While communities are to some extent defined by distinguishing themselves from those who do not belong to the community, they are not necessarily isolated from other communities. The ivory tower is a myth precisely because it assumes that the academic community is self-sufficient: if it were true, universities would not have survived as an institution for close to a millennium.

While there is a clear historical basis for referring to the academic community as such, it is less clear to what extent this community should still be considered as one today. The diversification of knowledge has led to different profiles and orientations within the academic community and so has the diversification of higher education, where classical university study programmes have been supplemented by shorter and more professionally oriented programmes, and where for-profit institutions have also been appearing. It is questionable whether the priorities and orientations of a research group in an applied natural science are the same as those of researchers – less likely to form a group – in humanities. The diversification of study programmes has many positive aspects but in our context, it may make it less obvious to speak about a single academic community.

A community of values

If there is an academic community, it should be a community of values. The phrase is heard quite frequently, at least on festive occasions, but there is less exploration of which values such a community should further. Nevertheless, this has a direct bearing on the topic under consideration: safeguarding values and ethics only makes sense if these values are worth safeguarding. It is therefore worth exploring what the values of the academic community might be and, inevitably, what follows will have the character of normative more than empirical statements.

The exploration might properly start with two closely linked yet distinct values: which are more often than not mentioned in the same breath and sometimes even confused: academic freedom and institutional autonomy. Academic freedom applies to the individual members of the academic community and concerns their right to pursue their research and teaching unhindered, whereas institutional autonomy applies to the institutions at which the individual members of the academic community work and describes the right of institutions to define their own priorities and policies. While the two are often thought of as inseparable and ideally should be, it is possible to imagine a high degree of freedom for individual members of the academic community even in situations where institutions have little autonomy and it is perhaps less difficult to imagine an institution with a strong leadership which zealously protects the institution's autonomy yet allows little academic freedom within the institution.

With this caveat, however, these two values are linked and should be thought of as complementary. At the same time, none of them is unrestricted. Even if European thinking around academic freedom and institutional autonomy has above all focused on legal provision, other elements are equally relevant. Since these have been explored elsewhere (Bergan 2009), a summary overview will suffice. Funding is one of the most important constraints and it is legitimate for funders, whether public or private, to stipulate reasonable conditions for the use of the funds provided. Interpretations of what is "reasonable" may give rise to discussion and it is impossible to provide anything like an exhaustive definition of the term but as an example, it is entirely legitimate for public authorities to provide more funding for areas they consider to be a priority and also to decrease or cut funding for areas that are not considered a priority. At the same time, however, public authorities have an overall responsibility for funding a diverse higher education system and to ensure a broad diversity of disciplines within the system if not necessarily within every institution (Bergan 2005). Both individuals within the academic community and institutions need to comply with the legislation of the country in which they work and this applies not only to specific provisions concerning higher education and research but also to general provisions like safety regulations, rules and regulations on public accounting and labour legislation. Academic freedom should also not be confused with freedom of speech, even if the two have common elements. Genuine academic freedom is perhaps unimaginable in societies where there is little or no freedom of speech but, at the same time, academic freedom is different from the right to simply express an opinion. Academic freedom does, for example, not free academics from the demands of their discipline in terms of substantiating their claims through valid research methods. Thus historians who would deny the Holocaust would not only be constrained by the limits of free speech but also by the demands of their disciplines since the reality of the Holocaust is well documented. If a linguist or a lawyer held that the earth is flat, their opinion would be censured by common sense rather than the limits of free speech or of academic freedom but it would certainly not be an acceptable opinion, according to the academic standards of their disciplines, if held by an astronomer or a geographer.

Research methodology and the academic standards of individual disciplines are intended to further another key value of the academic community: the search for truth. This search is difficult to imagine in the absence of academic freedom and institutional autonomy but also does not automatically follow where these values exist. The search for truth depends on an ethos of enquiry unbound by conventions and accepted dogma and a willingness to assess ideas and evidence on the strength of their own merits. It requires a will to reopen debates and question received truths. The move from an earth-centric to a heliocentric world view and the development of medicine beyond the dogmas of Gallen are classical examples (Hannam 2009) which also illustrate the importance of academic freedom. History also shows that the freedom of enquiry needed to search for the truth is not always accompanied by the freedom to disseminate the results of the search or even to raise the basic questions with one's students. As an example, in the 16th century, scholars were obliged to transmit the sacrosanct belief of Antiquity in their lectures while arriving at quite different convictions through their own research in areas like natural sciences and technical disciplines (de Ridder-Symoens 2006).

Academic freedom and institutional autonomy are key values in democratic societies, and democracy and participation should be key values to the academic community. Even if the definition of the academic community has varied over time and its different categories of members do not have the same representation in institutional governance (Bergan 2004, Persson 2004), the principle that the academic community plays a key role in the governance of their institutions is well established. The academic community should, however, also value participation in the life of society as a whole and here the record is less encouraging (Plantan 2004) even if there are many encouraging examples of individuals and institutions that engage very closely with society. As one example, the University of Pennsylvania conducts extensive outreach activities in its immediate neighbourhood of West Philadelphia. The importance the university gives to its outreach activities in a socially and economically disadvantaged part of the city is even reflected in its most recent financial report (University of Pennsylvania 2009: 3-9) and in statements by its president (Campus Compact 2010).

If we take the slogans about the knowledge society seriously, it is difficult to see how higher education institutions could choose not to engage on a wide range of societal issues. This touches on the very role of higher education in modern societies and on the responsibility of the academic community towards the broader community of which it is a part.

A responsible community

For higher education to play an important role in safeguarding values and ethics, the academic community must be conscious of its responsibility. The question is not only about safeguarding values and ethics in higher education, but equally about safeguarding values by and through higher education and research.

Ethics is, of course, a discipline taught and researched at universities. That is not disputed but that is also not what is under consideration. Rather than the role of a specific academic discipline, the question is what responsibility the academic community might have for transmitting values and developing the ability to think ethically in all higher education graduates regardless of their academic specialisation and regardless of whether they graduate with a first, second or third degree.[47] Ethics should not be considered the preserve of philosophers, theologians and graduates of a limited number of other disciplines, one of the common denominators of which seems to be that graduate pay is relatively low.

Rather, a concern for ethics and values must be a task of the entire academic community, which must identify with it and not consider it an added burden imposed from outside. Ethics and values must be an integrated dimension of all study programmes, not as a separate course to be taken and then forgotten about but as a dimension that permeates the whole study programme. The reason is that ethics and values are not issues to be mulled over at leisure. Rather, they confront us in

---

47. Frequently referred to as Bachelor's, Master's and Doctoral degrees, but since these terms – with the possible exception of Doctoral – are specific to certain systems, the generic terms as developed within the European Higher Education Area are preferred.

our everyday lives regardless of our professional and personal activities. Engineers, doctors, financial officers, political scientists, social workers, teachers, biologists and historians are all at some point in their careers likely to be faced with dilemmas of ethics and values, as are graduates of any other academic discipline one can think of – at least it is difficult to think of a discipline whose graduates will not at some point be faced by such issues. The issues may vary from profession to profession and from situation to situation, but they have one thing in common: there are few ready-made answers. There is no "frequently asked questions" service that graduates can consult for quick answers to difficult issues. In most cases, they will need to work out the solutions for themselves, hopefully in discussion with colleagues and friends, but ultimately the responsibility for the decisions made will be theirs, alone or as part of a professional team. Higher education must develop the ability in its graduates to find answers to questions of ethics and values as well as to identify potential issues in the first place. Future graduates may well be criticised for the decisions they will make in concrete situations but higher education should at least put them in a situation of not being criticised for not being aware of the issues or of being unable or unwilling to address them.

Educated persons

Ultimately, the question of the responsibility of the academic community for ethics and values may come down to our vision of what an educated person is. Different societies and ages have had different views of what an educated person is. European societies of a century ago valued classical education in a way that finds little echo today, whereas the literacy we take for granted and no longer even consider a distinctive feature of education except in the relatively rare cases where literacy is utterly lacking may not be considered of great importance in societies whose culture is primarily oral – including those of our own ancestors of a few centuries ago.

The first point to be made in seeking to refine our vision of the educated person is perhaps to distinguish between education and training. Training develops very useful skills and the ability to carry out specific tasks. The importance of training should not be underestimated or belittled. Our societies depend on the skills thus developed and we are all likely to undergo training numerous times in the course of our lives, from cleanliness training as toddlers through computer training at various stages of our lives to preparation for retirement as mature adults. Nevertheless, training is not education. Education concerns the ability not only to develop skills but also to identify the need for skills, to analyse the processes involved, to question whether the skills we set out to develop are the ones that we really need and in what circumstances we need them and to ask the fundamental questions of life. If we jump back to our discussion of the audit society for a second, training may be compared to the audit and education to the more fundamental questions the audit too often fails to ask.

Higher education graduates must be fully literate for modern society. That of course includes the ability to read and write, but well beyond the traditional definition of literacy as mastering the alphabet. Traditional literacy, incidentally, is a far steeper challenge for those whose languages, like Japanese or Chinese, use non-alphabetical writing systems with hundreds and sometimes thousands of distinctive characters. Literacy in the broader sense includes being able to read sophisticated texts as well as the ability to write such texts oneself, in a way that makes one's texts stimulating and interesting to read. If this author were allowed a sigh of frustration after many years of working with highly educated people, it would be that the ability to write clearly, intelligently and reasonably elegantly is alas not something to be taken for granted in higher education graduates, nor does it seem to be much valued in our broader society. Whenever higher education is accused of not living up to the expectations and priorities of broader society, its inability or unwillingness to develop the writing skills of its graduates comes to mind as a readily available example.

Literacy for modern societies also, in this author's view, encompasses numeracy and an understanding of natural sciences and social sciences as well as of one's own past and that of others. This author also cannot conceive of literate graduates unable to make good use of computers or to work fluently in a language other than the one in which they were raised, of graduates uninterested in other cultures and beliefs or unconcerned about the environment. Whatever their professional or personal activity, the resolutely monolingual, monocultural and monoperspectival[48] will be lacking not only in training but in education.

As societies, we need highly developed competence in as many areas of knowledge as possible. As individuals, we need to develop advanced competence in at least one area. However, even though advanced specialised competence is important, it is not sufficient. We need subject specialists but we also need intellectuals: those who are able to put their advanced competence in one or more subject areas into a broader context, to identify not only solutions to specific problems but also whether those solutions are beneficial to broader society and tenable in the long run as well as in the immediate future and to consider whether the action to be taken is morally justifiable and whether it is in line with the values on which we wish to build our societies.

This is a formidable challenge but who will rise to it if not the higher education community? If we agree that we should learn *non scholae sed vitae* – not for school but for life – these are among the key competences that higher education must provide and the academic community needs to define the institutional policies required to meet the challenge.

Institutional policies for ethics and values

The policies and practices of higher education institutions must promote values. The link between the two is important: in the same way that democratic culture cannot be developed through lecturing if one's practice is authoritarian, a concern

---

48. Probably not a dictionary entry but a useful term nonetheless.

for values and ethics cannot be transmitted unless institutional practice reflects this concern. Institutional practice affects the credibility of institutional policies. Higher education institutions which were unethical in their practice or failed to take action against students and staff who act unethically would lose credibility in the same way as a police force riddled with corruption. Developing the ability of graduates to reflect on ethics and values should therefore be a part of the mission statement of higher education institutions and they should recognise the imperative for their own policies as well as their own staff to meet these high standards.

In the institutional context, study programmes are the main tools for developing the competences of learners. As already mentioned, the most effective measure to instil all graduates with a concern for ethics and values is probably not to require them to take mandatory ethics courses. A course on "ethics and values for all" could easily have the effect of a course in "Pragmatism 101" – one does not care whether one understands it as long as one knows enough to pass the exam. All study programmes should encourage students to think about values and ethics in relation to their studies and to situations they may face as professionals and as citizens. This dimension of ethical reflection should be introduced at an early stage of a study programme and should remain present throughout and at all levels. It should be integrated into the descriptions of learning outcomes, which at least in the European context are likely to be an important part of the institutional policy agenda over the next few years where it has not become one already.

At all levels, study programmes must challenge students to think about ethics and values and the programmes must aim to develop the ability to weigh consequences in the long term as well as the short term, for broader society as well as for one's immediate environment. Clearly, long-term survival is a moot point if short-term survival is endangered but short-term survival or the flourishing of one's immediate neighbourhood is of limited value if those very policies doom our broader society in the longer term. Reflection on ethics and values requires the ability to see an issue from different points of view: what the Council of Europe in its programme on history teaching has come to term "multiperspectivity" (Council of Europe 2001, Stradling 2001). The ability to look at an issue from several angles is not the same as accepting all views as valid, but in order to influence as well as learn from others, we must understand their points of view. In a different order, an attempt to explain why outrageous events such as ethnic cleansing took place in given circumstances is not the equivalent of condoning the actions of the transgressors. Rather, to prevent repetition we must seek to understand the reasons why the transgressions occurred. These are abilities that study programmes must develop.

Institutional policies for research programmes are inherently difficult to devise. On the one hand, the academic community is committed to the freedom of research and rightly so. Discovery cannot be pre-programmed but that is not to say that institutions and public authorities cannot legitimately have policies for the areas for which funding will be provided as well as standards for ethical issues. Some are self-evident: plagiarism or falsification of experiments or results are unacceptable, full stop.

However, transgression may often be difficult to detect since this may require competences that few except the transgressors possess. Sometimes cheating is discovered by chance, such as when a medical researcher who had falsified data was uncovered not because the results seemed improbable but because someone happened to notice that the researcher claimed to have obtained data from a register that had not yet been established at the time when he claimed to have received the data. In spite of the difficulties involved, institutions would most likely gain from assigning institutional responsibility for research ethics to elected officials, such as vice rectors or vice deans, supported by some administrative staff resources. These must be reasonable: the purpose is not to install an all-powerful body that will quench research initiatives.

The same applies to arrangements for funding. Few higher education institutions can realise their ambitions through classical, non-earmarked funding alone and there is a need for reasonable oversight of institutional funding to ensure compliance with ethical standards but at the same time it is important that this oversight is not intrusive and that it does not discourage institutions, departments and individuals from seeking funding from bona fide partners. External funding is of course not suspect in itself; some sources of funding may, however, prove problematic and could cause the institution considerable damage. Therefore, institutions should have policies that prevent funding from questionable sources or from sources that could tarnish the reputation of the institution. One good example would be the institutions that severed relations with funders that violated the international sanctions of apartheid South Africa; another would be vigilance against funders involved in child labour or illicit trade.

Institutional arrangements for such oversight would probably not be able to root out all cases of fraud or questionable funding but they would probably help reduce the number of cases. They would also send a strong signal to the academic community as well as to broader society that higher education is focused on ethics and values.

Conclusion

In his *Devil's Dictionary*, the US journalist Ambrose Bierce defined responsibility as

> A detachable burden easily shifted to the shoulders of God, Fate, Fortune or one's neighbor. In the age of astrology, it was customary to unload it upon a star (Bierce 1983: 271).

This is, of course, not a definition with which higher education can identify. Ethics and values are not a burden detachable from the mission of higher education. Rather, the higher education community may need to identify with Garrison Keillor's imagined Mid-Western community of Lake Wobegon, where the local church is named Our Lady of Perpetual Responsibility. The responsibility of higher education extends to all its purposes:

- preparation for the labour market;
- preparation for life as active citizens in democratic society;
- personal development;

–   maintaining and developing an advanced knowledge base (Bergan 2005, Council of Europe 2007).

This cannot be accomplished without devising institutional policies that take a holistic view of higher education; that aim to develop future citizens and ethically conscious individuals as well as future economic actors – and that do not seek to develop these qualities and competences in all their graduates as well as in all their staff.

This author's native language, Norwegian, has the term *helstøpt*, which literally means "moulded in one piece" and which denotes an individual of unquestionable character and integrity and conveys connotations of a holistic view of the person. This must be a key goal of higher education: to develop citizens with ethical awareness, an understanding of values and commitment to society.

To the classical definition of learning outcomes – knowledge, understanding and the ability to do – higher education must add a fourth dimension: the ability to be.

References

Anderson B. (1983), *Imagined Communities. Reflections on the Origin and Spread of Nationalism*, Verso, London.

Bergan S. (2004), "Higher education governance and democratic participation: the university and democratic culture", in Bergan S. (ed.), *The University as* Res Publica: *Higher Education Governance, Student Participation and the University as a Site of Citizenship*, Council of Europe Higher Education Series No. 1, Council of Europe Publishing, Strasbourg.

Bergan S. (2005), "Higher education as a 'public good and a public responsibility': what does it mean?", in Weber L. and Bergan S. (eds) (2005), *The Public Responsibility for Higher Education and Research*, Council of Europe Higher Education Series No. 2, Council of Europe Publishing, Strasbourg; reproduced in this volume.

Bergan S. (2009), "Public responsibility and institutional autonomy – Where is the balance?" in Bastian Baumann et al. (2009), *Past, Present and Future of the* Magna Charta Universitatum. *Celebrations of the XX Anniversary of the* Magna Charta Universitatum, Bononia University Press, Bologna; reproduced in this volume.

Bierce A. (1983), *The Enlarged Devil's Dictionary*, edited by Hopkins E. J., Penguin American Library, London (first published in 1911, as *The Devil's Dictionary*).

Bologna Process (2001), Prague Communiqué.

Bologna Process (2010), "Budapest-Vienna Declaration on the European Higher Education Area".

Campus Compact (2010), "Penn President Amy Gutmann's passion for engagement", in *Compact Current*, Summer 2010, pp. 1-2.

Council of Europe (2001), Recommendation Rec(2001)15 of the Committee of Ministers to member states on history teaching in twenty-first-century Europe.

Council of Europe (2007), Recommendation CM/Rec(2007)6 of the Committee of Ministers to member states on the public responsibility for higher education and research.

Hannam J. (2009), *God's Philosophers. How the Medieval World Laid the Foundations of Modern Science*, Icon Books, London.

Persson A. (2004), "Student participation in the governance of higher education in Europe: results of a survey", in Bergan S. (ed.), *The University as* Res Publica*: Higher Education Governance, Student Participation and the University as a Site of Citizenship*, Council of Europe Higher Education Series No. 1, Council of Europe Publishing, Strasbourg.

Plantan F. (2004), "The university as a site of citizenship", in Bergan S. (ed.), *The University as* Res Publica*: Higher Education Governance, Student Participation and the University as a Site of Citizenship*, Council of Europe Higher Education Series No. 1, Council of Europe Publishing, Strasbourg.

de Ridder-Symoens H. (2006), "The Intellectual Heritage of Ancient Universities in Europe", in Sanz N. and Bergan S. (eds), *The Heritage of European Universities*, second edition, Council of Europe Higher Education Series No. 7, Council of Europe Publishing, Strasbourg, pp. 79-89.

Sanz N. and Bergan S. (eds) (2006), *The Cultural Heritage of European Universities*, second edition, Council of Europe Higher Education Series No. 7, Council of Europe Publishing, Strasbourg.

Stradling R. (2001), *Teaching 20th-Century European History*, Council of Europe Publishing, Strasbourg.

University of Pennsylvania (2009), *2008-2009 Financial Report.*

II. Public responsibility

Higher education as a "public good and public responsibility": what does it mean?[49]

Introduction

The right to education is fundamental, an integral part of our European heritage values,[50] and one that is included in the European Convention on Human Rights. In European countries, it is, in fact, not only a right but also a legal obligation for certain age-groups, and the average grade school student may well emphasise the aspect of obligation rather than that of right. There is general agreement that public authorities have a duty to provide education for all at basic level, and the interpretation of what basic level means has been expanding. As a result, the length of mandatory schooling has tended to expand over the past couple of generations – but not to the level of higher education.

The situation with regard to higher education, then, is somewhat less clear, even if the concept of public higher education is very strong in Europe. Today, there is a high level of public involvement in higher education in our continent, and this was reflected in the communiqué adopted by the "Bologna" ministers at the Prague Higher Education Summit:

> As the Bologna Declaration sets out, ministers asserted that building the European Higher Education Area is a condition for enhancing the attractiveness and competitiveness of higher education institutions in Europe. They supported the idea that higher education should be considered a public good and is and will remain a public responsibility (regulations etc.), and that students are full members of the higher education community (Bologna Process 2001).

On the face of it, the statement by the Bologna ministers would seem to reaffirm a well-established European practice. However, we also know something about

---

49. This article was published in Weber, Luc and Bergan, Sjur (eds) (2005): *The Public Responsibility for Higher Education and Research*, Strasbourg: Council of Europe Publishing. Council of Europe Higher Education Series No. 2.

50. The point can be illustrated by two quotes from Sanz and Bergan (2006): "In terms of cultural heritage, the university presents itself as an actor of collective responsibility guaranteeing the sense of certain moral, intellectual and technical values. Freedom of belief, freedom of teaching and the preservation of memory – physical or intellectual – teach values for life and for respect between generations. The project embarked from an attempt at defining a conceptual and contextual framework for the concept of university heritage as well as for considerations deriving from the role of universities as heritage in Europe. In addition, the university appeared as a space for reflection on the delimitation or enlargement of the term 'heritage'. This programme was inserted into a discussion already under way concerning a heritage that was constantly widening its definition and its basis for social, cultural, economic and symbolic action" (p. 11); and "Heritage is conceived of as an inheritance, as a cultural product and as a political resource. This practice includes more possible kinds of usage, not only those aiming at improving our knowledge of the past, as in the case of history. Rather, heritage conveys contemporary economic, cultural, political or social use" (p. 13).

the context in which the statement was made, which is one of stagnating or even diminishing public budgets combined with increased claims on the public purse, an increase in the provision of private higher education and in higher education with no link to public higher education systems (transnational education) and a general debate on the proper role of public authorities, generally cast as a debate on the role of the state.[51]

This context warrants the question of whether the statement in the Prague Communiqué should be seen not primarily as a statement of fact but as an expression of concern. When you need to state the obvious, it may be an indication that it is no longer obvious. The communiqué also provides an opportunity to explore what the ministers' statement could actually mean, as the concept of higher education as a public good is less straightforward than it would seem at face value. In order to do so, I shall seek to outline some questions raised by the statement and then try to identify some common ground before exploring a number of "twilight zones" where the debate deserves to be phrased in shades of grey rather than stark contrasts of black and white. We are at the beginning of a debate, and my ambition is limited to discerning some areas where we might move toward agreement as well as outlining some issues for further discussion.

Some questions

Beyond the question of why ministers felt the need to underline that higher education is a public good and a public responsibility, a number of questions could be asked about the statement. The first one is in what sense the term "public good" is used.

The problem here is that the term is well established in economic theory, where it denotes a good that is freely available to be enjoyed by all. In more technical terms – and that may be a risky undertaking on the part of a non-economist – a public good has been described as non-rival and non-excludable, meaning that one person's consumption of the good does not prevent that of others, and that it is not possible to exclude anyone from enjoying the good (Stiglitz 1999). It follows that public goods are not readily tradable, whereas their opposites – private goods – are essentially sold on the market for exclusive consumption by one person or a group of persons paying for the privilege.

While widespread access to higher education is a cornerstone of higher education policy in most European countries, unrestricted and free access is not a realistic description of the situation: higher education – whether in the form of higher education provision (courses and study programmes) or its outcomes (diplomas and qualifications) can actually be traded and people can be excluded from higher education. In fact, in our societies, concern about the knowledge or qualifications gap is an indication that exclusion is to some extent the real situation today, and

---

51. In this article, I shall prefer the term "public authority" to "state" or "state authorities", as responsibility for higher education is in some countries located at other levels, for example in federal states.

experience from other political regimes past and present shows that undemocratic rulers will go to some length to exclude their subjects – "citizens" is hardly the word to use – from at least the kind of education that may awaken their curiosity and stimulate critical thinking. While these are perhaps extreme examples, the knowledge gap is of great concern also in democratic societies and may well be one of the most important social and economic divides in modern democratic societies. There is also solid evidence that higher education is tradable, hence our concern about the inclusion of higher education in the General Agreement on Trade in Services (GATS) and our distinction between non-profit and for-profit higher education providers. Therefore, higher education is hardly a public good in the economic sense of the term, and it is difficult to envisage policies that would render it so in the foreseeable future.

We are left, then, with an economic term used as a political statement. It is of course not unusual for terms to mean different things in different contexts, or even to change meaning in the course of time,[52] and life is certainly much more than economics. Yet, using a well-established term from one area of knowledge in a different context is not unproblematic, and this shift in usage from the domain of economics to that of a political and social context is perhaps a part of the reason for the confusion. Reality does not always correspond to ideal types, and higher education is probably situated somewhere in between public and private goods, or has elements of both (Quéau 2002, who uses the term "global common good"). In this sense, one is also reminded of the biblical parable of the talents.[53] While the talents were given to individual servants by a demanding master – and were thus eminently private goods – the parable does underline the obligation to put these to good use. This aspect may not be a part of the economic definition of a public good, but it underlines an obligation incumbent on public authorities as well as on individuals: not to let their resources and talents lie idle but to use them in a beneficial way and for the greater good.

The most reasonable interpretation of the term as used in the Prague Communiqué seems to be that good quality higher education should be enjoyed by as many qualified persons as possible on equal terms, and that is a goal that would meet with approval in much of Europe.

If a public good is not marketable, does it also mean it is free of charge? This seems to be a common assumption, and the assumption is reinforced through association with the concept of public service, or rather the French concept of *service public*, which, at least in France, has strong connotations of non-payment. However, even this needs to be nuanced. At least in some countries, services that are regarded as public are in fact performed for a fee, which is normally quite modest. Passports would be

---

52. The obvious example from English is "gay", which in the space of a generation has gone from describing a mood to describing sexual orientation, and the opposite of which is no longer "sad" but "straight".
53. Matthew 25, 14-27.

one example. More importantly, all goods or services come at a price – the question is, who pays? Even where modest fees are charged, a substantial part of the real cost is borne not by individual users in accordance with their actual use of the service, but by a collective through other payment mechanisms – typically taxes – and where wealth or ability to pay is as likely a criterion as actual use of the service.

However, the ministers do not only refer to public good; they also speak about public responsibility. The next question is, therefore, why the two terms have been coupled. I take the explicit connection between the two as an indication that the ministers are in fact concerned that higher education may not be a public good after all or – more to the point – that higher education may not be accessible on equal terms to all qualified candidates. Public responsibility is in a sense an instrument or a precondition for such a system of higher education, and the more relevant issue for the European Higher Education Area may be to explore the implications of a public responsibility for higher education. I will seek to do so by first outlining some areas on which I believe there is general agreement and then address some points on which opinions are likely to diverge.

Yet another possible question is, what is meant by public?[54] In the widest sense, the public encompasses all members of society and the public sphere encompasses what is done collectively or on behalf of at least a large part of society. For the purpose of this article, however, I will focus on public authorities, as the operationalisation or agent of society.

Some common ground

Higher education framework

Given that there is agreement that public authorities have some kind of responsibility in higher education, this responsibility should at the very minimum extend to the make-up of the education system or, if you prefer, the framework within which higher education is delivered, regardless of by whom.

One important part of the higher education system is the qualifications framework. There is agreement in Europe that public authorities decide the degree structure and its requirements. If this were not to be the case, one of the key goals of the Bologna Process – a three-tier degree structure – would be difficult to implement, as would the goal of transparency. Nor can it easily be argued that public responsibility for the degree structure makes it too rigid, as there is considerable scope for variation within the overall qualifications framework. There seem to be two conflicting tendencies today: on the one hand, study programmes give individual students possibilities to choose combinations that appeal to them for various reasons, whether of personal interest or judgments about career perspectives and, on the other hand, there is increasing awareness that this diversity has to be fitted to an overall framework that

---

54. I am grateful to Birger Hendriks for making this point.

can be described in a transparent way. These two tendencies can only be combined within a transparent degree structure with a limited number of levels, but one that allows flexible combinations of credits and courses at each level. Establishing and maintaining this framework is a public responsibility.

Another important element of the higher education framework is quality assurance, where there now seems to be agreement that public authorities are responsible for ensuring that there is adequate provision for transparent quality assurance, whether they themselves carry it out or not. Quality assurance is also an example of how the perceptions of the proper role of public authorities in higher education may change quite rapidly. As late as 1997, when the Council of Europe/UNESCO Recognition Convention (Council of Europe and Unesco 1997) was adopted, the need for formalised quality assurance was still disputed, and the convention had to circumscribe references to quality assurance by referring to institutions and programmes making up the higher education system of a party. We also had to include separate provisions for parties having a formalised system for the assessment of institutions and programmes and those that did not.[55] Today, the discussion is no longer of whether but of how, and public responsibility for a transparent quality assurance system is one of the cornerstones of the Bologna Process.

Autonomy

University autonomy[56] is another key element of the Bologna Process and would in the first instance seem to have more to do with public authorities keeping out of matters beyond their competence than interfering with them (Magna Charta Observatory 2002). This is in a certain sense true, but university autonomy is an important part of the higher education framework and can only exist if public authorities make adequate provisions for autonomy in the legal and practical framework for higher education, that is, if public authorities not only ensure laws that guarantee autonomy but also ensure that these laws are implemented. The same is true for higher education governance – balancing concerns of democratic participation, academic competence and stakeholder interests – which has to be implemented at institutional level but which cannot exist without an adequate framework, which again is the responsibility of public authorities.

Equal access

Another point on which there is general agreement and which again concerns the higher education framework rather than case-by-case implementation of the policy is the equal access of all qualified candidates to higher education. Here, the responsibility of public authorities really extends to two aspects of the same policy framework. Firstly, public authorities are responsible for ensuring that qualified

---

55. Cf. Section VIII of the convention.
56. It may be argued that institutional autonomy and the freedom of individual academics are at the very least two sides of the coin, possibly separate if related issues, and it may be asked whether universities and non-university higher education institutions should have the same kind of autonomy.

candidates are treated equally, that is, that the access process corresponds to the Weberian definition of the much-reviled term "bureaucracy": impartial decisions made according to transparent procedures and with predictable outcomes (Weber 1982: 105-157). In other words, whether you are admitted to higher education should depend solely on your qualifications and not on who assesses your qualifications, at what time your qualification is considered (as long as you apply within the published deadlines), your opinions, beliefs or other characteristics or what favours you might do the person handling your application, generally referred to as corruption.

This is the classical conception of the rule of law,[57] which is essentially that of passively ensuring equal treatment on the basis of the applicant's current situation. However, contemporary European societies tend to agree on a more activist approach under which public authorities are not only responsible for watching over the equitable application of rules but also ensuring equal opportunities through other means, in this case by taking measures to increase the number of qualified candidates through improving educational opportunities for underprivileged groups. The task, then, is not simply to administer an equitable procedure for qualified candidates, but also to increase the pool of candidates, for example through providing better education opportunities at lower levels of the system. Here, we are rapidly approaching the limits of consensus and the discussion may more appropriately be resumed under the consideration of the "twilight zones".

Higher education subject to general laws

A final example, which is not a minor one, is that higher education is subject to a good number of general laws intended to apply to society at large, and which influence the activities of higher education institutions. Examples include health regulations, for example on hazardous materials in laboratories, accounting practices, salaries or labour regulations, such as the maximum hours an employee can be required – or indeed is allowed – to work per week. Some of these measures are controversial – academic staff do not take lightly to attempts to curtail their working hours – but the principle that public authorities have a right and duty to regulate such matters and apply these regulations also to higher education is hardly at issue.

Absence of public monopoly

The "common ground" includes not only a set of responsibilities for public authorities but also the recognition that, in some areas, there is no public monopoly. Here, of course, we are beginning to address the limits of public responsibility. The most obvious of these is that there should be no public monopoly on higher education provision.[58] Higher education institutions may be required to operate within the framework established by public authorities but as long as they do so, it is difficult

---

57. Possibly more precisely conveyed by the German term *Rechtsstaat* or the Norwegian *rettsstat*.

58. Non-public higher education provision may be non-profit or for-profit; the former seems more readily accepted than the latter, but both forms are a part of the current higher education scene, if not in every country.

to argue that they have to be publicly run and financed. To me, the issue is not whether higher education institutions are public or private, but whether they are of good quality, are subject to quality assessment, offer programmes leading to recognised qualifications, offer equal access and ensure academic freedom for staff and students. To paraphrase two dictums of a now outmoded ideology, what matters is not the ownership of the means of education, but whether the cat catches mice.[59]

Secondly, public authorities have no monopoly on defining knowledge or truth. There is no lack of examples from both ends of the political spectrum to show what happens when the attempt is made or, less dramatically, of what happens to the development of research in an environment where, even on an apolitical basis, new and alternative ideas are frowned upon.

Some "twilight zones"

Anything goes in the name of autonomy?

However, there is a caveat to this assertion, and this takes us from the common ground of consensus to the "twilight zones" of controversy. Saying that there is no public monopoly on the definition of truth or the content of teaching is not equivalent to saying that all views are acceptable or that higher education staff may teach anything they want. For one thing, higher education staff also have to abide by laws prohibiting racial discrimination or slurs or incentives to violence and crime. There is, of course, in any society an inherent danger that such laws may be interpreted too narrowly, but as long as they are reasonably interpreted, such laws also clearly serve a noble purpose.

Secondly, higher education staff are required to be competent in their field, and this competence is defined by their peers even if the definition can sometimes be formally approved by public authorities. History teachers who make denial of the Holocaust an element of their courses could probably be prosecuted for breaking laws against inciting ethnic hatred, but they could also be attacked on the grounds of incompetence, since the reality of the Holocaust is not in doubt. Similarly, the medical profession has established criteria for what are academically accepted doctrines and practice, and these would normally be confirmed in legal terms by public authorities. Teaching medical students to treat patients by methods judged to be hazardous would invite disciplinary proceedings. Research is another matter, and the point is perhaps that while seeking new knowledge, and hence a redefinition of truth is acceptable and even laudable, this new knowledge has to be accepted by peers before it becomes a part of the teaching canon. This is nevertheless not an unproblematic point, as is shown in medicine by the case of Semmelweis, the current debate on human cloning and in more general terms by the tension between teaching and research in 16th- and 17th-century European universities, where teachers often had to lecture according to the established canon but disseminated new knowledge through their publications (de Ridder-Symoens 2006).

---

59. From Marx and Engels and Deng Xiaoping, respectively.

Funding issues

A characteristic element of what I have called the "twilight zone" is that it concerns the details of implementation more than the framework and it concerns what is negotiable in view of a compromise rather than absolute principles. An important part of it is made up of funding issues, the foremost of which is how much funding is reasonable for higher education. The absence of a public monopoly implies that public authorities will not fund all higher education provision, but it is equally clear that public authorities cannot reasonably run away from an obligation to provide substantial funding. That private provision is a part of the higher education system in many countries does not mean that public provision is no longer required. The difficult part is identifying how much public funding is reasonable, and on what conditions.

Public responsibility should extend to funding teaching and research in a wide diversity of academic disciplines, which is something market-driven higher education is unlikely to do. Many disciplines will have low staff and student numbers, but cultural, political, economic or other reasons will dictate that a society have a certain academic activity in these areas, which may concern less widely spoken foreign languages, less studied periods of history, relatively neglected fields of art or areas of mathematics and natural science currently out of vogue. Part of the point is that even areas that seem less important today may suddenly find themselves in the focus of public attention a few years down the road, as when many European countries scrambled to upgrade their meagre knowledge of Arabic language and culture in the wake of the oil crisis in the 1970s. An even stronger reason, however, is that areas that may not be important in numbers may be very important for our cultural identity or as a basis for developing the key concepts on which more applied knowledge is based. These are areas in which our societies need advanced competence, but they may not need large numbers of people with this knowledge.

The fact that public authorities provide significant funding for higher education institutions does not mean, however, that all higher education institutions fulfilling defined minimum quality standards have a claim on the public budget. Firstly, public authorities should have the right to distinguish in funding terms between public institutions, which public authorities fund entirely or substantially, and private ones, for which they provide much less funding or none at all. Secondly, in the same way that public authorities make judgments about the need for higher education institutions and programmes when they decide on the level and distribution of public funding for these institutions, they should be in a position to make similar judgments about public funding for private institutions. A decision that private institutions and programmes are recognised because they are of sufficient quality should not automatically mean they have a right to receive public funds. Needless to say, this is an important point in the context of GATS.

Student support

Student support is another key economic issue where no ready-made answer exists, but which is intimately linked to the public responsibility for making higher education accessible to wider groups and more individuals. The basic principle seems clear: it is a public responsibility that no qualified candidate should have to abstain from higher education because he or she lacks the means to study. This principle, however, raises a number of questions, such as how "qualified candidates" should be defined. Are we talking only about the academically promising ones or also about those who may barely make it through a study programme? Is public responsibility limited to funding some kind of higher education for qualified candidates, or does it extend to giving them access to and funding for the discipline and level of their choice? Is there a free choice of institution or should public student support be given a maximum price tag? Not least, should it be given as scholarships or loans, and if the latter, at market rates or more favourable student rates?

One argument has it that students should bear a substantial part of the cost of their studies because higher education will most likely give them access to more highly paid jobs, so that over a life time investment in higher education will pay off in pure economic terms. That may be so, although I suspect it is not true for all academic disciplines in all European countries. Some higher education graduates – lawyers would be an obvious example – may reasonably expect a high financial return on their investment of time and money, whereas others – schoolteachers would probably be a valid example – would not. An argument in favour of a high level of student support would be that if society believes higher education is vital to its development, and that a country as a whole should have advanced knowledge of a wide area of disciplines, society should also stimulate its members to seek higher education in as many fields as possible. Another argument is that even where there may be lifetime economic gain in pursuing higher education, not all qualified students will actually be in a position to raise the money needed to study in the first place.

If higher education is to be made more widely accessible, a reasonable student support scheme therefore seems to be vital, but there may be a case for designing it in such a way that it caters in particular to less favoured students. This is, however, a difficult discussion that goes well beyond the scope of this article, and it touches on such issues of principle as individual versus group rights and the legal relationship between young adults and their parents.

Direct student support through loans and scholarships is, however, only a part of the discussion. To the extent students do not pay the full cost of their education, they receive public support, and the question is how much such support they should receive or – to phrase it in more controversial terms – whether they should pay study fees. Traditionally, at least in many European countries, public higher education does not charge fees, and the issue is highly charged, even if – or perhaps precisely because – the issue is now being raised in some countries. In considering the issue of fees, it should be kept in mind that higher education is generally considered to be of benefit to the individual, even where it does not demonstrably increase overall lifetime earnings, and that access to higher education is not unbiased, in that young people from families of higher socio-economic status whose parents have higher education degrees are more likely to take higher education than those of lower socio-economic status with little or no education traditions in the family. Granted, this argument again raises the question of individual versus group rights, but it should at least serve to illustrate the fact that higher education free of charge to the individual is not an issue to be phrased in black and white.

The point is also illustrated by the opposite possibility: students paying the full cost of their education. Apart from the fact that the full cost of some study programmes would be prohibitive and could cut society off from certain kinds of much-needed competence, this model is also untenable on reasons of principle. While the benefits of higher education may be most immediately felt by those who graduate from it, all members of society benefit to some extent from a high general level of competence in that society. Certainly, the benefits of a medical education are not limited to doctors.

Funds from other sources

If it is recognised that public authorities do not have a monopoly on funding higher education, and indeed that they are unlikely to be able to provide funding at anything like the aspirations of higher education institutions, what is the role of private funding? This is, in my view, not a discussion of whether there should be private funding, but of whether there should be conditions for such funding. Where is the balance between the priorities decided by the governing body of a university and the power of outside funding to modify those priorities? If some academic disciplines will easily attract funding and others not, should a part of external funds be redistributed within the institution through some kind of "internal taxation", or would this be unfair on those who are able to raise money and discourage external sources from contributing because the priorities of those contributors will not be fully respected? Could external funds be used not only to improve the working conditions in certain fields, for example by financing advanced equipment or travel, but also to improve salaries of staff or scholarships for students? In the latter case, access may be improved, but students' choice of academic field may be influenced as much by immediate possibilities for financing their studies as by their own interest in the disciplines or by considerations of future earnings.

This is of course not a new issue: in past centuries, the seminary was often the only possibility for sons of poor families to break out of a cycle of poverty and low status and to satisfy intellectual curiosity, even if they did not all have a burning vocation for the priesthood. Military academies have also been engines for social mobility. However, there are also examples of selection procedures for military training that aim to ensure that control over the armed forces rests with the dominant parts of society (Rouquié 1987: 84-93).

Funding from private sources is a valuable and much-needed supplement to public finance, but it should be subject to conditions. The precise implementation of this principle, however, implies a delicate balance between ensuring that public and institutional priorities are not unduly skewed through the power of external finance and avoiding setting up rules that would deter potential contributors.

Access policies – How directive and activist?

We considered that the role of public authorities in ensuring equal access to higher education was a part of the consensus, but we also indicated that there were limits to this consensus, and that the degree to which public authorities can direct institutions in their access policies is a part of the "twilight zone", as is the extent to which such policies should be "activist".

If it is recognised that educational opportunities at least to some extent depend on place of residence and socio-economic or cultural background, public authorities could take steps to ensure favourable access for members of underprivileged groups if these are considered to have the potential to do well in higher education even if they might not satisfy all access requirements at the time of application, or, if access is restricted and competitive, a certain number of qualified candidates from disadvantaged backgrounds may be given preference over better qualified applicants from more classical higher education backgrounds (Council of Europe 1997 and 1998).

Such measures, often referred to as "positive discrimination" or "affirmative action", are often controversial, as proven by the discussions in many countries about favouring access of women applicants to study programmes in which they are under-represented or measures in favour of ethnic minorities. The latter has frequently been a bone of contention in United States higher education, where the Bakke case is possibly the best-known example since *Brown v. the Board of Education*,[60] and where the Bush administration is now seeking to have current practice at the University of Michigan declared unconstitutional on the grounds that it discriminates against members of the majority.[61] In another case, Norwegian universities were directed to review policies favouring qualified women candidates for academic positions, in an attempt to recruit more women in fields where they are under-represented, in particular at the highest levels, because this had been judged unacceptable under the non-discrimination provisions of the European Economic Area.

Ultimately, the main argument in favour of activist public authorities in the domain of access is that the public responsibility for ensuring fair and equitable access to higher education is an important instrument in making higher education something close to a public good. However, exactly where the right balance is to be found between this highly important concern and other policy goals is likely to continue to be a matter of debate.

Consequences of quality assurance

As we have seen, a consensus on the need for quality assurance has emerged over the past five years or so. However, this consensus does not – at least not yet – extend to an agreement on what should be the consequences of quality assurance. At one level, while

---

60. In this landmark case from Topeka, Kansas, the US Supreme Court struck a decisive blow against the segregation of US schools.
61. See the *International Herald Tribune*, 17 January 2003, p. 3.

accreditation is in many countries given on the basis of quality assurance, the concept of accreditation is not accepted in all countries. Beyond the concepts, however, there is considerable discussion of what the goals and consequences of quality assurance should be. If an institution or programme receives a negative assessment, should it be closed, should it be given a deadline to bring its house in order but otherwise be left alone, or should a sustained effort be made to turn it into a good quality institution or programme? Most likely, the answer will depend on circumstances. An institution that is seen as important to the development of an underprivileged part of the country is likely to be looked at with more lenience than one that is located in an area where there are many alternatives, and the only study programme in a discipline public authorities consider important is more likely to receive the benefit of the doubt along with an infusion of funds than one that is considered expendable.

Nevertheless, some would go further and reject the notion that a quality assurance process could be linked to decisions concerning funding or licences to operate a given institution or programme. There may be a case for carrying out quality assurance solely with a view to improving existing higher education provision,[62] but in my view it is unreasonable to say that this must in all circumstances be the only purpose of quality assurance. Public funds for higher education are limited, and it would seem unreasonable to spend them on programmes of unsatisfactory quality unless other concerns would dictate a sustained effort to improve those programmes. Likewise, students would be badly served by funding policies that simply aimed to maintain programmes regardless of their quality.

Information

This brings me to my final point in this far from exhaustive overview of the "twilight zone", namely the responsibility of public authorities with regard to information to students, employers, parents and others. We all agree that they should receive correct and comprehensible information provided in good faith (UNESCO/Council of Europe 2001), and that for many kinds of information, this is primarily the responsibility of the education provider. However, what responsibility do public authorities have to oversee the information given by institutions? On the one hand, public authorities should not unduly interfere with academic autonomy and the right of institutions to provide the particular kind of information known as advertising, but on the other hand, public authorities do have some responsibility for ensuring that citizens are not led astray by patently untruthful publicity material.

Again, suggesting an overall rule of thumb is difficult, but I would suggest that public authorities should be responsible for providing information on the higher education

---

62. The European University Association institutional review programme is intended to support universities and their leaders in their efforts to improve institutional management and, in particular, processes to face change. The emphasis is laid on self-evaluation and allows the institutions to understand their strengths and weaknesses. Such reviews may make specific recommendations to institutional leaders regarding the internal allocation of budgets, but since the evaluation is independent of national or other funding sources there is obviously no link to decisions concerning such funding.

system, including its degree structure and on the institutions and programmes that make up the higher education system of a given country,[63] which also implies that the results of quality assurance exercises should be made public and easily accessible. Public authorities should also be able to suggest models for how institutions could provide information, and in some cases they should be able to enforce a specific format for the provision of information. Thus, I am fully in line with the authorities of those countries that have included in their laws an obligation for institutions to provide students with a Diploma Supplement[64] and/or have made the European Credit Transfer System mandatory. I also believe that public authorities should keep an eye on the overall information provided by institutions operating on their territory and that they should have as much power to act against systematic misinformation by higher education providers as against any other kind of false advertising.[65]

Right to university heritage

Finally, I would suggest that students, staff and society at large have a right to the heritage of universities, that this heritage should be a factor in shaping current policies, and that public authorities share a responsibility for making this right real. As we stated in a different context:

> The university heritage is not a story of immediate gratification, nor is it one of constant and unfailing success. Its importance is of a different order: the heritage of European universities is one of the most consistent and most important examples of sustainable success and achievement that Europe has ever seen. The university is a part of our heritage, and its future is decided now ... Our reflection on the university heritage coincides with a time when cultural heritage policies are no longer only identified with a typology or with a prescriptive approach to tangible and intangible resources, but are also aimed at valorising problems of heritage policies that also have to do with filiation and affective ties (cultural, sociological, confessional, territorial). From these ties a specific kind of current relationship to the ways of establishing memories can be defined, based on what is lived today (Sanz and Bergan 2006: 176).

The Bologna Process builds on the heritage of European universities, and the ability to adapt to changing circumstances is very much a part of this heritage. The public responsibility for higher education also includes conserving and building on this heritage and to transmit it to future generations. A medieval scholar might not recognise organised higher education exchange programmes; even if Dom Sancho I of Portugal set up a kind of mobility scholarship scheme as early as the 12th century (Saraiva 1978: 109), he would be surprised at the range of today's

---

63. In this respect, the European Network of National Information Centres on Academic Recognition and Mobility (ENIC) information centres and the National Academic Recognition Information Centres (NARICs) play an important role.
64. In 2005, ministers of the European Higher Education Area committed to issuing the Diploma Supplement automatically, free of charge and in a widely spoken European language.
65. In discussions at the conference for which this article was written, the need for proper guidance to students was strongly emphasised and, I believe, rightly so. However, the main responsibility for guidance would seem to lie with the institutions rather than with public authorities as considered here.

academic disciplines and the fact that academic discourse is no longer in Latin, and he would probably consider the idea of a Socrates Office in Athens as an unnecessary bureaucratisation of philosophy. Yet, the idea of a European Higher Education Area is not only one he could easily identify with, but probably one he would take for granted.

By way of conclusion

As the ambitions for this article were limited to outlining the issues and identifying some areas of consensus as well as for further discussion, the conclusions can hardly be final. They are made up of four elements.

Firstly, I believe public authorities have exclusive responsibility for the framework of higher education, including the degree structure, the institutional framework, the framework for quality assurance and authoritative information on the higher education framework. The framework cannot be left to others.

Secondly, I would maintain that public authorities bear the main responsibility for ensuring equal opportunities in higher education, including access policies and student finance. This is a crucial area in making higher education as much of a public good as possible, and the overall goal for public authorities in this area must be to make sure that any person living in the country[66] be able to make full use of his or her abilities regardless of socio-economic and cultural background, financial possibilities and previous education opportunities.

Thirdly, I believe public authorities should have an important role in the provision of higher education. While there should be no public monopoly on higher education provision, public authorities should be heavily involved not only in designing the framework but also in the actual running of higher education institutions and programmes, to contribute to good educational opportunities on reasonable conditions and to ensure that higher education encompasses a wide variety of disciplines and levels.

Fourthly, and this point is in part a consequence of the other three, public authorities in my view have an important financial responsibility for higher education. Public funds may and should be supplemented by money from other sources, but these alternative funding sources should never be a pretext for public authorities not to provide substantial public resources.

In thinking about higher education as a public good, I was reminded of an illustration in one of the first books I can remember reading. Snorri Sturluson was an Icelander, but he wrote the sagas that have now come to be considered as one of

---

66. To avoid misunderstanding, I deliberately use the more cumbersome formulation "any person living in the country" rather than "citizen", as I believe this obligation extends not only to those who are citizens in the legal, "passport" sense of the term, but to all those who are citizens in the larger sense as members of a given society. For this, residence is a surer guide than cultural or political identity. Besides, at least in some contexts, "citizen" is now used as the public policy equivalent of "consumer".

the main items of Norwegian literature and the first attempt at writing Norwegian history. In one of his illustrations of Olav Haraldsson's – Saint Olaf's – final battle at Stiklestad on 29 July 1030, Halfdan Egedius showed a steady stream of people bearing arms and moving in the same direction. In the laconic style of the sagas, the caption to this particular drawing simply states that "all paths were filled with people" (Snorri Sturluson 1964: 453). My vision of higher education as a public good is something like this, except that the arms are to be replaced with a desire for learning and that the people on the paths are on their way not to battle – an extreme form of competition – but to higher education institutions and programmes based on competition but even more on co-operation, where they will find a wide variety of offers on terms that will not exclude any qualified candidate, and that will:

– prepare them for the labour market;

– prepare them for life as active citizens in democratic society;

– contribute to their personal growth;

– maintain and develop an advanced knowledge base.

This is no small challenge, but it is vital to our future that we meet it. I am convinced it is one that can be met, and that public authorities bear the main responsibility for meeting it. Public authorities cannot do this alone, and they need to draw on the combined efforts of higher education institutions, students and staff, the private sector, and other members of society. However, the overall responsibility for the exercise and for its success or failure remains in the public domain – which is to say it is a collective responsibility for all of us as citizens of democratic societies.

References

Bologna Process (1999), Bologna Declaration, "The European Higher Education Area. Joint Declaration of the European Ministers of Education, 19 June 1999".

Bologna Process (2001), "Towards the European Higher Education Area". Communiqué of the meeting of European ministers in charge of higher education in Prague on 19 May 2001.

Bologna Process (2003), Berlin Communiqué, "Realising the European Higher Education Area", adopted by European ministers of education on 19 September 2003.

Council of Europe (1997), Recommendation No. R (97) 1 of the Committee of Ministers to member states on private higher education.

Council of Europe (1998), Recommendation No. R (98) 3 of the Committee of Ministers to member states on access to higher education in Europe.

Council of Europe and UNESCO (1997), Convention on the Recognition of Qualifications concerning Higher Education in the European Region.

Magna Charta Observatory (2002), *Autonomy and Responsibility – The University's Obligations for the XXI Century. Proceedings of the Launch Event for the Magna Charta Observatory 21-22 September 2001*, Bononia University Press, Bologna.

Quéau P. (2002), "Global governance and knowledge societies", *Development*, Vol. 45, No. 4, pp. 10-16.

de Ridder-Symoens H. (2006), "The intellectual heritage of ancient universities in Europe", in Sanz N. and Bergan S. (eds), *The Heritage of European Universities*, pp. 79-89.

Rouquié A. (1987), *The Military and the State in Latin America*, University of California Press, Berkeley and Los Angeles.

Sanz N. and Bergan S. (eds) (2006), *The Heritage of European Universities*, second edition, Council of Europe Higher Education Series No. 7, Council of Europe Publishing, Strasbourg.

Saraiva J. H. (1978), *História concisa de Portugal*, Publicações Europa-America, Lisbon.

Snorri Sturluson (1964), *Snorres kongesagaer*, Norwegian translation by Anne Holtsmark and Didrik Arup Seip, Gyldendal, Oslo/Stavanger.

Stiglitz, J. E. (1999), "Knowledge as a global public good", in Kaul I. Grunberg I. and Stern M. A. (eds), *Global Public Goods: International Cooperation in the 21st Century*, Oxford University Press, New York.

UNESCO/Council of Europe (2001), Code to Good Practice in the Provision of Transnational Education.

Weber M. (1982), *Makt og byråkrati,* Gyldendals Studiefakler, Oslo; based on the 1922 edition of Weber M., *Wirtschaft und Gesellschaft*.

Public responsibility and institutional autonomy: where is the balance?[67]

Introduction

University autonomy is, along with academic freedom, one of the cornerstones of the European university heritage as well as of democratic society. For good reasons it is one of the underlying values of the European Higher Education Area. That university autonomy is enshrined as a core value is of course a good thing, but this has its own risks. Fundamental values are often taken for granted, carted off to ritual or harmless declarations and brought out in daylight on festive occasions but not given the oxygen that comes with daily use. Democracy itself is an example: 20 years ago, Europe was excited about democracy as the Berlin Wall fell and along with it the authoritarian regimes that were the Wall's only defenders. Today, democracy is largely taken for granted in Europe and it suffers its share of lost illusions, even if we also understand better than we did 20 years ago that democracy is not only about institutions, structures and laws. The structures can only work in a society imbued with democratic culture. This is one of several reasons why the work of the Magna Charta Observatory is fundamental, and it is one of the reasons why the Council of Europe, as an organisation devoted to democracy, human rights and the rule of law, is also an education organisation.

In the framework of the Council of Europe, the clearest formal statement on university autonomy and academic freedom is Parliamentary Assembly Recommendation 1762 (2006) (Parliamentary Assembly 2006), which was proposed by Josef Jařab, and he was well seconded by the Magna Charta Observatory, in particular by Andris Barblan. Josef Jařab proposed the recommendation in his (then) capacity as a Czech Senator and a member of the Council's Parliamentary Assembly but Senator Jařab has much more direct experience of the importance of university autonomy and academic freedom to democracy than most of us. He is not only a scholar of English literature and a former member of the Collegium of the Magna Charta Observatory. He was also a long-time dissident under the communist regime of Czechoslovakia, he was a university rector in the early days of democracy after the Velvet Revolution and his experience of the totalitarian regime did not shake his commitment to humanist values.

Even if the importance of university autonomy is not challenged by words, there is every reason to consider whether it is not challenged by silent practice. The

67. This article was originally published in Baumann, Bastian et al. (2009): *Past, Present and Future of the* Magna Charta Universitatum. *Celebrations of the XX Anniversary of the* Magna Charta Universitatum, Bologna: Bononia University Press. It is reproduced by kind permission of the Observatory for Fundamental University Values and Rights (Magna Charta Observatory).

"ivory tower" model of the university has, I would argue, never been an adequate description of reality – if it had, the university would not have survived as an institution for centuries – and it certainly is not today. The fact that higher education is part and parcel of broader society makes the question of autonomy a particularly urgent one.

University autonomy and academic freedom are closely related but they are nevertheless distinct concepts (Bergan 2002). Institutional autonomy refers to the freedom of institutions to carry out their mission of research and teaching, whereas academic freedom refers to the freedom of individual academics to teach, research and publish. Both are essential to democratic societies as well as to the university as an institution, but none is unrestricted. There may be valid reasons for restricting university autonomy and academic freedom, in the same way that there may be valid reasons for restricting the freedom of the press or the general freedom of expression in democratic society. These restrictions, however, should be exceptional and they should be limited to situations where the freedom itself may severely damage others or even endanger society.

Official secrets acts fall into the latter category, and the difficulty of drawing a clear line is illustrated by the potential for abuse of such acts, which are only valid if they genuinely protect the vital interests of a society and not merely protect the government in place from hostile press. Laws against denial of the Holocaust or against racial discrimination fall into the former category. Quite apart from the fact the reality of the Holocaust is not in doubt and that there is no factual basis for asserting that a person's value or abilities depend on race – which is in any case a nebulous concept – the damage caused to individuals through denial of the Holocaust or through racial discrimination is in most European societies considered more weighty than the possible restrictions on the freedom of expression caused by the laws in question. While most citizens would agree with the laws, they also need to be applied reasonably. Laws against pornography are yet another example. The majority of citizens see pornography not as a natural manifestation of one's liberty of expression but as an affront to human dignity. Nevertheless, society's understanding of what constitutes pornography evolves over time and is not the same in all societies.

A traditional view of autonomy

While university autonomy at first sight may have little in common with the preceding examples, I would argue that we need to reconsider our concept of autonomy. Traditionally, Europeans have had a legal view of autonomy, and it is one that does not distinguish very clearly between university autonomy and academic freedom. The traditional view has been that autonomy was guaranteed through laws, and the value of the law has tended to be taken at face value except in cases of fragrant violation (Bergan 2002). Examples of violations were mainly to be found in authoritarian regimes, where the lack of university autonomy and also of academic freedom were often seen as but one aspect of a general lack of freedom of expression or of freedom *tout court*. In our recent past, the Soviet Union was a clear example, and Belarus is, sadly, a current example that shows that even if university autonomy is a more widespread feature of European societies today than it was 20 years ago – as witness by the many universities who were able to sign the *Magna Charta Universitatum* only after the regime changes of the early 1990s – it is not a universal feature. Serbia of the Milošević years provides a particular example in that the 1998 Serbian Law on Universities included provisions that were clearly at variance with the basic principles of autonomy, including the appointment of rectors and deans by the government. In one case, a rector was also dismissed and a new one appointed by the minister for education even after the fall of Milošević and the introduction of democratic reforms in Serbia.

This means that the reality of university autonomy has not been widely questioned in democratic societies. The emphasis on legal provision and structure is not unique to considerations of university autonomy. Rather, democratic societies in Europe as well as in North America have tended to have a relatively formal view of what constitutes democracy. There has often been more emphasis on legislation and institutions than critical questioning of whether the laws and institutions functioned as intended. There were cases in which laws and institutions were clearly not democratic and that gave rise to reform movements, of which the Civil Rights movement in the United States in the 1960s is a vivid example. This movement led to legal reform, in particular in the south, and the Black population obtained the right to vote in states where this right had previously been curtailed. Even after the reforms, however, Blacks participated far less actively in political life than the White population. In the same sense, democracy was widely seen to have been established in the countries of central and eastern Europe once laws and institutions had been reformed in the wake of the regime changes of the early 1990s. These reforms were of course fundamental and their importance should not be underestimated. Legal and institutional reform were a necessary condition for democracy, but there was relatively little debate of whether they were sufficient conditions. As an example, it was only at the Third Summit of Heads of State and Government of the Council of Europe,[68] in Warsaw in 2005, that the concept of democratic culture was taken up in official texts adopted by the highest level of the Organisation, *in casu* in the Action Plan.[69] Democratic culture designates the set of attitudes, skills and understanding that make democratic laws and institutions work in practice, and it is therefore an essential condition of democracy.

The legal approach to autonomy has been combined with a strong emphasis on public financing of higher education. This is a characteristic that distinguishes higher education in Europe from that in the United States, even if the element of public financing has varied over time as well as between European countries. Public funding has been seen as a guarantee of independence and public authorities have been seen as neutral arbiters defending the public interest, or at least as more neutral than

---

68. See www.coe.int/t/dcr/summit/default_EN.asp?
69. www.coe.int/t/dcr/summit/20050517_plan_action_en.asp.

non-public actors. Again, this view is not unique to issues of university autonomy. A very illustrating example was the debate on broadcasting regulations in the Nordic countries in the 1980s, when moves were made to abolish the public monopolies on broadcasting and the legislation was amended to allow private broadcasting physically based on the territory of the country concerned. While the resulting liberalisation of broadcasting is uncontested today, in the 1980s there was a minority opinion which saw the public broadcasting monopoly as a guarantee of objectivity, a view that of course contrasted sharply with the strong emphasis on the diversity of the written media – a diversity cherished by all parts of the political spectrum.

New challenges to university autonomy

The preceding paragraphs lead us to a consideration of the environment in which university autonomy is exercised today. A part of that context has not been modified substantially over the past generation or two. European societies are democratic, and if anything, the main change has been the extension of democracy to parts of Europe that were under authoritarian rule until some 20 years ago. The ideological commitment to democracy is strong in most European countries. Belarus is a spectacular exception in terms of its official ideology, but also in Belarus democracy is a strong ideal for the opposition to the current regime, which includes a significant part of the academic community. The ideals of university autonomy and academic freedom are strong, as are the ideals of human rights, the rule of law and the freedom of expression. The changes over the past generation or two do therefore not alter the fundamental ideological basis for university autonomy.

What has also not changed is the fact that autonomy is not absolute, and that universities must relate to the societies of which they are a part. Nevertheless, European societies have changed in ways that may challenge university autonomy and lead us to rethink the concept as well as the ways in which it may be implemented.

Legal considerations

Even if university autonomy is not merely a legal issue, it is important that the principle of autonomy be included in national legislation. This is, however, not a major concern, as it seems to be well covered and as there seems to be no reason to expect that political authorities would want to take away provisions concerning university autonomy.

However, higher education legislation is not the only kind of laws that may impact on university autonomy. Like other organisations, universities are bound by a range of laws and regulations of more general scope and these will normally not have been devised with a particular view to their possible impact on university autonomy. Two trivial examples are safety regulations for laboratories and public accounting rules. University autonomy cannot be invoked to claim that there is no need for university laboratories to be protected or that there is no need for a university to keep accounts, nor would any university leader make such claims.

Other areas may be more problematic. Let me point to two in particular: immigration rules and labour legislation.

Most countries would like to increase academic mobility, and European ministers have made this one of the main goals of the Bologna Process. At the same time, however, many European governments aim to reduce migration and they have shown little inclination to exempt students and faculty from a general tightening of the regulations covering visas and work permits. I am personally not convinced that European countries have the policies we would need to attract many of the foreign students that have not been admitted to the United States following 9/11. European countries are less vocal about their restrictions, but they have restrictions all the same. The effect of these is that while university autonomy is a key principle of our societies, universities cannot make autonomous decisions on what students to admit and what faculty to hire. If their preferred candidates do not obtain visas and work permits, university autonomy in admissions and hiring remains theoretical.

Most countries have laws regulating working hours, and in many countries, these stipulate the maximum amount of hours an employee may work in a given period, such as a week, a month or a year. It is of course difficult to see how certain activities could be regulated, since some research is carried out by individual researchers and is not necessarily restricted to their offices. Inspiration may come and ideas be formulated at any time of the day and writing may be done in any suitable place. Nevertheless, some kinds of research activities could be regulated. If no special provision is made for university staff, this could reduce the ability of universities to conduct certain research activities (for example, laboratory experiments) or provide certain kinds of intensive teaching (for example, intensive courses on campus or during field trips). Depending on the provisions, labour legislation could also make it more difficult for universities to run schemes under which faculty may take on increased teaching loads in one period in order to have more sustained time for research in another period. The point is not that university employees have no need for labour protection and some regulation of working hours, but rather that such regulations must be flexible enough to allow a trade-off between periods of intense activity and periods of less intense activity, and that they must take account of the fact that many university employees choose to work more than a standard working week of 35, 38 or 40 hours.

Labour legislation must, in brief, take account of the fact that universities are not ordinary companies run on a classic company model. They are places at which people choose to work because their motivation lies in their commitment to a set of ideals or their personal interest in a discipline rather than in more classic motivations like remuneration and career perspectives, even if these motives are of course also present and even if remuneration is not the only motive for those working in more classical business companies.

In order to illustrate some of the possible impact of general laws on institutions that carry out a specific mission that may require specific legal provisions, it may be of interest to look at a recent court ruling concerning the Catholic Church. The details of the case have only partially been made public, and they are of little importance to this article. For our purposes, it is the principles of the case that matter. In summary, a lower level court – *tingrett* – in Norway found the Catholic Diocese of Oslo at fault for having removed a parish priest from his functions,[70] and the court bases its ruling on labour legislation protecting employees from dismissal except in strictly defined circumstances. The diocese argues that only the Church – through the local bishop – has the authority to decide who can rightfully be a priest. It follows that only the bishop has the authority, under Church law, to decide who can be a priest in a parish under the jurisdiction of the bishop. The priest in question is a member of a religious order and was recalled to his country of origin by the superior of his order. However, he refused the order and rather than bringing an appeal within the Church, according to Church law, he brought a civil case arguing he was wrongfully removed under Norwegian labour legislation. It is this line of argument that the *tingrett* decided in favour of.

The diocese appealed this verdict to a higher court and the higher court ruled in favour of the diocese. The case is, however, of great interest because it concerns the freedom of religion, guaranteed by the constitution as well as by international conventions to which Norway is a party, and its limits as well as the competence of religious bodies to define doctrine and requirements for employment. The Catholic Church is a minority church in Norway, but it has a high public profile in part because many of its members have or have had high profiles in Norwegian society and in part because it plays an important role in catering for immigrants. It is of course also a Church with a well-developed doctrine, Church law and structures and with a stronger international dimension than almost any other institution one can think of, with the much more loosely structured institution of the university as one of the very few possible "rivals". It may also be worth noting that the right to select candidates for ordination is not at issue: the priest has been rightfully ordained. The diocese does, however, maintain that by disobeying the bishop as well as the superior of his order, he cannot, according to Church law, administer the sacraments and he therefore cannot fulfil the functions of a parish priest. The case therefore concerned the right of the Church to decide who is a priest in good standing, which is a precondition for serving as a parish priest.

While this case concerns the Catholic Church, one could well imagine cases in which universities could justifiably argue that a given provision of a general law prevents the university from fulfilling its key functions. Even if the principle of university autonomy is enshrined in national law, other legal regulations may conflict with this principle and in effect reduce or threaten university autonomy. How would a court rule in the case of, say, a professor who had been duly appointed 20 years ago but who had not keep abreast of development in his or her field and could therefore no longer teach competently?[71] Would it be for a court or for an autonomous university to decide whether or not competence once held had been lost?

---

70. See www.katolsk.no/nyheter/2008/07/15-0001.htm; accessed on 16 July 2008. The court ruling, by the *tingrett*, was issued on 15 July.
71. Which is not to suggest that this was the issue in the case just referred to.

Increasing demand on public authorities and institutions

There may have been a view in the past that universities were beyond doubt useful to society in the long run, even if their usefulness may have been difficult to demonstrate in the short run. That view is not predominant today, when all sectors of society are faced with the question of their "added value" and demands for "value for money". Governments depend on the continued confidence of votes as expressed through elections but also strongly influenced by a public debate that rarely views higher education and research as absolute and unquestioned values. Public debate is even contradictory: higher education and research institutions are expected to provide answers to current problems and challenges, yet there is little understanding of the fact that immediate solutions are rarely possible and that even relatively quick solutions depend on sustained research in areas that may have been considered peripheral but that suddenly come into the spotlight. Many European countries had little competence on the Arab world prior to the oil crisis of the 1970s and an understanding of Arabic societies and political culture could not be developed overnight. Climate change is probably the most serious challenge we face today and while there is increasing awareness of the importance of facing up to this challenge, it can only be achieved through a combination of the political will to make difficult choices and competence developed though basic research in a wide range of disciplines as well as the ability to work across traditional academic disciplines.

Today, higher education works in an environment characterised by increasing demands on public institutions. The point here is not whether a higher education institution is publicly or privately owned and operated but rather that European public opinion tends to see beyond formal ownership and consider that higher education institutions fulfil public functions.

The public aspect of higher education has also been underlined by European ministers of education in the context of the Bologna Process. Twice – in Prague in 2001 and Berlin in 2003 – the ministers underlined that higher education is a public good and a public responsibility (Bologna Process 2001 and 2003). The operational part of their statement concerns the public responsibility, and it can be analysed from several angles. One question is whether the ministers were stating the obvious or expressing their concern that what has been an essential element of the European academic heritage is no longer a truth held to be self-evident. My view is that ministers were not stating the obvious. If we want public responsibility for higher education and research to remain a key feature of European policies, we also need to reconsider how this responsibility should be defined and implemented in our modern, complex societies. The Council of Europe has taken up this challenge, and the result of our reflections has been published (Weber and Bergan 2005) as well as given rise to a formal policy recommendation (Council of Europe 2007).

There is, then, an increasing demand for return on public investment and a decreasing willingness to spend public funds on purposes that are not seen as providing tangible return in the near to medium term. The increasing demands on public authorities gave rise to "new public management", which was intended to make public authorities more responsive to political priorities as well as more efficient in their management. From the vantage point of someone working in public administration, it is questionable whether actual practice corresponds to the intentions. Rather, the "new public management" seems to have provided non-public actors with greater freedom of action through deregulation of several sectors, whereas for public institutions the effect seems to have been the opposite: more bureaucracy[72] and more detailed management by public authorities.

The clearest example is perhaps what has come to be called the "audit society", where considerable time and efforts are spent on reporting and verification rather than on activities that are directly beneficial to the target groups concerned. For higher education institutions, this means that time and effort that could have been devoted to research, teaching and service to the broader society are spent on reporting and justification of activities. This is a phenomenon that most faculty would immediately recognise, and the demands for reports and justification come from within as well as outside of the institution, even if some of the "internal" requirements have "external" sources. It is also important to underline that the alternative is not to abolish all requirements for reporting and audit. The issue is not eliminating reporting and verification but finding reasonable control mechanisms that allow competent authorities to verify that funding is well spent according to intentions while ensuring that institutions and faculty are able to spend a sufficient proportion of their time and resources on their primary tasks. While the issue may seem technical, it directly concerns the principles of university autonomy. How can universities be autonomous if a significant part of their resources are spent fulfilling reporting and audit obligations imposed by outside authorities? My point is not that external control is illegitimate. Rather, what has come to be called the "audit society" illustrates two important points: firstly, that any good idea can be perverted and, secondly, that nothing is as elusive to regulation – and perhaps also to regulators – as common sense.

A diversity of actors and sources of finance

One characteristic of modern societies is the diversity of actors. At one level, one might question the scope for political decision making. With a high number of diverging agendas and interests and a stronger role of economic actors as well as of sector organisations, one may question whether the ability of political authorities to make and implement decisions that bind all of society is not less today than it was a generation ago. This is of course not to say that political decision making is irrelevant or unimportant, but political decision makers today do seem to face stronger competition from decision makers in other areas. In part, this is linked to the seemingly increasing complexity of individual societies and in part it is linked to internationalisation and the decreasing importance, in many areas, of national borders and

---

72. In the popular rather than the Weberian sense of the term.

national legal space. Not least in the economic area, actors unhappy with conditions in one country may have a rich choice of alternatives, which may again be used to influence conditions in the first country. The government of country A may decide that corporations of a given kind should pay a 25% tax on their earnings and may have valid reasons for its decision, but corporations may leave country A if country B is a viable location and only imposes a 10% tax. In modern societies, the public sphere seems to be shrinking and the private sphere expanding. Whether this is seen as a positive or a negative trend of course depends on one's vantage point, and the trend most likely has positive as well as negative effects. At the very least, however, there is reason to be concerned about our civic culture.

There is also reason to reflect on how, as societies, we can deal with the divergence of political, legal and economic space. The economy is largely global, politics is anything but local,[73] but our legal space is mostly national, with the notable exception of EU legislation and some international standards like the European Convention on Human Rights. It may well be argued that some of our most important advances in improving social conditions were made at a time when the economic, political and legal space largely overlapped. Therefore, social legislation and policy could be enforced within a single framework. At the time, this framework was the nation state, but a return to the nation state is neither possible nor, most likely, desirable. Rather, the challenge is creating a new political and legal space to match the global economic space.

Universities, therefore, need to relate to a diversity of actors, only some of which are public authorities. This has a direct impact on university finance. While classic public financing of higher education and research is important in Europe and is likely to remain so, this kind of basic financing is less important than it used to be. Few higher education institutions can fulfil their ambitions through classic public financing alone, and public financing is becoming more diversified and more strongly linked to projects and/or earmarked for specific purposes and objectives. If a university receives a grant from the ministry responsible for technology, foreign trade or industry, this is still public funding but unlike traditional block grants through the ministry responsible for higher education, this kind of public funding is likely to be given for carefully defined purposes. The same is likely to be true for most finance available from non-public sources, whether from business companies, large health organisations such as those combating cancer or cardiac disease or even private donors who may be generous in their support but are likely to have precise views of the academic disciplines on which they would their money to be spent. The trend, therefore, is for a higher proportion of overall higher education to be earmarked, which means that institutions have less influence over their use. They have a choice of whether to accept such funding or not, but they have less influence over actual use than they have with traditional allocations through the ministry responsible for higher education.

---

73. In contradiction to the famous dictum by former Speaker of the US House of Representatives "Tip" O'Neill to the effect that "all politics is local".

The traditional view of public authorities as neutral and disinterested funders is overly naive and underestimates the potential risks of relying on single-source funding. A development towards a diversity of funding sources could therefore potentially strengthen university autonomy but this potential is largely undercut by the predominance of earmarked rather than "free" funding from other sources as well as by the conditions attached to some of this funding. As one example, project funding provided on the condition that the funder have the authority to decide whether research results from the project may be published according to the standards of the discipline is problematic in relation to university autonomy as well as academic freedom.

The primacy of the economy

Bill Clinton's 1992 campaign slogan "It's the economy, stupid" has been quoted so often that it may have become a cliché. It nevertheless seems to give an apt description of much of the public debate about higher education in Europe. Even someone who tries to follow the public debate in this area could easily be left with the impression that the sole purpose of higher education is to help improve our economy.

Since saying that man does not live by bread alone could be taken to mean that our daily bread is unimportant, I hasten to underline that contributing to economic well-being is an important purpose of higher education. My point is simply that the current public debate is too one sided and that by creating the impression that higher education has only one basic purpose, it contributes to reducing university autonomy. The Council of Europe has identified four main purposes of higher education:

– preparation for sustainable development;

– preparation for life as active citizens in democratic societies;

– personal development;

– the development and maintenance of a broad, advanced knowledge base (Council of Europe 2007).

If public authorities and funders see only one of these purposes – the one relating most clearly to the economy – as relevant and fail to appreciate the broader mission of higher education as well as the link between the purposes, universities will be strongly encouraged to give priority to programmes and projects contributing to this goal in the short run. While this may ultimately be for the university to decide, and the priorities of others may therefore not impinge on university autonomy in a formal sense, there can be little doubt that university autonomy would be much better served by public recognition of all four major purposes as being of equal value. Even if universities may be formally autonomous to ignore the priorities of public authorities and other funders, there can be little doubt that priorities for public funding strongly influence university policies.

Institutional differentiation

That brings us to a different consideration of priorities and funding. Europe today has a more diversified higher education landscape than it had the proverbial generation ago. This is partly because the number of private institutions has increased, even if public institutions are still more numerous and above all cater to a far greater number of students than do private institutions, at least in most countries. It is also because the typology of higher education institutions has diversified in many countries. In addition to comprehensive research universities, many countries have also seen the development of what is often but unsatisfactorily referred to as non-university higher education. These are, for the most part, institutions that provide more professionally oriented higher education and that offer a higher proportion of their programmes at first degree or short-cycle level, even if many also offer second degree programmes and some may even offer third degree (doctoral) programmes. Internationally, the German term *Fachhochschulen* is often used as a generic term for these institutions, many of which are members of EURASHE (the European Association of Institutions in Higher Education).

The diversification of higher education institutions raises a series of issues in relation to university autonomy. Clearly, *Fachhochschulen* were developed – and funded – by public authorities because there was felt to be a need for the kind of higher education these institutions offer. In terms of academic prestige, they have, however, not come to be seen as quite the equal of universities. Even if they offer higher education programmes of good quality and for which there is a clear need, some see them more as a second choice rather than as a real alternative, and prestigious academic careers are rarely built through *Fachhochschulen*. At the same time, our higher education landscape would be much poorer without the *Fachhochschulen*.

This illustrates the importance of criteria for funding and career development. Both universities and public authorities may underline that higher education has at least three main missions: teaching, research and service to the broader society of which higher education is a part. Both universities and public authorities may underline the importance of developing and maintaining excellence in teaching as well as the importance of high quality learning environment. Academic careers are nevertheless built primarily on research achievements. Unless excellence in teaching is made as rewarding as excellence in research, faculty and institutions will strive for key roles in research. Again, decisions by formally autonomous institutions will be strongly influenced by criteria set outside of the institutions.

The importance of considering these criteria is underscored by the beginning debate about whether the Humboldtian model is a viable model for Europe in the future. There is broad agreement that there should be a link between higher education and research, and the Humboldtian model assumes that university teachers are also active researchers. This is true for many European faculty, but it is not true for all faculty or even all universities. A different way of seeing the relationship between research and higher education would be to require that all higher education teachers have direct personal experience of research at some point in their training and/or profes-sional career, but also to say that not all faculty will necessarily be active researchers throughout their career. In the same way, some institutions may have only some or even very few faculty members conducting research and may instead offer good quality study programmes, which again would require staff with a personal experience of research at some point of their career. There seems to be increasing awareness in Europe that the Humboldtian model of the unity of research and teaching is not of universal validity in Europe today, and there is also an emerging awareness that we may have to face an uncomfortable debate on whether Europe can afford to assume that all universities will be good quality research institutions. The debate has already started in some countries and in Albania the government put forward a master plan for higher education that stipulates that public research funding will be available mainly for select areas that are either unique to the country, such as Albanian language, history or culture, or in which the country has specific needs in terms of its economic and social development. The plan also stipulates that publicly funded research be limited to three of the country's eight public universities.

The above paragraph refers to priorities set by public authorities rather than auton-omous decisions made by higher education institutions. However, unless higher education institutions set clear priorities for their own development, they may well be reduced to reacting to priorities set by public authorities and other funders without the benefit of a clear institutional strategy. Such a strategy does of course not offer full protection against priorities set by others, and any good university strategy needs to take account of the environment in which the institution operates. It is also a valid argument that it would be far easier for higher education institutions to adopt a strategy favouring excellence in teaching over excellence in research or emphasising the role of the institution in relation to its local community if public support for higher education were based on a broader set of criteria. Nevertheless, higher education institutions may strengthen rather than weaken their autonomy if they take the lead in a comprehensive debate on institutional profiles and structures as well as public support mechanisms rather than leave the initiative to public authorities and other funders or let it be dictated by ranking lists.

Time perspectives: the long run versus the short run

Time is, in my view, one of the most serious challenges to university autonomy. Public patience is in short supply, the demand for immediate results is increasing, and democratic societies do not seem to excel at long-term planning. Perhaps this is also a side effect of watching television more than reading books and of commu-nicating more by e-mail than by letter. Modern societies are fast moving, and that has many advantages, but they tend to leave insufficient time and space for deeper reflection. High quality research cannot be developed overnight, and neither can high quality study programmes providing society with graduates that have the kind of specialised competences in vogue at the moment.

The narrow time horizons of modern society are therefore a threat to university autonomy. How can universities set sustainable priorities and develop high quality teaching and research programmes if they cannot have a certain guarantee of sustainable funding and political support? How, ultimately, can societies ensure that their young people will aim for careers that may provide intellectually stimulating work but that are relatively badly remunerated in relation to the sustained effort required, lacking in positive media attention and devoid of immediate gratification?

In the difficulty of providing reassuring answers to these questions under present conditions, however, we may also find a germ of hope. Our societies need to move beyond the quest for quick fixes and look at longer term trends and solutions. Climate change is an enormous challenge, but it is also an interesting one in that it is at once urgent and long term. It is urgent to start to address the issue and to do more, but we will not know tomorrow whether the efforts we need today will be successful. What we do know with reasonable certainty is that if we do nothing today, our successors will be faced with even more unmanageable problems tomorrow. Those addressing climate change, but also other fundamental issues like democratic culture, social cohesion and intercultural communication, are perhaps modern societies' equivalents of the builders of cathedrals in the Middle Ages: they are convinced of the fundamental importance of what they set out to do, but they also know that they will very possibly not see their work completed. Autonomous universities should help our societies face up to this kind of challenge.

Public responsibility and university autonomy

At the outset, the balance between public responsibility for higher education and research and institutional autonomy is dictated by a paradox: the basic conditions for university autonomy are set by public authorities.

Higher education is fundamental to developing the competences our societies need to develop as humane and sustainable societies. This requires vision at political level as well as by university leadership. It requires co-operation between public authorities and autonomous institutions, and the role of both must be reconsidered to meet our current needs while also respecting the values on which European higher education is built. The Council of Europe recommendation on the public responsibility for higher education and research developed a nuanced approach to the responsibility of public authorities. They should have:

- exclusive responsibility for the framework within which higher education and research is conducted;

- leading responsibility for ensuring effective equal opportunities to higher education for all citizens, as well as ensuring that basic research remains a public good;

- substantial responsibility for financing higher education and research, the provision of higher education and research, as well as for stimulating and facilitating financing and provision by other sources within the framework developed by public authorities (Council of Europe 2007).

Only autonomous higher education institutions able to develop a clear view of their roles and missions in modern societies can go beyond our short-term concerns and help our societies find solutions to the more fundamental problems we face. Only autonomous higher education institutions able to take due account of all major purposes of higher education can provide the education and competences that modern societies need to be sustainable, not only environmentally but also economically, politically, culturally and socially. Addressing these issues requires sophisticated citizens able to analyse complex issues, often on the basis of incomplete evidence, and able to weigh priorities as well as long- and short-term benefits and risks. Public authorities should take the lead in creating the conditions in which fundamental issues become a key part of the agenda of our societies and in which the need for a broad and advanced knowledge base is not only recognised in rhetoric but acted upon in practice.

In return, public authorities have the right to expect higher education institutions to use their autonomy to define institutional priorities and strategies that help us create and then maintain the kind of societies in which we would want to live. It is worth recalling the words of the Chilean sociologist Eugenio Tironi: the answer to the question "what kind of education do we need?" is ultimately to be found in the answer to the question "what kind of society do we want?" (Tironi 2005). Higher education institutions have to engage fully in this debate, and they have to do so on the basis of their autonomy.

More than ever, in the age of the sound bite, where "novelty usurps beauty",[74] society needs institutions that by definition take the longer view. Our societies need highly competent specialists in a very broad range of disciplines, but we also need intellectuals, namely people who not only know a lot about a specific field but who have the understanding to put this knowledge into a broader context and to reflect and act critically on the basis of their understanding.

That, perhaps, is the essential mission of higher education and the ultimate justification for both public responsibility for higher education and university autonomy. This is too complex and important a task to be left to management and public relations consultants. Public responsibility for higher education and research as well as university autonomy are essential instruments to make the endeavour succeed. The Council of Europe has launched important work in this area, but the Council project and recommendation should be the start of a crucial discussion and not the end of it. Defining the responsibility and roles of the range of actors in higher education should be an important element of the European Higher Education Area beyond 2010.

References

Bergan S. (2002), "Institutional autonomy between myth and responsibility", in *Autonomy and Responsibility. The University's Obligations in the XXI Century*, Bononia University Press, Bologna, pp. 49-66.

Bologna Process (2001), "Towards the European Higher Education Area." Communiqué of the meeting of European Ministers in charge of higher education in Prague on 19 May 2001.

---

74. Pope Benedict XVI in an address to the World Youth Day in Sydney, as reported by the *International Herald Tribune*; www.iht.com/articles/2008/07/17/asia/catholics.php, accessed on 17 July 2008.

Bologna Process (2003), Berlin Communiqué, "Realising the European Higher Education Area", adopted by European ministers of education on 19 September 2003.

Council of Europe (2007), Recommendation CM/Rec(2007)6 of the Committee of Ministers to member states on the public responsibility for higher education and research.

Parliamentary Assembly of the Council of Europe (2006), Recommendation 1762 (2006) on academic freedom and university autonomy. Available at: http://assembly. coe.int/Mainf.asp?link=/Documents/AdoptedText/ta06/EREC1762.htm.

Tironi E. (2005), *El sueño chileno: Comunidad, familia y nación en el bicentenario* [The Chilean Dream: Community, Family and Nation at the Bicentenary], Taurus, Santiago de Chile.

Weber L. and Bergan S. (eds) (2005), *The Public Responsibility for Higher Education and Research*, Council of Europe Higher Education Series No. 2, Council of Europe Publishing, Strasbourg.

Academic freedom and institutional autonomy: impact on international students[75]

Academic freedom and institutional autonomy

Deists – or at least some deists – believe that God created the world and then stepped back to let things run their course, which in many ways means letting human beings do as they please. What does a belief that had prominent adherents in the 18th and 19th centuries but which is little known today have to do with academic freedom and institutional autonomy? Not a great deal, except as an image of the classical and perhaps caricatural form of these concepts in which the state guarantees academic freedom and institutional autonomy by law and then steps back and leaves the scene to the academics, with one important exception. The state is still responsible for financing higher education.

This is of course quite far removed from the actual situation. This article sets out to explore aspects of academic freedom and institutional autonomy today[76] and to consider the possible impact on international students. First, however, it may be useful to distinguish two concepts that are often confused. Academic freedom refers to the scope of action of individual faculty and students, and the most typical academic freedoms are those of research, teaching and publication. Institutional autonomy, on the other hand, describes the freedom of the organised academic community: universities and other higher education institutions.

We could perhaps add to these two concepts the broader freedom of expression, namely the freedom to participate in public debate outside of the institution, a point at which academic freedom becomes enmeshed with the freedom enjoyed by citizens of democratic societies. However, freedom of expression is distinct from academic freedom. The latter certainly concerns the right of academic staff and students to pursue their research without constraints of ideology, dogma or the inconvenience their findings may cause public or academic authorities. At the same time, however, academic freedom does not dispense faculty and students from the rigours of their discipline, which encompasses an obligation to follow sound research methods as well as ethical guidelines. Freedom of expression is not without limits, as shown by anti-defamation legislation, but it is considerably less constrained by rigours of methodology and ethics than is academic freedom. A quick look at the more

---

75. This article was originally published in Birtwistle, Tim (ed.) (2008): "Legal Aspects of Higher Education in an International Context: Disputes, Resolutions, Methods and Safeguards", Amsterdam: European Association for International Education, EAIE Occasional Paper 21, pp. 27-36. Reproduced by kind permission of the European Association for International Education.
76. The present paper draws on four earlier articles (Bergan 2002, 2003, 2004 and 2005). For an overview of the development of the concept of autonomy, see Lay (2004). The home page of the Magna Charta Observatory is www.magna-charta.org/home.html.

sensationalist parts of the press is sufficient to make the point. It is, however, also true that it is difficult to imagine academic freedom in a society without freedom of expression. The point is obvious for political science, history and perhaps social sciences in general, but also extends to other areas of intellectual pursuit, as shown by the example of "Lysenkoism"[77] in the Soviet Union of Stalin and German science under Hitler (Cornwell 2004).

While the two concepts of academic freedom and institutional autonomy are distinct, they are also linked. They both have to do with how the academic community interlinks with the broader community of which it is a part. In addition, academic freedom also has to do with how individual members of the academic community interact with academic institutions and their leadership.

Academic community

Hence, the concept of "academic community" is important to a consideration of academic freedom and institutional autonomy. This is also a concept that has evolved, and one effect of "1968" – shorthand for both massification and democratisation of higher education in Europe – is that the academic community has been widened to fully include students as well as the lower ranks of faculty and, perhaps more marginally, technical and administrative staff. The inclusion of students in the academic community is far from trivial. In my view, it is of fundamental importance to the future of higher education in Europe. The frequent reference to students as "clients" implies a fundamental change in the status and role of students. Clients are interested in final products and the price they pay for them. They have little interest in the "production process" and the internal arrangements of the producer.[78] If the end product is satisfactory and affordable, clients buy. If it is not, they go elsewhere for their preferred products. Members of a community, on the other hand, have an intrinsic interest in the development and well-being of their community. If citizens are unhappy with the state of their community, their first response should be to try to improve it. Finding a new community – permanent migration – should be a last resort. For the future of higher education, it is crucial that students engage in improving higher education institutions and systems rather than shop around for courses that satisfy their immediate desires. Students should make demands on their institutions, but they should do so as community members and not as clients. This also applies to foreign students, even if they will often find it more difficult to make their voice heard.

Legal issues

Discussions of academic freedom and institutional autonomy have often focused on legal issues, on the reasoning that legal provision is required to make both a reality.

---

77. Trofim D. Lysenko gained prominence in the final Stalin years by using political connections to promote views unsupported by scientific methods, see http://skepdic.com/lysenko.html, accessed on 30 June 2010.
78. Even if consumers may organise demonstrations against or boycotts of unethical producers.

This has landed us in the somewhat paradoxical situation that public authorities – in Europe often simply referred to by the imprecise term "the state" – have been called upon to offer institutions and academics explicit legal protection from … public authorities. The paradox is only a seeming one since public authorities play an important role in defining the framework within which institutions and academics work, and political support for university autonomy and academic freedom is essential (Council of Europe 2006). Nevertheless, the focus of discussions has often been too narrow in that issues of academic freedom and autonomy span far wider than legal issues and the role of public authorities.

Let us nevertheless start our consideration with legal issues. The principle of academic freedom and institutional autonomy will be found in the legislation of just about every European country as well as in very many countries in other parts of the world (Birtwistle 2004). Institutional autonomy is one of the underlying principles of the European Higher Education Area (Bologna Process 2004).

Yet, even if autonomy and academic freedom are protected by law, they are not absolute. Institutions cannot do exactly as they please without regard to the general legislation of the country in which they are located. If the country has legislation stipulating a maximum number of working hours per week or month and there is no exception under which academics may fall, the institution is bound by the general legislation. French academics are not more inclined to working short weeks than academics in other countries, but they are in principle bound by the 35-hour week even if their observance of this particular law may be difficult to verify. Institutions and academics are bound by general legislation in a whole range of areas, from financial issues through safety rules to libel and anti-discrimination clauses. For example, institutions and projects have to abide by rules and regulations for bookkeeping and financial reporting, however cumbersome they may be felt, and laboratories, libraries and all other university buildings must satisfy safety regulations covering the handling of toxic materials, fire escapes or accessibility for disabled students and staff. Many universities have historic buildings that have been declared heritage monuments and which therefore cannot be modified by the university without the agreement of conservation authorities.

Academic freedom, institutional autonomy and freedom of expression

The perhaps most difficult issues relate to areas where academic freedom may conflict with legislation protecting vulnerable minorities. Such legislation encompasses areas like hiring and housing but may also extend to speech and writing. For example, many countries have laws that make denying the Holocaust a crime. This is a clear-cut case, since the reality of the Holocaust is not in doubt and it is denied only by an extreme minority often referred to as a "lunatic fringe". A historian denying the Holocaust would not only fall foul of legislation but would also find it difficult to demonstrate the necessary academic competence to justify university

139

employment. The same would be true for a physicist insisting that the earth is flat[79] or a biologist maintaining that human intelligence is conditioned on race.[80] To my knowledge, no legislation exists that may be applicable to the former position, whereas many countries do have legislation covering the latter.

However, cases are not always clear-cut. There is disagreement between historians on how many Armenians perished in the Ottoman Empire from 1915 onwards and the extent to which Armenians were targeted because of their ethnicity or nationality. Hence, there is also disagreement on how to designate these events, with both historians and social scientists with good academic credentials taking different views. This would seem an issue where free academic debate supported by critical scholarship is required, yet in some countries, such debate may be curtailed by legislation. In October 2006, the French National Assembly adopted a legislative proposal that would make denying that these events constitute genocide a crime,[81] whereas in Turkey, the holding of an academic conference that invited participants to consider whether the events did or did not constitute genocide was met with considerable obstruction by courts and authorities.[82]

In the United States, there are currently strong controversies – in many cases between a fairly consensual academic community and strong economic and fundamentalist religious groups – on issues like evolution (the alternative to which is no longer "creationism" but "intelligent design"), global warming and environmental protection (Mooney 2006).

Autonomy and non-state actors

Whereas considerations of academic freedom and institutional autonomy have generally focused on the role of public authorities, there is every reason also to consider the position of non-public actors.

Many higher education institutions are private rather than public. In this case, the issue of institutional autonomy arises in relation to their private owners. Many private universities, of course, emphasise the institution's autonomy from the owner and their mission to foster the personal development of students and encouraging intellectual enquiry and open minds. Hence, Harvard:

> strives to create knowledge, to open the minds of students to that knowledge, and to enable students to take best advantage of their educational opportunities.

---

79. There is a Flat Earth Society, which maintains a website: www.alaska.net/~clund/e_djublonskopf/ Flatearthsociety.htm, accessed on 30 June 2010.
80. See for example the article on J. Philippe Rushton, www.psych.ucsb.edu/research/cep/rushton.html, and the home page of Richard Lynn, Professor Emeritus of the University of Ulster, who claims that average intelligence of humans varies according to race and gender www.rlynn.co.uk, both accessed on 30 June 2010.
81. www.iht.com/articles/2006/10/12/news/france.php, accessed 14 October 2006.
82. www.iht.com/articles/2005/09/23/news/turkey.php, accessed and http://news.bbc.co.uk/2/hi/ europe/4273602.stm, both accessed on 14 October 2006.

> To these ends, the College encourages students to respect ideas and their free expression, and to rejoice in discovery and in critical thought; to pursue excellence in a spirit of productive cooperation; and to assume responsibility for the consequences of personal actions.[83]

However, there are also other varieties. Oral Roberts University, a private institution affiliated with the Evangelical Right in the US:

> ... is a charismatic university, founded in the fires of evangelism and upon the unchanging precepts of the Bible. The University was founded as a result of the evangelist Oral Roberts' obeying God's mandate to build a university on God's authority and the Holy Spirit.

> It is the mission of Oral Roberts University – in its commitment to the Christian faith and to the University's Founding Vision – to assist students in a quest for knowledge of and relationship to God, humanity, and the universe. Dedicated to the realization of Truth and the achievement of one's potential life capacity, the University seeks to educate the whole person in spirit, mind, and body, thereby preparing its graduates to be spiritually alive, intellectually alert, physically disciplined, and socially adept.[84]

Chile saw a dramatic growth of private higher education provision from the mid-1980s onward, combined with a drastic reduction of public funding for the classical traditional universities – in particular the Universidad de Chile – as the Pinochet regime sought to refashion Chilean higher education in line with its own emphasis on liberalist economics and authoritarian politics. Many – but not all – of the new private institutions are owned and run by people with close connections to the Pinochet regime and UDI, the party that today is most closely associated with it. Many of these institutions are committed to the ideology of their owners and have low tolerance for alternative views among students and especially faculty. Thus, the teaching of economics follows the liberalist "Chicago School" that became one of the foundations of the regime. Universidad Gabriela Mistral, one of the earliest Chilean private universities and one which is traditionalist and confessional in outlook rather than related to the Chicago School, is run along the lines of a family business and has no room for student participation in institutional governance. Its founder and owner is on record as saying she sees education as an economic activity (Mönckeberg 2005: 393).

Autonomy and academic freedom in practice

It is important to keep in mind that laws are only effective to the extent they are put into practice. It is equally important to keep in mind that practice may restrict or expand autonomy and academic freedom in areas not covered by legislation. Academic self-censorship and conditions imposed by companies and bodies providing substantial outside funding of teaching and research are two examples, and the only ones that space allows me to touch on here.

Academics may well in the course of their teaching and research reach unpopular conclusions. In this case, should they teach and publish their findings or bow to the

---

83. www.harvard.edu/siteguide/faqs/faq110.php, accessed on 30 June 2010.
84. www.oru.edu/aboutoru/missionstatement.html, accessed on 14 October 2006.

majority view? A historic example is teaching at universities in the 16th century, where academics stuck to established dogmas in their teaching yet made the contrary findings of their research known through their published works (de Ridder-Symoens 2006). Currently, much of the discussion may be subsumed under the label "political correctness", which is a particular topic of contention at US universities but which may also be found in Europe. In this case, the academic community is accused of practising self-censorship or rather of trying to censor the scholarship of faculty proclaiming views at variance with the predominant views in a given discipline. While accusations of "political correctness" have in particular been made in humanities and social sciences, examples of peer pressure and censorship may certainly be found in all disciplines. Disputes over findings in medical research are one obvious example.

Today, few if any ambitious universities can work on public institutional funding alone. Much research and some teaching are funded by external sources, and this raises issues of the freedom to conduct research and publish research results. How do universities and academics act when a major funder wishes to restrict the publishing of research results or take ownership of data? One recent example is the case of Professor Aubrey Blumsohn and Sheffield University, which centres on researchers' access to and ownership of data under research funded by a major pharmaceutical company. The dispute led to Professor Blumsohn's dismissal from the university which, it can be argued, sided with a major research funder against a faculty member concerned with academic freedom (Birtwistle 2004).[85]

Issues concerning international students

So far we have been concerned with outlining issues of principle. Let us now look at three cases in which issues concerning institutional autonomy and academic freedom interact with other concerns and policies, and which particularly concern foreign students.

Immigration and social security

Autonomous higher education institutions decide on the admission of their own students, albeit within the broad framework of a duty to admit students on merit rather than, for example, favouritism or nepotism and in many cases also of broad public policies of facilitating access for disadvantaged groups.[86]

---

85. A brief description of the case will be found at www.slate.com/id/2133061, accessed on 30 June 2010. I am grateful to Tim Birtwistle for drawing my attention to this case.

86. Public policies in this area may of course vary over time, as exemplified by the United States where education provision for the black population was segregated in many states until the 1950s and 1960s. Later, federal authorities instituted a policy of "affirmative action" to encourage access for disadvantaged groups, but some admission decisions made under this policy were challenged in court, most famously in the Bakke case from California (*University of California Regents v. Bakke*). The Administration of George W. Bush seeks to reduce affirmative action, as when it sought to have University of Michigan admissions practices declared unconstitutional on the grounds that they discriminated against members of the majority (*International Herald Tribune*, 17 January 2003, p. 3).

Therefore, the principle of institutional autonomy would imply that higher education institutions are free to admit qualified students without regard to their origin or place of residence. However, students need visas to study in foreign countries, and visas are often made contingent on prospective students demonstrating that they have sufficient resources – including insurance policies against accident, illness and injury – to support themselves for the duration of their study programme, whether through their own or their family's resources or through scholarships or other support schemes. Students from certain countries may find it particularly difficult to obtain visas, as has been the case of students from some countries of predominantly Muslim culture since 11 September 2001 or students from countries from which there has been a high number of fraudulent applications or diplomas. European higher education institutions have talked about attracting students who now find it more difficult to obtain visas for the United States, but there seems little reason to believe that European immigration policies are more subtle than US ones, even if European countries may be less vocal about the point.

Higher education institutions are also free to hire their own staff within the same broad principles of non-discrimination and hiring based on academic merit, but again, foreign faculty need residence and work permits. In some countries, this may also apply to doctoral students, whose formal status may be that of temporary research staff rather than students. In the case of staff exchanges, rules and regulations concerning the portability of social security may also complicate institutions' autonomous decisions.

As we saw earlier in this article, university autonomy is tempered by universities' obligation to observe general laws and regulations, and immigration and social security legislation may overrule admission and hiring decisions made by autonomous institutions and de facto discriminate against foreign students and faculty. It is one of the paradoxes of the European Higher Education Area, which is built, *inter alia*, on the principle of university autonomy, that it seeks to stimulate academic mobility at a time when many European governments try to reduce professional mobility by tightening immigration legislation and policy. It is one of the most formidable challenges of the European Higher Education Area to resolve this paradox.

Confronting adverse opinion

Foreign students coming to European higher education institutions will come to autonomous institutions at which faculty and students enjoy academic freedom. For many foreign students, this will present no particular challenge and they will take open and free academic debate with few taboos for granted. For other foreign students, however, this debate may prove challenging and they may have to struggle to face opinions that go against their core beliefs in ways that would not be permissible in their home countries.

One obvious example is that of Muslim students, in particular from countries of traditionalist backgrounds and without significant groups of other beliefs. Not only will they live in societies in which public debate often questions fundamental tenets of Islam, as exemplified by the "cartoons" controversy in autumn 2005.[87] They will also attend institutions with a culture of challenging received beliefs and demanding verifiable proof, and at which subjects like history or political science will be approached from very different angles from their home countries. While European historians are, in most cases, committed to multiperspectivity (Council of Europe 2001, Stradling 2003) and may seek to avoid charges of Eurocentrism, their perspectives on issues concerning the Muslim world are likely to be some way from that of Muslim historians and social scientists, notwithstanding the fact that the latter are no more a monolithic group than their European colleagues. This is perhaps particularly true of issues in which Europe and the Muslim world interact.

Examples are, of course, not limited to Muslim students. US students from fundamentalist Christian backgrounds will find their beliefs challenged, and US students of all persuasions will often be confronted with courses, teachers and fellow students critical of key aspects of American society. Again, this is likely to extend beyond the area of general public debate into scholarly discourse, in particular in social sciences and history. Similarly, Japanese students of history will be likely to confront critical appraisals of Japan in the 1930s and 1940s and Chinese students will be confronted with a variety of scholarly opinion on issues like economic and political theory to which their home authorities might well have preferred that they not be exposed.

The point, of course, is neither that foreign students should be spared the rigours of scholarly debate nor that they should not be exposed to public debate in their host societies. Universities and individual academics should not compromise on institutional autonomy or academic freedom for the "benefit" of foreign students. They will, however, need to conduct debates with a measure of sensitivity that makes it clear that while academics may question key elements of some students' beliefs and values, they do so with respect and based on sound scholarly methods. Having one's values questioned may ultimately be a fruitful exercise but it is not an easy one, and it is doubly difficult when one's values are challenged by one's hosts.

Avoiding non-serious institutions

With the diversification of higher education and not least the rapid growth of institutions that are not affiliated with a national education system (Knight 2006), it is difficult for any prospective student to know the quality of institutions and study programmes, but this is particularly difficult if those institutions are located in a foreign country.

---

87. Launched when the Danish paper *Jyllandsposten* published cartoons critical of the Prophet in September 2005. Many in the Muslim world saw the cartoons as an attempt to humiliate Islam and the Prophet, and reactions led to large protests in many parts of the Muslim world. In many Western countries, it was acknowledged that the cartoons may have been in bad taste, but the case was widely seen as one in which the freedom of expression came under unfair attack. The timeline for the "cartoons crisis" is given in www.ft.com/cms/s/d30b0c22-96ee-11da-82b7-0000779e2340.html; a brief description in http://en.wikipedia.org/wiki/Jyllands-Posten_Muhammad_cartoons_controversy.

Prospective students would be well served if they could find reliable information on the status of higher education institutions and providers. As external quality assurance systems and procedures develop, it will hopefully be easier to find such information, but it will not be straightforward, and a great effort is still needed to make prospective students as well as employers looking to hire people conscious of the need to do background checks on higher education institutions.

The need for reliable information on institutions, however, to some extent runs counter to institutional autonomy. Is it legitimate for public authorities to close institutions that have not passed an independent quality assessment? Is it at least legitimate for public authorities to publish the results of quality assessments – positive as well as negative – as well as the names of institutions that have declined to undergo assessments, with an attendant warning to students and employers to beware that qualifications from such institutions may not deliver what they promise? This runs against two main concerns. On the one hand, the principle of institutional autonomy may be seen to justify the operation even of institutions that have not passed quality assessments, and on the other hand, some institutions claim the right to operate their business free from "state control" (Knight 2002a and 2002b, Mönckeberg 2005: 394).

In my view, this is an area in which we need to reconsider how the principle of institutional autonomy should be implemented to take account of the public's well-founded need for information. For study advisers and others counselling foreign students, it is particularly important to be able to give frank and transparent advice.

Conclusion

University autonomy and academic freedom are core values of higher education and research. To remain a reality, the concepts and practice of institutional autonomy and academic freedom need to evolve with the development of society. Legal provision is essential but also insufficient by itself: actual autonomy and academic freedom is determined by the implementation of formal regulations as well as by practice in areas not covered by legislation. Universities are not islands unto themselves, yet the academic community should insist that concerns of autonomy and academic freedom cannot be dispensed with lightly in face of broader concerns like labour legislation and immigration policies. On the other hand, the principle of institutional autonomy should not be interpreted to legitimise less than serious provision, which it may be particularly difficult for foreign students to detect. The academic community should stand firm in defence of autonomy and academic freedom, but it also needs to show consideration toward foreign students whose background may not have prepared them for the kind of intense academic and general debate found at many European universities. The ultimate piece of advice may be to approach these issues not with a legal frame of mind but in accordance with the title of one of the most important political pamphlets ever written: common sense.[88]

---

88. *Common Sense* is the title of Tom Paine's passionate pamphlet in favour of the independence of the American colonies, published in 1776.

References

Bergan S. (2002), "Institutional autonomy between myth and responsibility", in *Autonomy and Responsibility: The University's Obligations for the XXI Century. Proceedings of the Launch Event for the Magna Charta Observatory 21-22 September 2001*, Bononia University Press, Bologna.

Bergan S. (2003), "The responsible university", *Cuadernos Europeos de Deusto*, No. 29/2003, Universidad de Deusto, Bilbao.

Bergan S. (2004), "Higher education governance and democratic participation: the university and democratic culture", in Bergan S. (ed.), *The University as* Res Publica, Council of Europe Higher Education Series No. 1, Council of Europe Publishing, Strasbourg.

Bergan S. (2005), "Higher education as a 'public good and public responsibility' – What does it mean?" in Weber L. and Bergan S. (eds), *The Public Responsibility for Higher Education and Research*, Council of Europe Higher Education Series No. 2, Council of Europe Publishing, Strasbourg.

Birtwistle T. (2004), "Academic freedom and complacency: the possible effects if 'good men do nothing'", *Education and the Law*, Vol. 16, No. 4, pp. 203-217.

Birtwistle T. (2006), "Are we collectively guilty of complacency? An update on the continued confusion over what is academic freedom and what may become a battle for academic freedom", *Education and the Law*, Vol. 18, Nos 2-3, pp. 207-217.

Bologna Process (2004), Document BFUG B3 7 fin of 6 July 2004 on requirements and procedures for joining the Bologna Process.

Cornwell J. (2004), *Hitler's Scientists. Science, War and the Devil's Pact*, Penguin, London.

Council of Europe (2001), Recommendation Rec(2001)15 of the Committee of Ministers of the Council of Europe to member states on history teaching in twenty-first-century Europe.

Council of Europe (2006), Recommendation 1762 (2006) by the Council of Europe's Parliamentary Assembly on academic freedom and university autonomy.

Knight J. (2002a), *Trade in Higher Education Services: The Implications of GATS*, The Observatory on Borderless Education, London.

Knight J. (2002b), "The impact of GATS and trade liberalization on higher education", in Stamenka Uvailć-Trumbić (ed.), *Globalization and the Market in Higher Education: Quality, Accreditation and Qualifications*, UNESCO Publishing and Economica, Paris, pp. 191-209.

Knight J. (2006), "Programmers, providers and accreditors on the move: implications for the recognition of qualifications", in Rauhvargers A. and Bergan S. (eds), *Recognition in the Bologna Process: Policy Development and the Road to Good*

Practice, Council of Europe Higher Education Series No. 4, Council of Europe Publishing, Strasbourg, pp. 139-160.

Lay S. (2004), *The Interpretation of the* Magna Charta Universitatum *and its Principles*, Bononia University Press, Bologna.

Mönckeberg M. O. (2005), *La privatización de las universidades. Una historia de dinero, poder e influencias*, Editorial La Copa Rota, Santiago de Chile.

Mooney C. (2006), *The Republican War on Science*, Basic Books, New York.

de Ridder-Symoens, H. (2006), "The intellectual heritage of ancient universities in Europe", in Sanz N. and Bergan S. (eds), *The Heritage of European Universities*, second edition, Council of Europe Higher Education Series No. 7, Council of Europe Publishing, Strasbourg, pp. 79-89.

Stradling R. (2003), *Multiperspectivity in History Teaching: a Guide for Teachers*, Council of Europe Publishing, Strasbourg.

Institutional autonomy between myth and responsibility[89]

I welcome this opportunity to contribute to the inauguration of the Observatory of Fundamental University Values and Rights in Bologna, and I am particularly pleased to do so as a representative of the Council of Europe. The autonomy of higher education institutions and academic freedom are at the heart of democratic society and they are interrelated: democratic society is hardly conceivable without institutional autonomy and academic freedom but neither can institutions and academic staff be truly free in non-democratic societies. Autonomous higher education institutions are therefore also fundamental to the overall concerns of the Council of Europe: democracy, human rights and the rule of law. In this context, it is important that the title of the observatory includes a reference to values, since defining and defending values is one of the main tasks of universities as institutions playing an important role in developing the moral and ethical reflection without which democratic societies would cease to develop.

Autonomous universities are an integral part of the cultural heritage of Europe, an aspect that we have had an opportunity to develop in a previous Council of Europe project on the cultural heritage of European universities (Sanz and Bergan 2006). One of the meetings of the project was held in Bologna, in July 2000. Universities are among the very few institutions that have survived in continuity since the Middle Ages, and they have managed to do so not only by redefining their role in a changing society but by helping to change society and by finding the right combination of detached distance and active involvement. This heritage is at the basis of the *Magna Charta Universitatum* and of the new observatory.

The myth

Although I do not pretend to use the term "myth" in the scientific sense of the term, it might be useful to recall that the same myths tend to reappear in various circumstances and cultures, all of which identify with them. They may take slightly different forms, and the contents may also change somewhat, but the core elements recur. In addition, myths die hard and more often than not they contain a grain of truth. It is therefore interesting to look at what we may call the myth of university autonomy before considering how it is tempered by reality and responsibility.

---

89. The first version of this article was published in *Autonomy and Responsibility – The University's Obligations for the XXI Century. Proceedings of the Launch Event for the Magna Charta Observatory 21-22 September 2001*, Bologna: Bononia University Press, 2002. It is reproduced by kind permission of the Magna Charta Observatory. The author would like to thank Nuria Sanz, David Crosier and Angela Garabagiu for valuable discussion in the writing of the first version of this article.

The mythical academic is someone who follows his (unfortunately, less often her) own convictions, interests and priorities without outside interference. One story has it that a professor at a British university some time in the 1960s was asked why he was working on Icelandic, a language understood by few but its 250 000 native speakers, and he was given to understand that there were more useful things he could spend his time on. His answer was a simple "I beg your pardon, this is a university". There was no attempt to refer to the cultural treasures of Icelandic, such as the Sagas and the Edda, nor to the value of cultural and linguistic diversity,[90] because the professor saw no need to justify what a university does. Crudely put, the myth may be summarised as "you pay, I do the rest".

It may well be argued that what has just been described concerns academic freedom rather than university autonomy, and this is undoubtedly true. However, it is a part of the myth that it does not distinguish between these two related but distinct concepts, and that the myth describes university autonomy in similar terms. At least in a European context, the myth emphasises the role of the state in financing the university and the absence of any state role in running it. The state pays and then leaves the university to set its own priorities.

The myth is less clear when it comes to the relations between the higher education institution and its staff, although the balance tends to be towards as little interference as possible. At least in the countries of former Yugoslavia, this has translated into a weak central authority of the university and a high degree of faculty independence, including the recognition of faculties as independent legal entities, although the background for this may not solely be a concern with the individual freedom of academics but rather the fear on the part of Titoist authorities of the collective strength of the academic community. This argument was put forward forcefully by Professor Branko Jeren, then Rector of Zagreb University, in the closing discussion at the inauguration ceremony of the observatory. In the 2001 draft higher education law for Kosovo,[91] which the Council of Europe elaborated at UNMIK's request and in accordance with UNMIK policy, faculties were no longer foreseen as separate legal entities

The myth could perhaps also be described in terms of five freedoms. The first is freedom of research: no university or individual academic should be forced to refrain from doing research because of outside considerations. The second is freedom of teaching, and the two are closely linked, as research-based teaching is one of the fundamental aspects of the European university heritage. Therefore, researchers should not be forced to teach students in contradiction to the findings of their research.[92] The third and strongly connected is the freedom of publication

---

90. An eloquent defence of which may be found in Dixon (1997), in particular pp. 116-121.
91. All reference to Kosovo, whether to the territory, institutions or population, in this text shall be understood in full compliance with United Nations Security Council Resolution 1244 and without prejudice to the status of Kosovo.
92. This has not always been the case. At many 16th-century universities, scholars were obliged to transmit the sacrosanct belief of Antiquity in their lectures while arriving at quite different convictions through their own research in areas like natural sciences and technical disciplines (de Ridder-Symoens 2006).

of research results, while the fourth is the freedom of co-operation: a university as well as individual staff should be free to seek co-operation partners as they see fit.

These four freedoms are closely interrelated, they are generally agreed upon and they apply equally to institutions and individual staff. The fifth freedom is more controversial and more contradictory; it is what I would term the freedom from administration. Thus, it is negative rather than positive, and it applies to individual staff more than to institutions. While the research and teaching of individual staff will presumably be more productive if they are freed from administrative duties, the university as an institution or a collective body has every interest in taking care of its own administration as outside administration, namely by a ministry, would imply loss of university autonomy.

The anti-myth

In dialectics, if there is an A, there is also an anti-A, ultimately leading to a synthesis of the two. Let us therefore see if there is an anti-myth of university autonomy. If there is, it is in the form of direct state governance of, or at least interference with, higher education institutions. The clearest example in Europe after the Second World War is the 1998 Serbian Law on Universities, which stipulated that rectors and deans be appointed by the government and that the state would in general run the universities. Many Serbian academics, including those who took leadership of the Serbian Ministry of Education as well as of the Serbian universities in the immediate aftermath of the fall of the Milošević regime, took a clear stand against this aberration and suffered the consequences. Some of the academics who were fired or "voluntarily" left the Serbian universities in opposition to the law established the Alternative Academic Education Network (AAEN), which played an important role in keeping the academic community alive in the final years of the Milošević era and in preparing its resurgence in post-Milošević Yugoslavia. The 1998 law was also roundly condemned by the international community, admittedly at considerably less risk.[93]

A second example of the anti-myth was provided on the first day of the opening ceremony of the observatory, when the Comenius University of Bratislava acceded to the *Magna Charta Universitatum*, something that the then Czechoslovak Government had prevented it from doing in 1988. Another example is provided by the institutions belonging to the religious (that is, fundamentalist Protestant) right in the United States, such as Oral Roberts University,[94] which seek to ensure

---

93. Condemnations included those of the CRE (the European Rectors' Conference, which later became a part of the European University Association) and the Council of Europe's Higher Education and Research Committee; the reference for the latter is CC-HER(99)28. It is worth noting that since education was a republic rather than a federal responsibility in Yugoslavia, the 1998 law only applied to Serbia and not to Montenegro.

94. The mission statement of the Oral Roberts University may be found at www.oru.edu/university/mission.html. It emphasises that "Oral Roberts University is a charismatic university, founded in the fires of evangelism and upon the unchanging precepts of the Bible. The Board of Regents and the president and chief executive officer are dedicated to upholding the University's founding purpose."

that their students are protected from views that could challenge their faith in creationism or their allegiance to the Republican right-wing. This, however, is less an example of lack of university autonomy than abuse of it, and it should perhaps above all be used as a rare illustration of university autonomy combined with a relative lack of academic freedom. It should also be underlined that the latter is institution specific rather than system related, as the practice of Oral Roberts has little to do with that of Harvard, Stanford, Berkeley, MIT or other top US higher education institutions.

A particular example is Kosovo in the aftermath of the Kosovo war, where UNMIK, representing the international community, worked to re-establish institutional autonomy after the abuses of the Milošević era and its mono-ethnic university. Kosovo was therefore an example of a temporary administration which did not claim to honour the principle of university autonomy but which used its powers to reform the Kosovo higher education system by introducing new higher education legislation – an effort of which the Council of Europe was a part – modern university administration, a degree system conforming to the model of the Bologna Declaration and quality assurance mechanisms, and all of this with the stated goal of introducing university autonomy and a system that offers higher education provision for all qualified candidates in Kosovo regardless of their ethnic, religious or linguistic background. One of the most serious obstacles is ensuring higher education in languages other than Albanian within public higher education in Kosovo.

It may also be pertinent to raise two issues at this point. The first and most serious concerns the system found in some European countries whereby the Ministry of Education, the government or the sovereign de jure appoints rectors and some other university officials following their de facto election by the academic community. In most cases, this is a theoretical – one would be tempted to say "academic" – problem only, as in reality the appointments honour the outcome of university elections. Nonetheless, the potential for abuse is real, in at least two ways. Firstly, if the political circumstances change, a future undemocratic regime would not have to bother to change the legislation; it would be sufficient to change the established democratic practice and still appear to be in conformity with the letter of the law. Secondly, these examples from established democracies serve as tempting pretexts for regimes concerned with preserving the forms of democracy and autonomy while being unencumbered by their spirit. Would it not be worthwhile for the countries where such de jure practice is still to be found to reconsider their laws, not because of their current practice but as a safeguard against potential future abuse?

The second problem concerns the position of university officials, especially rector and dean. Clearly, a weak rector or dean is of little benefit to the institution, but what about the overly dominant variety? What is the right balance between authority on behalf of the institution or faculty and a capacity for consultation within it? How can a rector best lead and listen, represent and consult?

Elements of responsibility

Let us now confront the myth with reality, which can only be a perfunctory exercise within the space of a few pages. Institutional autonomy is a complex topic and it will be one of the major tasks of the observatory to explore its many facets. Some elements of responsibility can, however, briefly be discerned.

We have already touched upon the responsibility of higher education for the development of a democratic society built on active participation and consciousness of democratic values. A linked element is the increased demands on public service, and it does not matter much whether the university is public or private. Whatever the "ownership of the means of research and teaching", to borrow a phrase from an outmoded ideology, the perception is that of an institution with a public function, a responsibility towards society and subject to the general requirement of fairness and transparency, for example, in admissions procedures, grading, examinations and hiring of staff.

These considerations lead straight to an emphasis on the accountability of higher education. This aspect is richly covered both by the programme of the inauguration ceremony and higher education literature, so I will limit my comments to two points. Firstly, quality assurance, which is one of the key elements of the European Higher Education Area, is now a key concern of higher education policy. One crucial question is who should carry out the evaluation, and who should define the criteria for it. Should the universities evaluate themselves, or should they at least be evaluated by staff from other universities, or should they rather be assessed by outside agencies? We find both models, exemplified on the one hand by the EUA Institutional Evaluation Programme[95] and on the other by national quality assurance agencies. There are good arguments in favour of both approaches, and a combination of the two will give the best overall results but what is the right balance between internal and external assessment?

Secondly, some effort should be spent on answering the question "accountability – to whom?" To society, certainly, but "society" is a nebulous concept that needs to be dissected further in order to be meaningful. For public universities, and to some extent also private ones, accountability is to public authorities represented by, among others, the ministries responsible for higher education, national or regional legislative assemblies, political parties and their programmes, and even the press. Higher education institutions are also accountable to public and private bodies, who may choose whether or not to hire their graduates or make use of their competence in research and teaching, as well as to future, current and past students and staff. In this context, I would like to insist that students should not be seen as clients but as members of the academic community. The difference is far more than semantic; it is crucial. Whereas clients shop for the best offer at the lowest price and therefore easily move from one provider to another without an interest in either, members

---

95. www.unige.ch/eua.

of a community share responsibility for and a stake in the development of their community. Where dissatisfied clients leave the shop, dissatisfied members stay to reform their community and leave only in desperate circumstances, in which case we talk about emigration. Universities are therefore accountable to their students but the students share the responsibility and are in their turn accountable to society as members of the university.

Public policy is a further element of university responsibility. The university cannot lead an existence in isolation from public policy but at the same time it should not bend to public policy like a straw to the wind. As a former university administrator, I have recollections of adjusting not only annual budget proposals but also strategic plans to priorities that emerged from the latest government position papers without much consideration of the longer term implications of the adjustments or whether they were in fact consistent with the institutional policy of the university. Some adjustment is of course called for, but the decision to adjust should be a conscious one, and it should be motivated by a sustainable commitment extending beyond the annual budget.

The next in this chain of interlinked elements of responsibility is therefore the quest for funds, where it is important to bear in mind that strings are attached not only to public purses, but also to private ones. What conditions are there for funding of research and teaching? Are funds given for areas in which the university has a conscious interest, or are new courses developed simply to attract funds? Is research funding subject to limitations on the publication of the results and, if so, are these limitations acceptable? The university needs substantial funding to fulfil its tasks; increasingly these will have to come from a variety of sources. While there may be virtue in poverty, such virtue may not bring many results in terms of research and teaching. The point is therefore not that universities should necessarily refuse funding but that they should have a conscious policy of what kind of funding to accept on what conditions and that the observatory could contribute to such a discussion.

Universities are European and international institutions par excellence and therefore also have a responsibility with regard to international developments. To take just one example, the Bologna Process of higher education reform is the most important and comprehensive policy process in Europe for many a decade. While universities may theoretically be free to ignore it, for example by insisting on keeping "long" one-tier degrees[96] and refusing to issue Diploma Supplements, they would fail in their responsibility to their staff and students as well as to the society of which they are a part if they did so. For a university to choose not to be a part of the European Higher Education Area would mean that its students would find it more difficult to move around because their degrees would be less easily recognised, that its staff

---

96. To the extent that higher education institutions have a choice as to the degrees they offer. While the degree structure is decided by the ministry responsible for higher education, these may leave universities the option of choosing between different degree structures, as seems to have been the case in Russia at least in the early part of the 1990s, possibly as a transitional measure.

could encounter some of the same obstacles to mobility and that its students would find it more difficult to enter the labour market in competition with students with "Bologna" degrees. This is not to imply that universities are left no leeway: the Bologna Process is a framework which leaves ample room for adaptations, but the general direction is nonetheless very clear.

A particular challenge is known in the United States under the name of political correctness, which designates what many see as a severe constraint on teaching, research and publication, not through any law or formal regulation but through a particular form of peer pressure which aims at preventing the expression of views contrary to a narrowly defined list of acceptable views. While the extreme form of PC[97] may be peculiar to the US academic scene, elements of it can probably be found also in Europe, where peer pressure and self-censorship may prevent the expression of unpopular views even if backed up by personal research.

The issue of political correctness does lead, however, to the wider issue of the ethical and moral responsibilities of higher education. Even if the academic community tends to give a wide interpretation to the freedom of research, teaching, publication and expression, this does not imply that "anything goes". Is the revisionist historian protected by academic freedom or, if (s)he is employed by a university, institutional autonomy? Is a university free to sponsor a research programme in any discipline, or individual researchers free to carry out the programme, regardless of possible ethical misgivings? It is probably not difficult to agree that the answer is negative, but the discussion on cloning illustrates that the boundaries between the acceptable and the unacceptable are difficult to draw. The debate on euthanasia is perhaps not research related, but some of the key actors are former medical students and perhaps also current academic staff, and the debate again illustrates a lack of agreement on a fundamental ethical issue.

Nor are the boundaries static: what is acceptable to one age may not be to another. The University of Oslo returned two skulls from its anatomical collection to the families of the victims. The skulls were those of two of the executed leaders of a Sámi uprising in northern Norway in 1852, and it was now high time to correct the political and racial discrimination of previous generations. The ethical and moral responsibilities of higher education institutions, staff and students are of course not limited to refrain from doing things; they also have a positive responsibility to lead the way in ethical and moral reflection. An example of collective action in this sense is the university pension funds that withdrew their investments from companies working in apartheid South Africa, whereas one among many individual examples is the philosopher Fernando Savater, who is a leading voice against violence in the Spanish Basque country (Savater 2001). The latter can also illustrate the respon-sibility of higher education to a multicultural outlook, in an age where it makes little sense to see education, heritage, history, political science, physics or any other

---

97. It is perhaps an indication of the scope of the issue that PC, at least in the US context, no longer means only "personal computer".

discipline in a purely national perspective, and in which few if any universities worthy of the name employ only staff from the country in which it is located.[98]

If the examples given may seem reasonably clear-cut, they are nonetheless intended to show that the line of distinction between the "high road" of the moral and ethical responsibility of higher education and the "low road" of political correctness is not crystal clear. At what point does a legitimate concern for defending democratic values veer into the lane of political correctness? Is the right of an academic or an institution to teach, research or publish on any topic of its own choosing an absolute or a relative right?

A final element in this far from exhaustive list of elements of responsibility is far more prosaic but nevertheless very real: it concerns the total workload of academic staff and the distribution of their tasks. In particular, many academics worry that the load of administration comes in the way of their primary work and that research is relegated to whatever hours and energy are left when the teaching schedule has been completed. On the other hand, the institution surely has a responsibility to ensure a reasonable teaching offer for its students as well as to seek to give as many qualified young – and not so young – people as possible an opportunity to take higher education. It also has an institutional interest in taking care of its own affairs rather than leaving them to an outside body, and it has an obligation to abide by a number of general labour regulations and other laws, ranging from safety to equal opportunity. Since research is less easily quantifiable and the consequences of downsizing the research effort will not show immediately, the temptation to leave research for better times is often too strong to resist. Do autonomous institutions have a specific duty to ensure the core parts of their mission, and what should the consequences be in terms of institutional autonomy if they fail to do so?

Autonomy in the age of the sound bite

As will be seen, the challenges facing the observatory are many and multifaceted. Some of them can at this stage best be formulated as questions, as will already have been seen, and one of the most serious concerns long-term versus short-term priorities and considerations. How can university autonomy be maintained when the horizons of policy makers are limited by the end of their electoral mandate? How can institutional policies best be formulated under such conditions, and what should they aim to achieve? Put more directly: how, in the age of the sound bite, can it help defend and define an institution that by definition takes the long view?

The ivory tower may be a popular stereotype of the university, but it is hardly consistent with the idea of the university as a part of the European heritage and it is certainly not a model for university autonomy. Rather, the university has to be fully involved in modern society to ensure its own autonomy, which is also linked

---

98. Ironically, the concept of "national education" nevertheless survives in the title of some European ministries.

to its relevance. If no man is an island,[99] the same is true for higher education. The university should interact with society and its numerous groups and individuals, and not isolate itself from society.

No single institution is more important than the university for the defence and development of institutional autonomy and academic freedom. However, the university is not alone in defending these values, nor can it be alone in putting them into practice. Among the participants in the inauguration ceremony of the observatory were people who had first-hand experience of what can happen when the state authorities do not share the university's aspiration for autonomy, as shown through the examples of Comenius and Belgrade. University autonomy can only come about when the academic community, civil society and political authorities share this aspiration.

This was the background for a 2001 Council of Europe discussion document on higher education governance. In particular, it arose from the experience of the Legislative Reform Programme of the Council of Europe, which over a period of some eight years (1992-2000) sought to assist central and eastern European countries in bringing their higher education legislation in conformity with European standards, of which institutional autonomy and academic freedom are pillars. This was a discussion document, and it succeeded in raising discussion. This discussion was running high at the time the first version of this article was written but has long since died down. Nevertheless, it may be worth repeating some of the salient points.

Standards is a vaguer term than what is suggested by its legalist connotations. Standards can indeed be laws, conventions or set rules, but they can also be looser instruments like codes of good practice or simply a common understanding.[100] The purpose of any text, statement or declaration would not be to restrict institutional autonomy, but rather to have European governments enter into an explicit commitment to it. I feel uncomfortable when I hear arguments such as "autonomy is something the universities *themselves* should take care of" (italics added) because the statement betrays a defensive attitude which in its turn betrays an awareness of the fact that reality is somewhat more complex. University autonomy is something for both universities and public authorities, and in a democratic society they should define and defend it together. The Council of Europe is therefore committed to co-operating with the Magna Charta Observatory in this endeavour, which will be relaunched in a project starting in autumn 2010 and focusing on the specific role of public authorities in ensuring academic freedom and institutional autonomy.

---

99. "No man is an island, entire of itself; every man is a piece of the continent, a part of the main" John Donne, *Devotions,* XVII.

100. In the 1780s, the quality of Ottoman-produced gunpowder had declined so dramatically that gunpowder was imported from abroad while new factories were built to relaunch Ottoman gunpowder production toward what was commonly referred to as "European standards", cf. Mansel (1997: 254). "European standards" in this context were neither a law nor an ISO type industry standard, but simply an aspiration for high or at least improved quality.

This again ties in with the role of the observatory whose inauguration we celebrated in Bologna and which, as this article is being revised for republication, is close to celebrating its 10th anniversary. I would like to see a more active role for the observatory than its name implies, at least to northern European ears. Maybe it is appropriate that universities should gaze to the stars, but they should be much more than observers. I would rather like to see the observatory in the role of a forum and a driving force for university autonomy and I am pleased to see that in the first decade of the observatory's existence, it has indeed fulfilled this role. The Council of Europe welcomes this role for the observatory and will offer its continued co-operation in contributing to it.

References

Dixon R. M. W. (1997), *The Rise and Fall of Languages*, Cambridge University Press, Cambridge.

Mansel P. (1997), *Constantinople – City of the World's Desire 1453-1924*, Penguin, London.

de Ridder-Symoens H. (2006), "The intellectual heritage of ancient universities in Europe", in Sanz N. and Bergan S. (eds), *The Heritage of European Universities*, second edition, Council of Europe Higher Education Series No. 7, Council of Europe Publishing, Strasbourg, pp. 79-89.

Sanz N. and Bergan S. (eds) (2006), *The Cultural Heritage of European Universities*, second edition, Council of Europe Higher Education Series No. 7, Council of Europe Publishing, Strasbourg.

Savater F. (2001), *Perdonen las molestias*, Ediciones El País, Madrid.

Reflections on ranking in Europe[101]

Context

In 2009, the ministers of the European Higher Education Area adopted the following statement in their Leuven/Louvain-la-Neuve Communiqué:

> We note that there are several current initiatives designed to develop mechanisms for providing more detailed information about higher education institutions across the EHEA to make their diversity more transparent. We believe that any such mechanisms, including those helping higher education systems and institutions to identify and compare their respective strengths, should be developed in close consultation with the key stakeholders. These transparency tools need to relate closely to the principles of the Bologna Process, in particular quality assurance and recognition, which will remain our priority, and should be based on comparable data and adequate indicators to describe the diverse profiles of higher education institutions and their programmes (Bologna Process 2009).

This statement represents at least a temporary truce in one of the most animated discussions the Bologna Follow-up Group has ever had, where those who favoured work on institutional ranking and classification at European level and those who opposed it held strong views and expressed them vividly. The intensity of the debate reflects the saliency of the issue as well as the very considerable economic and political stakes at hand.

The "Bologna Ministers" were not alone in expressing a view on the issue: among others the Council of Europe's Steering Committee for Higher Education and Research (CDESR) adopted a statement at its 2009 plenary session a few weeks before the ministerial conference. This statement also reflects a compromise between quite diverse positions, even if discussions in the CDESR were less heated than they were at times in the Bologna Follow-up Group.

Ranking in Europe

The Leuven/Louvain-la-Neuve Communiqué and the CDESR statement reflect the fact that institutional rankings and classifications have become part of the higher education policy debate in Europe. There are numerous ranking and classification exercises and this article does not pretend to provide any kind of inventory. The rankings developed by the *Times Higher Education Supplement* and Shanghai Jiao Tong University are among the best known but are at the same time two among many. The QS World University Rankings, which was involved with the Times

---

101. This article was written specifically for the present volume. The author is grateful to Radu Damian, Ligia Deca, Hilligje van't Land, Viorel Proteasa and Virgílio Meira Soares for comments on a first draft of the article.

Higher rankings until 2009 but no longer is, recently sent out e-mails[102] asking for input to its rankings with the claim – probably correct – that the results will feature in many of the world's leading newspapers and be viewed by millions of people.

It may be useful to distinguish between rankings and classifications. Rankings aim to establish a qualitative order between institutions so that, according to the criteria of the ranking in question, institution A scores higher than institution B, which again scores higher than institution C. The ranking then assumes that the order of institutions expresses a qualitative difference between them, again according to the criteria of the ranking.

Classifications do not aim to establish a precise order between institutions in terms of quality. Rather, classifications aim to group institutions into broad categories grouping together institutions that share similar characteristics. These groups do not need to be defined on the basis of performance but as used in the higher education policy debate, the term classification also seems to allow for grouping together institutions that are broadly similar in terms of performance, and for example establish that a given institution belongs to the top 20% or is among those in the 50-75% range. The German CHE[103]/Zeit Online ranking, which calls itself a ranking, may thus be seen as classifying institutions in three groups – top, middle and lower – according to a quite broad range of criteria.

The rankings referred to so far have been developed and are run by non-governmental actors. News media, such as the *Times Higher Education Supplement*, *Die Zeit* and the US News and World Report, are actively involved in higher education rankings and give these broad publicity. The public interest in the results of the rankings is considerable and most likely far exceeds the public understanding of what the rankings really express. Many of those who read about the rankings seem to believe that they provide reliable information on "the best universities in the world" and use them with limited caution as to the reliability and relevance of the results in spite of the fact that the results often differ from one ranking to another. As an indication of the force of rankings, even institutional leaders who are sceptical of the value of rankings may well publicise their own institution's results if the institution comes out well in a given ranking and use this as an argument to attract students and funding.

There are, however, signs of greater public involvement with rankings. The European Commission has launched a project called U-Multirank,[104] which aims to provide a global ranking encompassing all types of higher education institutions and based on a variety of factors such as teaching and learning, research, knowledge exchange and internationalisation, among others. The project is carried out by a consortium of

---

102. By coincidence received by the author on 21 July 2010, as work on this article started.
103. Centre for Higher Education Development www.che-ranking.de/cms/?getObject=615&getLang=en; the ranking for 2009/10 is accessible at http://ranking.zeit.de/che10/CHE_en, both accessed on 21 July 2010.
104. www.u-multirank.eu, accessed on 21 July 2010.

institutions but the public financing of the project through the European Commission represents a new feature in relation to previous rankings. This project may be seen as a response to the desire by some European governments and other actors to develop criteria that better respond to the perceived strengths of European universities. This was, in particular, a prominent issue during the French presidency of the European Union in autumn 2008.

The heated debate in the Bologna Follow-up Group, as well as the public debate about rankings more broadly, show that there are very diverse views on the topic. The controversy of the issue is also illustrated by the fact that the request by ministers was for monitoring the development of "transparency instruments" and did not use the more controversial terms "rankings" or "classifications". The term "transparency instruments" may be given different interpretations and it could be argued that it should include instruments such as the Diploma Supplement, ECTS[105] and even qualifications frameworks but the term has come to be associated above all with the ongoing debate on the usefulness of rankings.

The controversial character of the issue was underlined at a session at the 2010 International Conference of the International Association of Universities in Vilnius in June 2010,[106] where three projects were presented and where the ensuing debate demonstrated that there is little consensus but considerable scepticism on the topic. The present article builds on the questions the author contributed to this debate. The questions raised apply to rankings as a whole rather than a specific undertaking and the questions will therefore not be illustrated with reference to specific rankings.

In this author's view, three broad questions are essential to forming an opinion on rankings and the rest of the article will be devoted to exploring these questions without necessarily arriving at a definitive position on each one.

Are rankings reliable?

The first question to be raised is whether the results of the rankings are reliable, in other words whether the indicators defined are meaningful, whether the data collection is carried out in satisfactory ways and whether those who undertake the rankings have sufficient technical competence. This is the easier question to answer: there is little reason to doubt that at least the more serious rankings are undertaken by competent professionals. The questions raised are a reflection of the complexity of the issue rather than the professional competence of its practitioners even if one might legitimately ask whether at least some practitioners would not have been well advised to exercise a higher degree of caution in presenting their results.

Some of the problematic issues are recognised by those responsible for rankings, as shown in an article by Phil Baty, editor of the Times Higher Education World University Rankings, on the Inside Higher Ed website. While defending the

---

105. European Credit Transfer and Accumulation System.
106. www.iau-aiu.net, accessed on 21 July 2010.

principles and purposes of rankings, Baty acknowledges that the ranking for which he is responsible has had serious shortcomings that those responsible are now seeking to remedy (Baty 2010). Methodological difficulties are also recognised by other practitioners, such as the IREG[107] Observatory on Academic Ranking and Excellence (IREG 2006).

That the issue of methodology is nevertheless a difficult one even for qualified researchers is illustrated by the fact that current rankings use a variety of methods. Few rely on a single method but the relative weight of factors varies significantly. Some rankings rely more strongly on citations, others give considerable emphasis to the opinion of peers and the selection of academic disciplines varies considerably. Some rankings assign an overall result to an institution, whereas others may emphasise the standing of an institution in a given discipline, either exclusively or as a complement to an overall result for the institution. If institution A is the third best in the survey, does that apply to all its academic disciplines or might it be number one in chemistry and number ten in mathematics?

This indicates that a more relevant question than whether a ranking is technically sound is whether its methodology is satisfactory in terms of the choices it makes. If institution A is number three overall in the survey, number one in chemistry or number ten in mathematics, what does it really mean? It may also be worth noting that measures such as opinion polls normally indicate a margin of error, whereas, to this author's knowledge, similar margins are not indicated in the case of rankings.[108]

It is likely to mean considerably less than what is often assumed. The results of any ranking exercise are only relevant in relation to the criteria employed. If a ranking emphasises peer-reviewed publications in certain academic disciplines, what the ranking will give an indication of is how institutions score in terms of peer-reviewed articles in these disciplines. It will not say much about the quality of the institution per se. The culture of publishing and the availability of peer-reviewed academic journals vary from discipline to discipline. They are characteristic of many natural sciences but less common in humanities. This criterion also favours those who write in the most widely read languages and in particular in English. It may also favour disciplines where research results are mainly published through academic articles rather than in academic books even if academic books are normally peer reviewed as part of the publication process. Even if quality may be more important than quantity, what is the relative value of an article of 30 pages and a book of 300? How can one indicate the relative quality of the outcomes of a three- or five-year successful research project and research conducted by an individual researcher over 15 years leading to a highly appraised book? The point is not that one is more valuable than the other but that the two are difficult to compare.

---

107. International Ranking Expert Group.
108. The author is grateful to Ligia Deca for making this point.

If the number of Nobel Prizes is included as a criterion, this again strongly favours natural and life sciences and the older and more established ones at that.[109] There are no Nobel Prizes in the humanities, theology, law or the social sciences. There is an economics prize that is usually counted as a Nobel Prize even if it was established only in 1968 by the Swedish Central Bank (Sveriges Riksbank), whereas the other Nobel Prizes were established through Alfred Nobel's will and awarded as of 1901, and is officially called the Swedish Central Bank's Prize in Economic Sciences in Memory of Alfred Nobel.[110] The Literature Prize is for authors rather than those who study their works and develop literary theory and even successful heads of the most conflict-ridden higher education institutions are unlikely to be considered for the Peace Prize. This criterion also illustrates the problem of time: a Nobel Prize won by a scientist or a research team who is still active at the university is clearly an indication of excellence in that particular area of research but how relevant is a Nobel Prize won half a century ago? Would the same university be able to win one today? Humboldt University, for example, won 29 Nobel Prizes in the first third of the 20th century (Litta 2010: 22), but this says very little – positively or nega- tively – about the university today. The Economics Department at the University of Oslo has obtained two Economics Prizes, both by scholars no longer active but who spent most of their careers at the department and had decisive influence on its development at the time. These prizes say nothing about the quality of teaching in the department or about the quality of other departments at the university. At the same time, the fact that a department obtained a number of Nobel Prizes years ago and none since does not necessarily imply it has lost in quality.

The examples above refer to research and that is not by coincidence: a frequent criticism of rankings is that they tend to measure research results rather than the quality of the institution as such. Good researchers may also be good teachers and good research institutions may also have excellent undergraduate study programmes but one does not automatically follow from the other. Research results also say little about the extent and quality of an institution's efforts to fulfil other missions of higher education, such as engaging with its local community, which is a mission that is perhaps given greater prominence in both Latin America and the United States than in most of Europe. In the words of the Council of Europe's Steering Committee for Higher Education and Research:

> Whatever their stated missions, higher education institutions should aim to carry them out with excellence, and public authorities and other stakeholders should encourage higher education institutions to develop and maintain excellence in their chosen

---

109. In the widely quoted ranking developed by Shanghai Jiao Tong University, the number of alumni winning Nobel Prizes and Fields Medals counts 10% and staff winning these prizes 20%, see www.universityworldnews.com/article.php?story=20100813204958643, accessed on 16 August 2010. However, the weight of an award in the ranking is reduced with time so that awards received recently carry a greater weight than those received less recently. Nobel Prizes in Peace and Literature are excluded (Billaut, Bouyssou and Vincke 2010, which offers a highly critical assessment of the Shanghai Jiao Tong ranking). 110. http://nobelprize.org/nobel_prizes/economics and www.riksbank.se/templates/Page.aspx?id=20192, both accessed on 22 July 2010.

missions. The criteria and indicators used for any type of evaluation must match the missions that the institution has defined for itself. In other words, the evaluation must fit the purpose of that institution (CDESR 2009).

Higher education rankings rarely apply to broader areas of an institution's activities and tend to measure research results. They also tend to favour a limited range of disciplines as well as results published in English, to a lesser extent in other widely read languages. It is therefore highly doubtful that rankings as they stand today give a meaningful impression of the relative quality of higher education institutions. Rather than measure what is important, current rankings seem to give importance to what is measurable. It is in the nature of research and higher education that methodologies can always be improved and one should not exclude the development of sounder and more relevant rankings over the next few years and decades. Nevertheless, it seems clear that most current rankings would need substantial improvement to make reliable statements on anything but the quality of research in specific disciplines at specific points in time.

Some of the proliferation of rankings may in fact be due to the difficulty of establishing sound or at least widely accepted criteria. In a Nordic context, it has been argued that indicators such as the ratio of full-time and part-time academic staff, the degree to which staff enjoy academic freedom, the degree to which staff participate in the governance of institutions and student participation in teaching and research as well as institutional governance should be given greater weight in ranking exercises (Öhlund 2010: 22).

Where the present author begs to differ with the ranking community is therefore not in accepting the need for improvement of the current rankings, which is nearly universally recognised, but – apart, most likely, from details of criteria and methods – on the chances of success and on the relevance of rankings if they were reliable.

Are rankings relevant?

If methodologically sound rankings were developed that made valid statements about the relative overall merit of higher education institutions or that made such claims about specific aspects of their activities, such as research in political science or linguistics, the teaching and learning environment for undergraduate studies in mathematics, outreach activities to the local community, developing a commitment to democratic participation, intercultural dialogue and ethical reflection in students at all levels, societal relevance locally and globally or a range of other aspects of the missions of higher education, would the rankings then be relevant? If the methodology and choice of criteria were right, would it be worth investing in rankings and paying attention to their results? To this author's knowledge, there has been little consideration of cost-benefit issues related to ranking, or satisfactory public information on the actual cost of the various exercises and sources of funding.[111]

---

111. The author is grateful to Hilligje van't Land for making this point.

In beginning to answer these questions, it may be useful to bear in mind the distinction made between ranking and classification in the first part of this article. Seeking to determine the individual merit of each institution in relation to all other institutions is a different undertaking from seeking to determine which institutions should be placed in which broad category of merit.

Any classification will raise debate about the precise cut-off points for each category. If institutions are classified into three, four or five broad categories, institutions that are close to the cut-off point but still fall into the lower category may legitimately challenge the choice of the cut-off point. This is not specific to higher education. If the authorities of a country wish to encourage settlement or economic activity in a specific part of the country, for example through tax incentives, those who live just on the other side of the administrative border may well ask why their neighbours and not they should be thus favoured. Questioning the choice of cut-off values for each category is, however, a different discussion from debating whether classification into broad categories is meaningful.

In this author's view, it is difficult to find arguments of principle against a broad classification of higher education institutions, also if broad classification is taken to mean giving an impression of order of magnitude without making overly ambitious claims about the precise position of an institution. For students, academics, employers, public authorities and others, it may be relevant to have an independent assessment of what institutions fall into which broad categories of quality.

There are, however, significant caveats. Classification is meaningful only if the methodology used is sound and as we have seen, serious doubts persist on the current state of the methodology. Saying that a broad classification may be useful provided the methodology is sound is therefore not saying that such a classification is available today. Saying that a broad classification may be meaningful is also not saying that the costs justify the measure – that must be assessed when both the costs and the potential merits of the exercise have been clearly established.

A second caveat is that the classification must measure what it claims to measure. If a classification exercise claims to measure the overall quality of the institution, it cannot limit itself to assessing research results. A classification of institutions based on overall quality would therefore be a much more ambitious exercise than classifying a specific department on the basis of its research results and/or its learning environment or an institution on the basis of its outreach activities. The broader the scope of the classification, the less likely it is that it can be based on existing methodology.

Ranking is a different exercise. Even if there were a methodology that allowed one to state reliably that institution A is number 20 in the world and institution B number 30 – whether in terms of overall quality or in terms of a specific criterion – would that be a meaningful claim to make?

Rankings implicitly assume that any difference between institutions, however small, is meaningful. That is, in this author's view, at best a highly questionable assumption. It amounts to saying that a temperature of 26 degrees is significantly higher than one of 25; that driving at 51 kilometres an hour is significantly more dangerous than driving at 50 – even if where, for practical reasons, the speed limit is 50, driving at 51 is a violation of the limit but that is an argument concerning the cut-off point for a classification – that someone weighing 80 kilograms is significantly heavier than someone of the same height weighing 79 or that a lawyer who obtained an overall grade of 2.78 is significantly better than a colleague who graduated with an overall grade of 2.79.[112] Whereas assigning institutions to broad categories of quality may be meaningful, with the caveats outlined above and granting that there may be legitimate discussion about the cut-off points, pretending to be able to rank each institution in relation to all other institutions in a meaningful way is in this author's view at best misguided and at worst misleading.

Any ranking or classification exercise will be a snapshot of the situation at a given moment in time. However, academic quality is not static: if it were, there would be no point in institutional development plans. The quality of the teaching and/or research of an individual, a team or a department may evolve positively or negatively over time, an institution may develop or reduce its engagement with its local community, it may decide to give higher or lower priority to some disciplines and key staff may move to other institutions or retire. The situation may therefore easily evolve between the time when the data are collected and the results are published. If classification is in broad categories, the consequences are perhaps not likely to be dramatic even if, as noted, institutions close to the cut-off point between two categories may evolve into one or the other, but it could easily change the order of institutions in a ranking. The more fine tuned the ranking and the louder its claim to make meaningful statements about small differences in quality, the more developments over even small periods of time will complicate its task and reduce its reliability.

This may be illustrated by another well-known quality guide, which is in our terminology a classification rather than a ranking. In France, the *Guide Michelin* is one of several quality guides for restaurants and even if there is mounting criticism against restaurant guides, they are still of considerable importance. A restaurant loses its status in the Michelin system of one to three stars when it changes owners and it would appear that many high quality restaurants time the change of ownership so they occur shortly after the data for the annual edition of the guide have been collected. This way, the restaurant retains its classification for another year and may have enough time to try to retain its classification in the following edition.

Should public authorities use and be involved with rankings?

One argument frequently heard in the debate is that rankings are here to stay and that public authorities therefore need to relate to them and even work to improve them.

---

112. The example is not fictitious; it refers to an older grading scale once used for law and economics at Norwegian universities. Since 3.15 was the lowest passing grade, mediocre lawyers were sometimes referred to as "pi lawyers", the value of ϖ being 3.14.

The first part of the argument is most likely correct. There are strong economic and political interests involved, the stakes are seen as high and the public interest in, if not understanding of, rankings and classifications is considerable.[113] There are, so far at least, few disincentives for those running the rankings and it seems likely they will be a long-term phenomenon.

The second part of the argument does not follow from the first, however. Public authorities need stronger reasons to engage with phenomena than the simple fact that the phenomena exist. There may be valid reasons for public authorities to use and even engage with rankings but they need to be stated. Surprisingly, this aspect has not been very present in the debate so far and this part of the article sets out to consider some possible arguments and their validity. Again, this is an invitation to further debate rather than an attempt to establish a definitive argument.

For public authorities to use or engage with rankings, they must be convinced that rankings serve a useful public purpose, which would most likely be that they either provide reliable and valuable information to important actors in society or that they are useful instruments of public policy. Public authorities will, or at least should, have little inherent interest in the economic well-being of the bodies that provide the rankings unless they are convinced that the rankings are worthwhile.

Public authorities may have an interest in encouraging transparent information but would need to consider whether rankings and classifications are suitable instruments. One aspect is the utility of rankings as information tools for students, where it is sometimes argued that rankings help students make informed choices about institutions and study programmes. There is, however, little indication that students in effect base their choices on rankings or that they can usefully do so in the future (Öhlund 2010: 18).

The information value of any ranking or classification[114] will depend on its reliability as well as on the public understanding of the information it conveys. The reliability issues have been addressed above and, as we saw, much work remains to be done before the reliability of existing rankings is anywhere near satisfactory. One can also question whether some factors that would be important in determining the quality of an institution are in fact measurable. In the words of Phil Baty:

> We always knew that rankings had their limitations. No ranking can be definitive. No list of the strongest universities can capture all the intangible, life-changing and paradigm-shifting work that universities undertake. In fact, no ranking can even fully capture some of the basics of university activity – there are no globally comparable measures of teaching quality, for example (Baty 2010).

---

113. In less than 24 hours, while working on this article, the author received two e-mails promoting two different rankings.
114. For the sake of easy reading, reference will in this part of the article be to ranking even if the arguments will also broadly apply to classification.

That some elements may not be measurable does of course not mean that none are and one could imagine more targeted rankings that expressly address only specific and measurable aspects of institutional performance. The value of ranking institutions according to these elements would then need to be assessed, but the issue also links to the other important question: public perceptions of ranking.

Presenting the results of current rankings correctly would require many footnotes and caveats and these are not the material of which general information to a broader public is made. Rather, general communication tends to simplify and identify major trends without providing detailed information on issues of methodology and nuances. Even where a ranking may not make an explicit claim to indicate the relative overall quality of institutions, the public perception seems to be that they do. The desire for information to be simple seems to be stronger than the desire for it to be meaningful and reliable. This is not an isolated phenomenon; it is for example exceedingly difficult to inform students and employers of potential quality issues in the choice of institutions and study programmes and hence in the validity of the qualifications earned, and this is an area in which, in the European context, there are reliable public bodies whose remit is to provide information on the recognition of qualifications.[115]

One may argue that the responsibility of those who develop rankings is limited to ranking institutions and does not extend to the use of the information provided. One may perhaps, but the argument is not convincing. Firstly, it is difficult to see what interest a body might have in providing a service that is likely to be misused and misinterpreted. This kind of body would be unlikely to score highly on a quality ranking. More importantly, societies cannot accept producers not taking responsibility for the use of their products. That would leave car producers with no responsibility for features that encourage irresponsible driving, food producers without responsibility for nutritional information and engaging in, for example, campaigns against obesity and makers of safety equipment without responsibility for the use of their equipment. At the very least, products that may be harmful if used incorrectly should come with "health warnings".

In the examples mentioned, public authorities play a role as overseers. Should they also do so with rankings? To the extent that institutions use rankings as part of their advertising, public authorities may well, depending on the country, already have a responsibility under current regulations on truthful advertising. However, claims made by providers may be on the limits of veracity and yet be phrased in such a way as not to overstep the limits of the law. It may well be argued that public authorities should take responsibility either for regulating rankings – although that is exceedingly difficult in a market that is essentially international and either is or can easily be converted to Internet delivery – or provide general information on ranking. Educating potential

---

115. Each country party to the Council of Europe/UNESCO Recognition Convention has a national information centre. For the convention, see www.coe.int/t/dg4/highereducation/Recognition/LRC_en.asp and for the ENIC Network, see www.enic-naric.net, both accessed on 22 July 2010.

users about the pitfalls of ranking may prove to be no easier than educating them about the potential pitfalls of institutional recognition and the validity of diplomas issued by non-recognised providers, but the argument also touches on another aspect of the role of public authorities: to what extent should they actively engage in the development of rankings? Before attempting to answer that question, however, let us briefly consider the potential role of rankings as policy instruments.

Public policy in higher education typically consists of legislation; providing over-arching frameworks, such as for qualifications and quality assurance; financing and actual provision (Bergan 2005, Council of Europe 2007). Quality assurance is recognised as a public responsibility but differs from ranking in that it "aims at ensuring the continuous improvement of the quality of higher education as well as at ascertaining whether a given higher education institution or programme meets a defined quality standard without weighting it and without comparing it to any other institution or programme" (CDESR 2009). Is the ranking of institutions, and not only ascertaining whether they meet established quality criteria, a task for public authorities? To use an analogy, should public authorities ascertain not only whether cars[116] meet safety criteria but also assess the relative merits of those that do and, if so, according to what criteria – speed, safety, comfort, fuel efficiency?

One may also imagine that rankings could be used in allocating public funding for higher education and research. Most public authorities wish to promote excellence and giving budget priority to those who perform well is in itself not an unusual thought. Using ranking for purposes of budget allocation does, however, encounter two major obstacles. Firstly, for rankings to serve as allocation instruments they must be reliable, so we come back to the severe doubts expressed concerning the quality of existing rankings. Secondly, allocation of funds on the basis of relative quality must be balanced against other considerations such as a desire to develop and maintain teaching and research capacity in specific fields, to provide higher education in all regions of the country or to develop new economic activity by developing new areas of teaching and research. Of course, public authorities would need very strong reasons to allocate funds to higher education institutions that would over a reasonable period of time not meet minimum quality standards. However, ranking is not about establishing minimum standards.

It is also worth underlining that rankings describe quality at the time the data were gathered rather than the effect of institutional policies to improve their quality. If rankings were used to decide allocations of funding without taking account of what an institution is doing to improve, only the institutions that fulfilled the criteria of the ranking at the time the data were gathered would survive. This would have a devastating effect if other factors were not considered. An institution that was not highly ranked but was working to improve its quality in several aspects could easily see its consistent efforts stopped.

---

116. Unlike higher education, which can be provided publicly or privately, cars are normally produced by private providers but this does not change the argument in relation to public oversight.

Public authorities may also well wish to provide extra funding to institutions, departments and individuals who provide outstanding teaching, research or community service. They may, however, do so on the recommendation of institutional leaders – presumably in the case of outstanding individuals or departments rather than entire institutions – or on the basis of recommendations from other sources. An elaborate ranking exercise is not necessarily the only relevant source of information. Considerations of quality may also well be linked to considerations of relevance. Public authorities may wish to encourage the development of alternative sources of energy, knowledge and understanding of Chinese language and culture or a better understanding of factors leading to economic growth and decline. In this case, additional public funding is more likely to be allocated to promoting excellence in these areas than in areas of lesser political priority. This point also underscores that excellence is not only a question of what already exists but also of what may be developed. Rankings or at least classifications may perhaps, if the methodological problems were resolved, be of use in identifying the former but less so in identifying the latter. Public authorities may also wish to fund institutions or study programmes that meet minimum quality standards without excelling for a variety of reasons, ranging from a desire to develop and maintain competence in a broad range of disciplines, not all of which will be provided at world class standards, to the desire to provide higher education in specific parts of the country.

Making rankings an important instrument for funding policies could therefore do considerable harm and could tempt public authorities to abdicate part of their responsibility for ensuring coherent overall policies in favour of indicators that are seemingly "objective" yet show considerable problems of reliability and relevance.

Beyond public policies for allocation of funding, it should also be noted that the impact of rankings to a considerable extent depends on its audience. If it reaches a broad audience, the ranking can become a "self-fulfilling prophecy" and highly ranked institutions will find it easier to attract funding, academic staff and students. Such policies could also have a harmful effect on institutional policies, which would most likely be reoriented toward the criteria used by the ranking(s) on which public funding would be based. If "you get what you measure" (Öhlund 2010: 17), what will be the impact on public and institutional policies for quality improvement and/or diversification?

It is therefore difficult to identify compelling reasons for public authorities to make use of rankings as an important policy instrument and good reasons why they should refrain from doing so. If there are insufficient reasons for public authorities to make use of rankings for the purpose of information or policy making, it follows that there are insufficient reasons for them to engage in the further development of rankings. Let us nevertheless consider this issue for a moment without taking into account the use public authorities may make of rankings, even if this may seem artificial.

As we have pointed to several times in this article, current rankings are problematic in terms of the quality and relevance of their methodology and results. If so, should public authorities play a role in improving them? The answer depends in part on what improvements are needed and whether they are realistic, in part on the stakes of public authorities in rankings. As far as the need for improvements are concerned, they have been addressed above and this consideration will also have made it clear that this author, at least, is sceptical about the prospect of establishing reliable and meaningful rankings within reasonable time.

That is in itself a considerable stake for public authorities. Should they decide to engage in the development of rankings in spite of the very real risk that rankings will remain considerably less than satisfactory, public authorities will run the risk of being firmly associated with a controversial measure the success of which is far from certain and very possibly unlikely. What will public authorities be able to do to make the difference in developing rankings that meet the concerns in terms of relevance and reliability outlined in this article that the current developers of rankings seem unable to do? This question needs a convincing answer for public authorities to engage. If public authorities were to engage in an exercise that led to unsatisfactory results but the public authorities nevertheless felt obliged to use them because of the funds and prestige invested, we would truly obtain perverse results of public policy.

Given the shortcoming of current rankings, one might expect that even if it were eventually possible to establish reliable rankings, and even if these were to play a meaningful role – in themselves very significant caveats – this would take considerable time. In the meantime, less than satisfactory rankings would flourish and by engaging with the development of rankings by using their results even if the rankings are unsatisfactory, public authorities would lend legitimacy to rankings as a phenomenon. Even if it were possible to arrive at reliable and meaningful rankings at some point in the future – and it remains to be proven that it is – the damage made along the road could be considerable.

Unsatisfactory rankings developed with the participation of or even simply used and hence implicitly approved by public authorities would also expose these authorities in a different way. Methodologically deficient rankings used for example in resource allocation or as an indication of the value of a diploma would seem very likely to lead to litigation. Decisions on the recognition of individual qualifications have already been brought to court in several countries even in cases where quality criteria have been far simpler than an assessment of relative merit would be, for example by identifying a diploma mill as such or by indicating that if an institution or programme is not recognised by the competent authorities, there is reason to be wary and at least investigate further before enrolling in such a programme or accepting the qualification emanating from it (Hunt 2010: 119). There is little reason to doubt that some institutions or individuals who would feel aggrieved by faulty rankings would seek redress through the judiciary.

Conclusion

We seem to be faced with something of a vicious circle: the more use public authorities make of rankings and the less determination they show in the face of the reality of unsatisfactory rankings, the higher stakes public authorities will have in trying to improve rankings, perhaps even when confronted with evidence suggesting that the effort is ultimately futile.

Rather than stimulate the use and development of rankings, public authorities should therefore have an interest in reducing the focus on ranking. Public authorities cannot stop rankings. However, the very considerable methodological problems, the limited value of rankings, which seek to establish a precise order of merit between institutions – here, there are arguments for seeing classifications in a somewhat different light – and the stakes of public authorities as well as an understanding of their proper role in quality assurance suggest that public authorities should neither make use of nor encourage the development of rankings. The request by ministers of the European Higher Education Area to monitor the development of the transparency mechanisms seems reasonable; efforts by public authorities to develop rankings or to fund their development do not.

Higher education in Europe is likely to be faced with difficult decisions on the profile, variety and missions of higher education in the years to come. The Humboldtian assumption that all institutions carry out research may not be sustainable and Europe needs a diversified higher education system that caters to all major missions of higher education. We need higher education policies that cater to the diverse needs of society and that prepare not only for the labour market but also for democratic citizenship and that further the personal development of learners as well as the development in our societies of a broad and advanced knowledge base (Bergan 2005, Council of Europe 2007). Rankings are unfit to further these essential policy goals today and they seem unlikely to be able to do so in the foreseeable future. In the words of the CDESR:

> [W]hile criteria and indicators must both cover the whole scope of higher education as laid down in the Recommendation cited above[117] and in their application fit the purpose of the individual institution, they must also be such that they are not a straitjacket for the institution. Even the best constructed system is of little use, and can potentially be harmful, if it encourages institutions to chase after rankings rather than focus on their core mission (CDESR 2009).

The stakes are considerable for public authorities as well as for institutions, staff, students and broader society. It is therefore important that the debate on ranking continue and that it not be taken for granted that because rankings exist, they must be used by public authorities or institutions. Rather, the debate must examine the problematic issues around ranking, identify the improvements needed and assess whether these improvements are likely or even possible. The debate must assess whether and how rankings might serve a useful purpose and be open to drawing the conclusion that they might not.

---

117. The reference is to the Council of Europe (2007).

A cynical view would be that since rankings are unlikely to disappear, at least in the short run, there may be advantages in having a thousand rankings bloom. The coexistence of many exercises using different methods and arriving at different results should at least diminish the impression that rankings may be reliable, objective indications of the relative quality of institutions. Whether public authorities should contribute to watering the thousand flowers is, however, more than questionable.

References

Baty P. (2010), "Ranking confession", Inside Higher Ed website, 15 March 2010, available at www.insidehighered.com/views/2010/03/15/baty, accessed on 22 July 2010.

Bergan S. (2005), "Higher education as a 'public good and a public responsibility' – What does it mean?", in Weber L. and Bergan S. (eds) (2005), *The Public Responsibility for Higher Education and Research*, Council of Europe Higher Education Series No. 2, Council of Europe Publishing, Strasbourg; reproduced in this volume.

Billaut J.-C., Bouyssou D. and Vincke P. (2010), "Should you believe in the Shanghai ranking? An MCDM view", *Scientometrics*, Vol. 84, No. 1, pp. 237-263.

Bologna Process (2009), "The Bologna Process 2020 – The European Higher Education Area in the New Decade". Communiqué of the Conference of European Ministers Responsible for Higher Education, Leuven and Louvain-la-Neuve, 28-29 April 2009.

CDESR (2009), "Quality Assurance, Ranking and Classification in the Light of the Missions of Higher Education", statement by the Steering Committee for Higher Education and Research (CDESR), adopted on 5 March 2009.

Council of Europe (2007), Recommendation CM/Rec(2007)6 of the Committee of Ministers to member states on the public responsibility for higher education and research.

Hunt E. S. (2010), "Qualifications from non-recognised institutions: an overview of the issue", in Hunt E. S. and Bergan S. (eds), *Developing Attitudes to Recognition: Substantial Differences in an Age of Globalisation*, Council of Europe Higher Education Series No. 13, Council of Europe Publishing, Strasbourg.

IREG (2006), "Berlin Principles on Ranking of Higher Education Institutions", adopted by the International Ranking Expert Group at its second meeting, Berlin, 18-20 May 2006.

Litta S. (2010), "Celebrating 200 years of Humboldt University", *International Higher Education*, No. 60, Summer 2010, The Boston College Center for International Higher Education, Boston.

Öhlund U. (2010), *Sammenfattande rapport från konferensen: Profilering av nordisk högre utbildning och forskning. Klassificering och ranking på nordisk dagordning* [Summary Report from the Conference: Profiling Nordic Higher Education and Research. Classification and Ranking on the Nordic Agenda], TemaNord, 20910:556, Nordic Council of Ministers, Copenhagen.

III. Qualifications
and recognition

Qualifications: purposes, functions and contexts[118]

Qualifications and the purposes of education

Qualifications are a fascinating phenomenon. Nevertheless, it is important to keep in mind that qualifications are not only fascinating in themselves. They contribute to a broader goal – that of preparing learners for whatever activities they will pursue once they have completed the course of learning they have embarked on, whether that activity be gainful employment, a deeper understanding of themselves or the world in which they live, or a contribution as citizens. Hopefully, learners will be engaged in all three kinds of activities, and other activities as well. Qualifications also allow others to understand and assess the competences acquired by learners. We should be careful to specify that this course is a specific "piece" of learning, and not the end of all learning. The day a learner completed all kinds of learning would be a sad day indeed. In the perspective of lifelong learning, this would be the end of life itself.

Qualifications, then, cannot be seen in isolation from the society in which they prepare us to work and live. As this society evolves, so must the form and content of qualifications. Yet, qualifications should be much more than the end point of a course of learning, the only purpose of which is to prepare learners for a specific job or even for a broad segment of the labour market. Qualifications are important in preparing for work, but if that were their only objective, they – as the education that leads to the qualifications – would miss their mark. Qualifications must be seen in relation to the purposes of education (Bergan 2005 and 2006).[119] Preparation for work and the economic function of higher education are clearly of great importance, and this is recognised in current debate. The other main purposes of higher education – including that of promoting citizenship – are far less clearly recognised in current debate, and the present chapter aims to put the concept of qualifications into this broader context of the purposes of higher education.

As these lines are written, we are already a few years into the 21st century, yet there is every reason to wonder whether our higher education qualifications are adapted to this fact. Have our descriptions of the knowledge, understanding and skills that higher education should develop been adapted to the likely requirements of the future, or are we still looking back towards the past century? Alternatively, have we been too eager to adapt our qualifications to our immediate concerns without asking

---

118. The first version of this article was published as Chapter 15 in Sjur Bergan (2007): *Qualifications: Introduction to a Concept*, Strasbourg: Council of Europe Publishing. Council of Europe Higher Education Series No. 6.
119. This article draws in particular on the 2006 article.

ourselves the difficult but crucial questions about the values on which we would like our societies to be based and how our qualifications help promote those values?

The concept of an educated person has shifted over time, and so have the purposes of study – whether in generic terms or in terms of studying a specific discipline. Just think of Latin. At the time of the Roman Empire, the purpose of learning Latin was for many to master their native language and for many others to gain fluency in the foreign language considered most useful for professional and social advancement. Latin was a lingua franca long before the emergence of the language that gave rise to the term. It had the function that English has gained today, that of the most important facilitator of communication between people from a variety of linguistic and cultural backgrounds. However, a working knowledge of Latin as a foreign language was reserved for an elite, much more so than a similar level of fluency in English today. In geographical terms, the elite who mastered Latin was also concentrated on a much smaller territory than those who master English today.

In the Roman Empire, public speaking or eloquence was an important part of education and served to prepare young men for careers as politicians and lawyers. Later, when schools became attached to the Church in western Europe, while the language of education was still Latin, the main goal of formal education was religious (Janson 2002: 103-104). Today, those who study Latin are less numerous, and their reasons for studying what is often referred to as a "dead language" are mostly either cultural enrichment, to use Latin as a support discipline for scholarly work in disciplines that require a knowledge of this language or – for a smaller minority yet – as an academic specialisation in its own right.

Yet, even if the specific objectives of education have changed over time, the deeper purposes seem fairly constant. Their relative importance may also have varied somewhat, but it would be difficult to find a time when education did not, at least to some extent, have the following purposes:

– preparation for the labour market;

– preparation for life as active citizens in democratic societies;

– personal development;

– the development and maintenance of a broad, advanced knowledge base (Bergan 2005, Council of Europe 2007).

These purposes are not mutually exclusive. Rather, they tend to reinforce each other. I also tend to consider them equally important for contemporary society, even if much of the current debate centres on the first of them: preparation for the labour market. The order in which they are listed should therefore not be seen as an expression of values or relative importance. Yet, the order is not entirely coincidental: it goes from the purpose that is the most debated through one that is increasingly emphasised in public debate through the one that is the least prominent in current discourse to the one that most clearly combines education and research.

Preparation for the labour market

From following current debate, one could easily get the impression that preparation for the labour market is the main or even the only purpose of higher education, but also that it is a relatively new purpose, a consequence of modern society and mass higher education, as opposed to the leisurely times of elite education when personal development was the main purpose. This impression is at considerable variance with reality.

The reason why the early universities focused on the *studium generale*, followed by theology, law and medicine, is not that these were the disciplines most conducive to personal development, but that they prepared learners for the kind of jobs for which higher education was required in medieval society. The earliest universities were strongly orientated to the labour market, but the academic labour market has changed radically since the late Middle Ages, and so has higher education. The *studium generale* was considered to provide the necessary background for undertaking professional studies, and it is perhaps not a coincidence that those three broad fields of professional studies are today typically among the regulated professions in most countries.[120] That the *studium generale* was so considered had partly to do with the emphasis on general culture in a society in which formal learning was the preserve of an elite, and partly with the fact that the opportunities for formal study enabling students to acquire such learning before they entered higher education were not well developed.

However, academic qualifications were not necessarily required even for these professions. In the Catholic Church, systematic academic training for all clergy came in the wake of the Council of Trento in the mid-16th century, as a part of the Counter-Reformation, and led to the establishment of seminaries (Launay 2003). Medicine was long thought of in more theoretical terms, with the hands-on parts left to practitioners with strong arms but little or no academic training. As late as 1789, one of the leaders of the early Brazilian independence movement, Joaquim José da Silva Xavier, went by the name of Tiradentes (Tooth Puller), which reflects the contemporary approach to dentistry, a trade he practised along with medicine and commerce.

Today, the labour market demands highly qualified persons to an unprecedented extent. Whether that has to do with the development of mass higher education or whether, on the contrary, mass higher education is a response to the labour market may be of theoretical interest, but need not concern us here. Probably the two reinforce each other and both are linked to the development of society, which is becoming increasingly complex technologically, but also politically and socially. Sometimes, the emphasis on specialisation – not least technological specialisation – can give the impression that the needs of the labour market are limited to increasing specialisation with little or no need for a broader view.

---

120. In a legal sense, this is not true of theology in all countries. Nevertheless, to enter the priesthood or to practise as a minister, ordination is required in most churches.

In this case, we would be talking about training and not education. Or, using the language of qualifications and competences, we could say the needs of society were for subject-specific rather than transversal competences. This would be a very narrow concept of the needs of society as well as of the purposes of education and both kinds of competences are needed. Most readers will probably have no problem remembering teachers or colleagues who had insufficient command of the specific subjects or disciplines that were essential to the job. At the same time, most readers will probably also have met the opposite case: teachers or colleagues who knew their field very well, but were lacking in transversal skills. They were unable to communicate their highly specialised knowledge and understanding to others or to apply it in practical terms.

Preparation for active citizenship in democratic societies

This may seem like a new purpose of education, and if we emphasise the terms "active" and "democratic", it probably is.[121] Yet, if we drop the adjectives, this purpose is probably as old as the notion of education, since the socialisation of children and young people has always been a key concern of both formal and informal education.

The emphasis on active citizenship and democracy reflects profound changes in society and the need for higher education to respond to them. How higher education responds, as well as the extent to which it responds, varies enormously from country to country and even from institution to institution.

"Citizen" and "citizenship" have a double meaning. In strictly legal terms, they denote "belonging" to a state. We may be citizens of Slovenia or of Greece, meaning we carry a Slovenian or Greek passport and expect to exercise certain rights, such as voting, in Slovenia or Greece as well as to enjoy a measure of protection from the government of our country of citizenship if we get into trouble abroad. We also have certain duties in regard to the country of our citizenship, the emblematic one being military service, even if many countries have now abandoned conscription in favour of professional and voluntary armed forces.

The other meaning of "citizen" and "citizenship" is a societal one, and this is the one that is relevant to our concerns with qualifications. It denotes a set of skills, attitudes and values related to how one perceives oneself as a member of society, and since we are concerned with democratic citizenship, they are the skills, attitudes and values that members of a society should have, for democratic societies to function as such.

If we think back to our school textbooks in civics and related subjects, the chances are that they described democracy in terms of institutions. Citizens elect parliaments,

---

121. It may be argued that active democratic citizenship was a feature of Athenian society and is therefore not a new feature of education. Even if Athenian democracy was of fundamental importance as a model for European democracy, its democratic character can be contested in our view on grounds of eligibility and participation.

the government is formed by the party or coalition of parties with the highest number of votes and parliaments enact democratic laws by voting, in which the majority decides. Of course, institutions and laws are important, and democracy would be inconceivable without them. They are absolutely necessary, but they are not sufficient. They will not function unless they are embedded in democratic culture.

Democratic culture has to be developed anew in each generation, and education at all levels, formal as well as informal, plays a key part in developing this democratic culture. Emphatically, developing democratic culture is not just a concern for new democracies: we do not need to read many newspapers to see that the old democracies also face formidable challenges in developing and maintaining democratic culture. It includes values as well as commitment. It cannot be developed by those who identify with democratic ideals in principle, but are unwilling to engage in the public sphere. The importance of democratic culture, as well as the essential role of education in developing and maintaining it, was recognised by the heads of state and government of the Council of Europe at their 3rd Summit in May 2005 (Council of Europe 2005).

The concepts of subject-specific and transversal competences are relevant also to this purpose of education. Active citizens in democratic societies need to know something about political theory, as well as about democratic institutions and how they work. They also need to develop a basic knowledge and understanding of a wide range of subjects, from economics through natural sciences to history, political science and language. History has no shortage of examples of what can happen when citizens are tempted by easy and fast solutions, whether it be to unemployment, wealth distribution, environmental problems, immigration or other issues.

Our consideration of qualifications is highly relevant to considerations of democratic culture. To be sustainable, democratic culture depends on well-developed transversal skills:

– analytical ability;
– the ability to present an issue clearly;
– the ability to identify alternatives;
– the ability to see an issue from different angles;
– the ability to step outside one's own frame of reference;
– the ability to solve and preferably to prevent conflicts;
– the ability to debate, but also to draw conclusions and put them into practice;
– even the ability to read between the lines – to read the unstated as well as the stated.

One important transversal skill is the ability to identify and then resolve paradoxes; and, as societies, we are not particularly good at it. How else would we strive to make our country ever more attractive, yet be very upset when it becomes sufficiently attractive for people to want not just to visit, but also to stay in our country to live and work?

It is also disturbing to observe the seeming inability of political debate in many of our societies to look beyond the immediate issues. What is expedient in the short run may not be right in the long run. If you are on a diet, it is normally not for the pleasure of starving, but because you think you will be better off in the long run. Yet, while diets are popular, transferring the same kind of reasoning to political debate is decidedly less so.

Education, at all levels, plays an important role in developing the skills and competences needed to develop democratic citizenship, and this purpose of education is not confined to primary level or even to compulsory education. Higher education is an integral part of the effort, and higher education qualifications are not a guarantee that the holder will have democratic attitudes. True, it is not difficult to think of academics who have done a lot to further democratic culture and who stood up for democracy at great personal risk. These examples include the Weisse Rose, the student group around Hans and Sophie Scholl, as well as the theologians Dietrich Bonhoeffer (Protestant) and Alfred Delp, SJ (Catholic) (Gotto and Repgen 1990) in Nazi Germany; Portuguese students under Salazar, especially from the 1960s onwards; Chilean students under the Pinochet regime; Greek students under the regime of the Colonels; Academician Andrei Sakharov in the Soviet Union; and the Alternative Academic Education Network under the Milošević regime. The list could be made much, much longer.

However, it is also easy to think of a list of counter-examples of academics who have led or assisted oppressive and dictatorial regimes. This list includes many right-wing German academics and students in the 1930s (Hammerstein 1991); many of the leaders of the Salazar regime, who had their roots at the University of Coimbra (Torgal 1999); the "Chicago boys" – the economists who hailed from the University of Chicago and the Universidad Católica de Chile – who played an important role in the Pinochet regime (Huneeus 2001, Mönckeberg 2005); academically trained judges in the German Democratic Republic and other communist states (Mählert 1999); the leaders of far too many universities and academies of science who served the same regimes; the teachers and students at the University of Ayacucho who founded the Peruvian left-wing terrorist movement Sendero Luminoso and those involved with European left-wing terrorist groups like the Rote Armee Fraktion (Baader-Meinhof) in Germany or the Brigati Rossi in Italy. Alas, this list, too, could be made much longer.

Developing and maintaining democratic culture is therefore a double task for the higher education community. It must do so for itself and it must do so for the benefit of others.

For itself, the higher education community must pursue its research and teaching in all areas of importance to sustaining our societies. That includes the ethics, values and principles on which we found our societies as well as the mechanisms that make them work. For itself, higher education must also live by the principles it proclaims. *Orthodoxia* – correct thinking – must be complemented by *orthopraxis* – sound practice.

With the wider society, the higher education community must engage. The image of the ivory tower is, I believe, a considerably exaggerated image. Had it been exact, it is difficult to believe that universities would have survived for several centuries. Yet, we often talk about the "society surrounding higher education" and forget that this is not an ocean surrounding an island. It is the very society of which higher education is a part. Our views of qualifications must reflect that, as must the definition of learning outcomes and other essential ingredients of qualifications.

Personal development

In current debate about higher education policies, it is almost never stated that higher education should contribute to the personal development of learners, nor does much thought seem to be given to what, in today's society, should be the characteristics of an educated person. In current debate, the importance and legitimacy of personal development is about as easy to argue as the indispensable role of coffee breaks at conferences to allow participants to network and discuss informally. Yet, we need not go many generations back in time to find that personal development was recognised as an important characteristic of education. This was not entirely disinterested, however, as education entailed social status and was key to the ideal of a gentleman. It was inconceivable that a gentleman could have no or little education, and the gentleman pursued education primarily for his personal development and the maintenance of his social status. It should also be noted that while "education for education's sake" may have been an ideal of high society, many of those thus educated did feel a strong obligation to put their knowledge to use at the service of society's less fortunate members or in pursuit of more immediately applicable knowledge.

The ideal of pursuing knowledge for its own sake is still alive, even if it is rarely applied in its purest form. The perhaps most extreme example of which this author is aware is that of Henry Cavendish (1731-1810), who made important discoveries in natural sciences but published only a part of them, so that later scientists made the same discoveries and published them much later (Gribbin 2002: 262-275).[122] Today, the personal development of students is a stated goal of education in many countries, as exemplified by the Norwegian law on primary and secondary education:

> Secondary education aims to … assist students in their personal development (Utdannings- og forskningsdepartementet 1998; author's translation).

Even if the value of personal development is not acknowledged much in public debate, individual citizens recognise it by taking courses at different levels of education and in all kinds of subjects and disciplines with no explicit aim other than personal development and enrichment.[123] These courses are often organised by bodies other than traditional schools and higher education institutions, such as the French *universités populaires*. Students normally pay fees for such courses,

---

122. One theory is that Cavendish may have had traits of autism.
123. Given current trends, it may be worth underlining that "enrichment" is here to be taken in the sense of enriching their knowledge and personal development rather than material enrichment.

which are often offered by bodies that do not belong to the education system of the country in which they operate nor lead to qualifications that are recognised within that system.

Incidentally, there is at least one sector of great importance to modern societies for which training in most European countries is entirely or almost entirely offered by private, profit-making providers: drivers' education. This contrasts with the United States, which has a larger private education sector than most European sectors, but where drivers' education has in most states been made a part of the high school curriculum. High schools may, of course, be public or private, but they are a part of the US education system, which is a public responsibility.

While personal development does not play a prominent role in any current policy debate of which this author is aware, it is at least implicit in the concept of liberal arts education in the United States. In the context of the European Higher Education Area, the Bologna Declaration strongly emphasised preparation for the labour market, the Prague Communiqué (Bologna Process 2001) clearly brought in the role of higher education in preparation for citizenship, and the Berlin Communiqué (Bologna Process 2003), by emphasising the link between higher education and research, brought in the development and maintenance of an advanced knowledge base. Personal development has so far not been mentioned explicitly as a goal of higher education in any of the political documents of the Bologna Process. An early draft of the Bergen Communiqué (Bologna Process 2005) contained a reference to the four major purposes of higher education, but it was not retained. The reason was not that there was any opposition to any of the four purposes, but rather that the text needed to be shortened and the reference was not considered essential.

Yet, there is at least occasional debate on whether some national education systems are geared more towards teaching students how to do well in examinations rather than to encourage a broad approach to learning and, for that matter, learning how to learn. There is also debate on the purposes of education, with encouraging attempts to emphasise that education is not purely about teaching students a set of technical skills, but also about helping them develop their personalities and the transversal skills that will enable citizens to discern connections and consequences, and to take a holistic view of society and of human existence. It should be an issue for modern societies that while we get more and more highly trained subject specialists, we seem to be getting fewer and fewer intellectuals, that is, people who can put knowledge and understanding in their proper context and subject received truths to critical examination. It may be worth keeping in mind William Butler Yeats' words that "education is not the filling of a bucket but the start of a fire".

As is the case with preparation for the labour market and preparation for citizenship, both subject-specific and transversal competences are important to personal development. The desire to learn is often subject-specific, such as a burning interest in history, physics or a foreign language. Developing transversal competences like communication and analytical skills along with well-reflected attitudes and values

– not least intellectual curiosity – are important to developing personalities. They are of course also useful for other purposes, and there is certainly no contradiction between personal development and other purposes of higher education. There is, however, every reason to be explicit about personal development as a main purpose of higher education. Besides, it is only through personal development that all other purposes can be fulfilled, starting with our earliest childhood experiences, which are very much in the realm of informal learning.

Developing and maintaining a broad, advanced knowledge base

In the Humboldtian tradition, on which much of European higher education is based, education and research are two sides of one coin. They go together, and the development of higher education in Europe since the early 19th century would have been very different without this tradition. Today, there is development towards a more differentiated view of the relationship between higher education and research.

The relationship is still essential, but higher education can be research based in one of two ways. There can be a direct link in that higher education teachers are also active researchers and bring the results of their research into their teaching. Alternatively, the link can be somewhat less direct in that higher education teachers have personal experience of research through their training and perhaps also through earlier stages of their careers, and they are therefore able to follow and make use of research results in their teaching, but they may no longer be personally engaged in research. One could also identify a third way in which research and teaching are linked, in which institutions ensure that the contents of teaching and learning are kept up to date by active reference to contemporary research. This relies less on individuals transferring their own research and more on a collective culture of feeding the teaching environment with active research issues.[124]

In reality, higher education in Europe is research based in all three ways, and there seems to be increasing willingness to acknowledge this. While the development will not be easy, it does in the longer run seem likely that Europe will move from officially having a system of universities that marry research and teaching to one where some universities are active research universities, while others are mainly teaching universities with limited research of their own, but where staff still have had personal experience of research at some point in their career.

Whatever the model, research is essential to modern societies, which could not have developed without advanced knowledge in a variety of fields. Technologically advanced knowledge is the example that most easily comes to mind, since our contemporary societies would be inconceivable without information technology, advanced production technology, infrastructure for road, sea and air transport, the technology that allows companies to supply goods on demand rather than maintain large stocks, the technology that makes it possible to perform various operations at

---

124. I am grateful to Lewis Purser for this observation.

a distance (Friedman 2006), the technology and knowledge needed to predict the weather and a long list of other technologies. Yet, contemporary societies would also be inconceivable without advanced knowledge and understanding in other fields. We need to understand how societies function, how the human mind works and how language works. We need to understand the consequences of given policies as well as the basic mechanisms governing the relationship between states and other political entities, how these influence co-operation and conflict, and what influences the decisions of voters.

Certain primates spend more than half their time looking for food. When they are held in captivity and fed regularly, they have much "spare time" on their hands, and the effect is often that they are bored and get either apathetic or aggressive. For humans, however, dramatically reducing the time needed to ensure subsistence has had the opposite effect. It has created opportunities for intellectual development or what Lisa Jardine has called "ingenious pursuits" (Jardine 1999) and, in many ways, this is what has made us human beings.

Humans develop and transmit knowledge, and research is an advanced form of knowledge development; but not all development of knowledge is research, nor is new knowledge necessarily developed within higher education. A farmer, a gardener or an artisan may acquire and further develop highly advanced knowledge within their specialisation and would normally do so without much contact with the world of higher education and research. Nevertheless, maintaining and developing advanced knowledge in a broad variety of fields is an important characteristic of higher education. Transmitting the knowledge and skills required for research is also one of the main tasks of higher education.

The need for advanced knowledge is, therefore, apparent. However, modern societies need a knowledge base that is not only advanced, but also broad, and that is partly because it is impossible to predict what knowledge will be key to our needs and desires five or ten years from now, not to speak of in the longer term. When the need arises, it will often be too late to develop the basis that will enable us to rapidly develop the precise knowledge we need.

The borderline between basic and applied research is not always clear in practice, but the concepts are nevertheless useful. Exactly what basic research will give rise to a practical application is not easy to predict. From natural science, one frequently mentioned example is Guglielmo Marconi's work leading to working radio transmission. At the same time, Ernest Rutherford was doing theoretically more important work on radio waves, but Marconi's work led to more immediate application (Gribbin 2002: 500-502). From humanities and social sciences, an example is the oil boycott of the early 1970s, when Arab countries substantially reduced their export of oil to North America and western Europe for political reasons. While some European countries had strong traditions of research in Arabic language, culture and history, many did not, and there was little broad understanding of the reasons for the boycott, and few if any in the countries subjected to the boycott had predicted that this could be the result of their policies in the Middle East. The point here is not whether those policies were justified or not, but rather that, whatever their justification, advanced knowledge and understanding of Arabic language, culture, history and contemporary society would have been of great use in assessing possible consequences of those policies and in seeking to diminish the consequences of them.

Challenges in terms of qualifications

Those concerned with the response of higher education to developments in modern societies and the implications for qualifications are living in interesting times.

This book has largely been concerned with exploring the concept of qualifications and its various components. Our understanding of the concept has improved significantly, and in the next few years we can hope to improve this understanding further. In particular, I am hopeful that we will better understand learning outcomes, that the description of learning outcomes will improve and not least that this competence will be developed among many more higher education policy makers and practitioners in many more countries. To an extent, the development of the European Higher Education Area depends on it, as do the possibilities for improving the movement of learners and holders of qualifications between Europe and other parts of the world. It is important that increasing numbers of policy makers and practitioners in more and more countries move from a legalistic interpretation of concepts to one that focuses on content. Such a move will also facilitate the recognition of foreign qualifications.

Qualifications are not unlike higher education institutions themselves: their forms and the details of their contents need to be adapted to reflect the changes in the societies of which they are a part, but their basic values must be safeguarded. Safeguarding the values is indeed only possible if the form and content are adapted; otherwise higher education qualifications would become obsolete. However, higher education should not only adapt to changes imposed by others. Higher education should influence and even lead the development of society. This is a formidable challenge, but one to which higher education has risen in the past and to which it must continue to rise in the years to come.

That qualifications must adapt is easy to see if we compare the needs and functions that higher education qualifications were required to meet at the beginning of the 19th century with those it was expected to meet at the close of the 20th century. There is little reason to expect that society will not continue to develop, and there is every reason to assume that the development of society will be more and more rapid.

One important challenge is to make sure that higher education qualifications are suited to addressing all four major purposes of higher education. Qualifications that have addressed only one aspect – as can be seen from many examples of qualifications over-focusing on supposed labour market needs in the past – have become obsolete much more quickly than qualifications with a balanced approach to the four purposes. As we saw, there is no fundamental contradiction between the four purposes. Rather, they complement each other: the knowledge, understanding and abilities that help prepare for citizenship or contribute to personal development can also help prepare for the labour market.

It follows that qualifications that focus only on subject-specific skills, without placing them in a broader context and seeking to develop transversal competencies, are likely be short-lived and insufficient. It would indeed be difficult to find such qualifications at higher education level, but there may nevertheless be good reasons for asking whether some higher education programmes provide students with too narrow specialisations. However, the example may be useful in order to underline that the opposite kind of qualifications would also fail the mark.

Transversal competences are important, but they are not everything. The gospel preached by some management specialists – self-appointed or otherwise, in the private sector as well as in the public – maintaining that managers should be generalists and need not know much about the specific areas in which their organisation or team is working, is hardly conducive to sustainable qualifications, or for that matter sustainable corporations. It reminds one of the quip about a journalist being someone who knows less and less about more and more. Taken to the extreme, this attitude would hold that the less a manager knows about the content of the core area of the organisation's activity, the better. What our societies will continue to need, at all levels, for all purposes and in all walks of life, is well-qualified citizens with solid subject-specific as well as transversal competences.

These, however, will not be written in stone, and they will not last a lifetime. They will need to be updated much more often than in the past, and this is another challenge in the area of qualifications. The development of qualifications frameworks and the concept of learning paths should facilitate this development, but a political will is needed all the same. Our education systems will need to provide ample opportunities to earn qualifications in different ways, at different times, and at different stages of life. This is true for "first" qualifications, but it is equally true of opportunities to update qualifications. This simple statement raises a good number of questions that go well beyond the scope of this book, including the provision for and financing of frequent return visits to higher education by learners who want to update their qualifications or to earn new qualifications in new areas of knowledge, and who will need to combine work and learning in a way that the traditional student would not, in most cases. The fact that many other factors are involved, however, is no excuse for not making the qualifications frameworks more explicit in their functions and purpose, and reviewing those which already formally exist, including the way we allow learners to earn qualifications. Without innovation in this area, the best financial provision in the world to help learners alternate between work and learning at different ages might be to little avail.

Technological developments are likely to change the ways in which we learn and to diversify the typical learning experience in ways that most of us will find difficult to imagine. Not all innovation is necessarily for the better, but it is certain that some innovations will be substantial improvements on the ways in which we learn today. As we develop qualifications, we must take account of and, if possible, foresee technological developments in order to make qualifications accessible to more learners. Again, it is a question of changing form and content while preserving values. Technologies that help learners earn qualifications with fewer limitations in time and space will be positive developments and should not only be welcomed, but also integrated into our concept of qualifications. Technologies that encourage unquestioning digestion of "facts" and do not contribute to developing learners' abilities to think critically, analyse information and place it in a broader context will do more harm than good. Technologies that further knowledge and skills without an understanding of what these really are should have no place in the education systems of tomorrow. Qualifications and the assessment processes that measure whether learners have achieved them should be designed to require a deeper understanding both of the specific subject and of its broader context.

The educated person of tomorrow will certainly be expected to master technology. Computer illiteracy may be a modern form of illiteracy, but in technologically complex societies it is a form of illiteracy all the same. In the same way, those able to work only in their native language will be severely disadvantaged in a world in which communication across borders is likely to increase. At the same time, cross-border communication is more than language – it is also intercultural competence: the ability to understand other points of view and to step outside one's own frame of reference.

Ultimately, the measure of whether qualifications are well suited to contribute to the development of society is perhaps whether they are suited to answering the seemingly simple question the Chilean sociologist Eugenio Tironi asked of education: "Educate – for what?" The author seeks the answer not in trying to identify trends in the labour market, but in trying to find an answer to the much broader question: "What kind of society do we want?" (Tironi 2005).

The ultimate measure of qualifications, then, is whether they contribute to developing the kind of society in which we would want to live. This is no small task, and it will challenge policy makers and practitioners alike. This book does not pretend to provide the answer to this challenge, but it will hopefully provide readers with a deeper understanding of the concept and contents of qualifications, so that they can better address the larger issues.

References

Bergan S. (2005), "Higher education as a 'public good and public responsibility' – What does it mean?", in Weber L. and Bergan S., *The Public Responsibility for Higher Education and Research*, Council of Europe Higher Education Series No. 2, Council of Europe Publishing, Strasbourg.

Bergan S. (2006), "Promoting new approaches to learning", article B 1.1-1 in Froment E., Kohler J., Purser L. and Wilson L. (eds), *EUA Bologna Handbook – Making Bologna Work*, Raabe Verlag, Berlin.

Bologna Process (2001), "Towards the European Higher Education Area". Communiqué of the meeting of European ministers in charge of higher education in Prague on 19 May 2001.

Bologna Process (2003), Berlin Communiqué, "Realising the European Higher Education Area", adopted by European ministers of education on 19 September 2003.

Bologna Process (2005), "The European Higher Education Area – Achieving the Goals", Communiqué of the Conference of European Ministers Responsible for Higher Education, Bergen, 19-20 May 2005.

Council of Europe (2005), Warsaw Declaration and Action Plan, www.coe.int/t/dcr/summit/default_EN.asp, accessed on 1 July 2010.

Council of Europe (2007), Recommendation CM/Rec(2007)6 of the Committee of Ministers to member states on the public responsibility for higher education and research.

Friedman T. L. (2006), *The World is Flat*, Penguin Books, London and New York.

Gotto K. and Repgen K. (eds) (1990), *Die Katholiken and das Dritte Reich*, Matthias-Grünewald-Verlag, Mainz.

Gribbin J. (2002), *Science: A History, 1543-2001*, Penguin, London.

Hammerstein N. (1991), "Universities and Democratisation: an Historical Perspective. The Case of Germany" (paper written for the Council of Europe Conference on Universities and Democratisation, Warsaw, 29-31 January 1992, reference DECS-HE 91/97).

Huneeus C. (2001), *El régimen de Pinochet*, Editorial Sudamericana, Santiago de Chile.

Janson T. (2002), *Latin: Kulturen, historien, språket*, Wahlström och Widstrand, Stockholm.

Jardine L. (1999), *Ingenious Pursuits: Building the Scientific Revolution*, Little, Brown & Co., London.

Launay M. (2003): *Les séminaires français aux XIXe et XXe siècles*, Les Editions du Cerf, Paris.

Mählert U. (1999), *Kleine Geschichte der DDR*, Verlag C. H. Beck, Munich.

Mönckeberg M. O. (2005), *La privatización de las universidades*, Copa Rota, Santiago de Chile.

Tironi E. (2005), *El sueño chileno: comunidad, familia y nación en el bicentenario*, Taurus, Santiago de Chile.

Torgal L. R. (1999), *A universidade e o estado novo*, Livreria Minerva Editorial, Coimbra.

Utdannings- og forskningsdepartementet (1998), "Lov om grunnskolen og den vidaregåande opplæringa (opplæringslova)", www.lovdata.no/all/tl-19980717-061-001.html#1-2, accessed on 1 July 2010.

The European Higher Education Area
in the global context: the case of recognition[125]

Context

It was perhaps natural that in its early years, the Bologna Process focused on its internal development, in other words on devising policies for the reform of higher education in Europe without giving extensive consideration to how these reforms would affect the relationship between European higher education and other parts of the world. Much of this work focused on reforming higher education systems, such as introducing three-tier degree systems in all "Bologna countries" and developing national qualifications frameworks and provisions for quality assurance. The first years of the Bologna Process were therefore quite inward looking.

At the same time, it is obvious that extensive reforms of an education system have implications for the relationship between that education system and the rest of the world. This is no less true if the reforms concern 47 countries,[126] since one characteristic of the Bologna Process is that major policies are agreed at European level and implemented nationally. As is well known, the European Higher Education Area does not aim at developing a single higher education system for Europe but rather at providing a framework for coherent development of our national systems.

The relationship between the European Higher Education Area and the rest of the world was for a long time referred to by the somewhat unfortunate term "the external dimension of the Bologna Process", and ministers put it squarely on their agenda at their meeting in Bergen in 2005. As is often the case, a working group was appointed to suggest a strategy, and the Bologna Follow-up Group appointed Toril Johansson of Norway as chair of an unusually large working group that comprised representatives of several "Bologna countries" as well as many of the consultative members, including the Council of Europe. In 2007, Barbara Weitgruber of Austria took over as chair of this group, which has continued to attract the participation of many member countries as well as of organisations.

One of the virtues of this working group was that it managed to find a better term for the "external dimension", so that we talked first about the global dimension and now about the international openness of the European Higher Education Area. Personally, I would have preferred to stick to the term "global dimension". More importantly, it developed a strategy for the global dimension of the European Higher Education Area (Bologna Process 2007a), and it also served as a reference group

---

125. The first version of this article was published in Bergan, Sjur and Rauhvargers, Andrejs (eds) (2008): *New Challenges in Recognition*, Strasbourg: Council of Europe Publishing. Council of Europe Higher Education Series No. 10.
126. Kazakhstan joined the European Higher Education Area as its 47th member in March 2010.

for Pavel Zgaga's impressive overview of the European Higher Education Area in a global context (Zgaga 2007).

At their meeting in London on 17 and 18 May 2007 the ministers of the Bologna Process adopted the strategy as proposed by the working group, and their decision is worth quoting in full:

> We are pleased that in many parts of the world, the Bologna reforms have created considerable interest and stimulated discussion between European and international partners on a range of issues. These include the recognition of qualifications, the benefits of cooperation based upon partnership, mutual trust and understanding, and the underlying values of the Bologna Process. Moreover, we acknowledge that efforts have been made in some countries in other parts of the world to bring their higher education systems more closely into line with the Bologna framework.

> We adopt the strategy "The European Higher Education Area in a Global Setting" and will take forward work in the core policy areas: improving information on, and promoting the attractiveness and competitiveness of the EHEA; strengthening cooperation based on partnership; intensifying policy dialogue; and improving recognition. This work ought to be seen in relation to the OECD/UNESCO *Guidelines for Quality Provision in Cross-border Higher Education* (Bologna Process 2007b).

And, as concerns priorities for the period 2007-09:

> We ask BFUG to report back to us on overall developments in this area at the European, national and institutional levels by 2009. All stakeholders have a role here within their spheres of responsibility. In reporting on the implementation of the strategy for the EHEA in a global context, BFUG should in particular give consideration to two priorities. First, to improve the information available about the EHEA, by developing the Bologna Secretariat website and building on EUA's Bologna Handbook; and second, to improve recognition. We call on HEIs, ENIC/NARIC centres and other competent recognition authorities within the EHEA to assess qualifications from other parts of the world with the same open mind with which they would expect European qualifications to be assessed elsewhere, and to base this recognition on the principles of the LRC [Lisbon Recognition Convention] (Bologna Process 2007b).

Thus, the strategy identifies recognition issues as one of the five core policy areas of the European Higher Education Area in a global context:

1. improving information on the EHEA;

2. promoting European higher education to enhance its worldwide attractiveness and competitiveness;

3. strengthening co-operation based on partnership;

4. intensifying policy dialogue;

5. furthering recognition of qualifications.

As we saw in the decision just quoted, the ministers also singled out recognition issues as one of two elements of the strategy that should be given particular attention.

Recognition in a global context

Ministers – as well as their representatives on the Bologna Follow-up Group – wanted a short and concise strategy rather than a full-fledged White Paper, and the strategy therefore does not go into great detail in any area. This, however, does not mean it does not send important political signals. It is also worth noting that the strategy was accompanied by an appendix called "Elements for further action". These elements are really suggestions for further action. They indicate some possible actions, and they also indicate how these activities could be carried out and by whom, often relying on existing structures and initiatives. The reason for this relatively cautious approach is that there is of course a potential overlap and even tension between possible actions to enhance the position of European higher education as such in a global context and measures individual countries may take to promote their own higher education. The internationalisation of higher education entails an important ideological commitment to co-operation, but it also constitutes an important commercial market. There is not necessarily a clear division between these two aspects of internationalisation, and the twain will often meet. The emphasis on building on current structures and initiative is also explained by concerns about the potential costs of large-scale new initiatives, especially as the Bologna Process as such has little funding of its own. As we have already seen, the Bologna Process essentially relies on agreed policies being implemented by competent national authorities as well as by consultative members.

The strategy confirms the crucial role of fair recognition in facilitating mobility to, from and within the European Higher Education Area. Therefore, also in a global context, recognition is far more than a technical element – it is a policy element of key importance. We cannot aim to attract more students from other parts of the world if we are not willing to consider their qualifications fairly. Stated very simply, European institutions and credentials evaluators must be willing – and able – to assess qualifications from outside the EHEA with the same fairness and openness of mind with which we would like others to approach our own qualifications. We cannot credibly complain about European qualifications not being recognised fairly unless we ourselves are willing to assess non-European qualifications on their merits. The recognition of qualifications must follow the Biblical injunction of "do unto others what you would have them do unto you", whereas one is sometimes left with the impression that the recognition of non-European qualifications is rather done according to the motto "do it to others before they do it to you".

Second, the strategy confirms the key role of the Council of Europe/UNESCO Recognition Convention as the legal framework for recognition as well as the role of the ENIC and NARIC networks in implementing the convention.

Third – and this is potentially the most important part of the strategy – it underlines the importance of the shift of emphasis from procedures and formalities to learning outcomes, and it links this to the need to develop a better understanding of the concept of "substantial differences". The latter is a key concept of the Council of Europe/

UNESCO convention, which stipulates that competent recognition authorities should recognise foreign qualifications unless they can demonstrate that there is a substantial difference between the qualifications for which recognition is sought and the corresponding qualification of the host country. However, no legal text can adequately describe what the term "substantial differences" means in practice, so it is important to develop a common understanding among credentials evaluators, and it is important that this common understanding be fairly generous. Not every difference is substantial, and an overly narrow interpretation of the concept will not further mobility.

Finally, the strategy underlines – as one of its five core elements – the need to intensify policy dialogue. The recognition of qualifications is one area in which such policy dialogue is important. In addition to the substantial issues – to which we shall return shortly – one challenge is finding the right partners for dialogue. The strategy stipulates that "wherever possible, the policy dialogue should be based on already existing and well-functioning fora". This is partly applicable to the recognition field, in that Europe has a well-functioning recognition forum through the ENIC and NARIC networks, but similar networks – and the national centres of which the networks are made up – do not exist to the same extent in other regions. The UNESCO regional committees have the potential to play an important role in this respect but the activities of the UNESCO regional committees are uneven. There is also a limit to the role public authorities can play. In the United States, in particular, the role of public authorities in higher education policy is far less important than it is in Europe, so that a strategy aiming at intensifying discussions between ministries responsible for higher education will be only very partially successful. There is no substitute for engaging in discussions with the higher education institutions and their organisations, and because of the number of institutions, this is a very demanding strategy. In 2009, the ENIC and NARIC networks took a first step by establishing a working group on recognition in a global context.

Some challenges

This section of the article aims to look more closely at the main challenges to recognition in a global context. It will draw on actions in the "Elements for possible future action" but also offer some thoughts beyond what is to be found in these. This section should therefore not be read as an exegesis of the "Elements".

The basic challenges that face those working with recognition issues on a global scale are basically the same as those facing recognition specialists working mainly at European level. Nevertheless, some of the issues at global level seem more difficult to resolve – as if they were magnified by the number of countries and institutions involved – and some are also specific to the global context.

The legal framework

One of the specific issues in the global context is the legal basis for recognition. In Europe, the Council of Europe/UNESCO Recognition Convention provides this legal basis, and separate regional conventions in the UNESCO framework provide a similar legal framework for Africa, the Arab region, Asia and the Pacific, Latin America and the Caribbean and, on an inter-regional basis, the Mediterranean area.[127] However, the UNESCO regional conventions date from the 1970s and 1980s and they are in need of revision, in the same way that the Council of Europe/UNESCO Recognition Convention, which was adopted in 1997 and entered into force in 1999, updated and in fact replaced a number of older conventions for the European region. The fact that the Council of Europe/UNESCO Recognition Convention now (as of July 2010) has been ratified[128] by 50 countries and signed by a further three clearly shows that it met a need for a better legal basis for the recognition of qualifications.

Some UNESCO regions are considering a revision of their respective conventions, and Europe should be prepared to support this work if the regions in question would like to draw on the European experience. Revising the UNESCO regional conventions now would give all regions a unique opportunity to establish an updated legal framework for recognition. Revised regional conventions could include provisions for co-operation between regions, and they include a number of issues that were not ripe for inclusion in the Council of Europe/UNESCO Recognition Convention. One prominent example is the role of quality assurance in recognition, where the wording of the Council of Europe/UNESCO Recognition Convention reflects the state of play in 1997 and hence also shows how far policy and practice have moved on since then. In 1997, there was still discussion about whether one needed a formalised system of quality assurance, whereas today, the discussion focuses on what that system should be like. In view of the developments in European policy and practice, I would argue that no party can fulfil its obligations under Section VIII of the Council of Europe/UNESCO Recognition Convention, which deals with information on the assessment of higher education institutions and programmes, without making reference to quality assurance. There is therefore no need to revise the convention, which would be a major undertaking, but it is also clear that the language on this issue would have been different had the convention been drafted today.

Quality assurance

The key role of quality assurance points to an underlying challenge of recognition: in order to assess an individual qualification, which is what recognition is all about, one needs to know something about the quality of the institution at which the qualification has been obtained. In other words, credentials evaluators need to make use of the results of quality assurance. At global level, this is something of a challenge because policy and practice with regard to quality assurance varies considerably. There is a general tendency to emphasise the importance of quality assurance, but actual practice varies substantially. Some countries, like the United States, have a

---

127. Links to the different regional conventions may be found at www.enic-naric.net/index.aspx?s=n.
128. A constantly updated overview of signatures and ratifications will be found at http://conventions. coe.int/; search for ETS 165. The full text of the convention as well as its explanatory report will also be found here.

long-standing system of institutional accreditation, which means that it is possible to obtain information on whether an institution meets the minimum quality criteria on which the accreditation is based.

With the adoption of European Quality Assurance Standards (Bologna Process 2005) at the meeting of Bologna ministers in Bergen in May 2005, members of the European Higher Education Area have also taken an important step towards providing reliable information on the quality of higher education institutions. This work was taken a step further in 2008, when the European Quality Assurance Register for Higher Education (EQAR)[129] was established. The intention is to provide an overview of agencies that operate in accordance with the standards adopted in Bergen. One possibility is to allow higher education institutions to apply for quality assessment from any agency included in the register, regardless of whether that agency is located or registered in the country in which the higher education institution works. However, it will be up to the competent public authorities whether they will allow institutions within their country to seek quality assurance from an agency in another country since there does not seem to be sufficient support for, as a general rule, allowing higher education providers to undergo quality assurance with the agency of their choice regardless of where the institutions and agencies operate.

In some parts of the world, however, an agreement on overall guidelines for quality assurance is still lacking, and in many countries, there are also no quality assurance agencies accepted as peers by agencies in, for example, Europe or North America. On the one hand, this leads to doubts about the quality of higher education institutions in some parts of the world, but on the other hand, this situation also makes it difficult for these institutions to demonstrate their quality unless they can seek and obtain quality assessment from an established agency that operates according to widely accepted guidelines. This is clearly an urgent issue to address, as lack of adequate quality assurance provisions opens possibilities for less than scrupulous agencies. In the same way that we have for many years been faced with degree mills – providers that issue diplomas against payment but that require little or nothing in terms of academic achievement – we are now also beginning to see the emergence of quality assurance or accreditation mills – agencies that sell quality assurance attestations without bothering to check the quality of the institution. Ultimately, the main victims of this situation will be those who depend on qualifications, primarily learners and the employers.

The ENIC and NARIC networks provide a partial way out of this dilemma, since national information centres with experience of specific institutions and qualifications may share their general assessment with other centres that have no knowledge of the institutions in question. For example, French higher education institutions have established extensive co-operation with higher education institutions in francophone African countries, and through the networks, the French ENIC/NARIC may share the knowledge and experience accumulated through this co-operation

---

129. www.eqar.eu/index.php?id=32, accessed on 1 July 2010.

with colleagues from other countries. This is of course no substitute for proper quality assurance but it is at least a partial solution until adequate quality assurance provision has been established.

Qualifications not belonging to a national system

While, traditionally, higher education institutions have operated within a clearly defined territorial jurisdiction, this is no longer always the case. The traditional institution operating in the country in which it is located is increasingly being supplemented with institutions providing higher education across borders. An institution located in country A may not even offer courses there but rather in countries B or C. Such an institution may not belong to any one national education system, in that it may not be accepted by country A as a part of its system, and it may also not be considered by countries B or C as a part of their respective systems. We are therefore faced with a number of institutions that do not belong to the education system of any country,[130] a phenomenon that is usually referred to as borderless, transnational or cross-border higher education (Knight 2006). We are not even always talking about institutions in the classical sense of the term, but rather about providers that offer courses through new means of provision such as the Internet. In these cases, it is often difficult to determine not only whether the provider belongs to a national system – which very often they do not – but even where they are physically located.

The main challenge in assessing such qualifications is that of determining whether the quality of the provision is sufficient to justify recognition. This is aggravated by the fact that many such providers appear to be less than serious, and credentials evaluators tend to treat this kind of qualification with justified scepticism. However, provision not linked to a national system is not inherently of low quality, and again such providers may face difficulties in finding a way of having their education programmes quality assessed. In this area, we are therefore faced with a double challenge: the firm impression is that there is an unusually high number of less than serious providers, but at the same time the serious providers face difficulties in finding an agency that can assess their quality.

Qualifications frameworks and learning outcomes

In 2005, ministers adopted an overarching framework of qualifications for the European Higher Education Area, and "Bologna countries" are now developing their national frameworks. Qualifications frameworks are not a specifically European phenomenon, and indeed the first national frameworks were developed in Australia, New Zealand and South Africa (Bergan 2007). Nevertheless, qualifications frameworks are a relatively new concept in many parts of the world, and we will need to invest considerable time and effort in explaining the overarching EHEA framework and its relationship to national frameworks. This is a double task: explaining the concept of qualifications

---

130. For the concept of "belonging to a national education system", see Section VII of the Council of Europe/UNESCO Recognition Convention and the explanatory report to this section.

frameworks and explaining the specificities of the EHEA frameworks. The task was not made easier by the fact that the European Qualifications Framework (EQF) for lifelong learning, which was launched by the European Commission, seemed, in its initial versions, to take a different track from the EHEA framework. However, the final version of the EQF is very close to the EHEA framework and co-operation between the two frameworks has been close since 2007. It is therefore not difficult to develop a national framework compatible with both overarching frameworks, and Malta has proven the point by self-certifying its national framework against both overarching frameworks in the same operation. At the same time, qualifications frameworks are now developing into a worldwide phenomenon with some 120 countries and territories having developed or currently developing their own frameworks.[131] Qualifications frameworks should be a major help in facilitating recognition since they provide a good framework within which to situate a specific qualification, and it is important that there be broad co-operation in developing qualifications frameworks in different parts of the world.

An increasing emphasis on learning outcomes (Adam 2006) is an important part of the development of qualifications frameworks in Europe, since frameworks not only provide a coherent description of qualifications within a system and of how these different qualifications interlink, but also aim to describe these qualifications in terms of learning outcomes. Again, learning outcomes are not a specifically European phenomenon, but the understanding of and familiarity with learning outcomes are very uneven throughout the world. In many countries – including some European countries – the concept of learning outcomes represents a break with a long-standing tradition of describing qualifications in terms of procedures and length of study, and this transition is not easy to make. There is a strong need for workshops with participants from both Europe and other parts of the world to develop a common understanding and practice with regard to learning outcomes. This is a wider issue than merely recognition, since learning outcomes need to be developed and described before they can be recognised. Workshops of this kind therefore need to reach out to a broad range of participants, including institutional policy makers and practitioners, curriculum developers and representatives of public authorities, but they also need to include credentials evaluators. It is also important that credentials evaluators in countries that have so far not progressed far in the description of learning outcomes participate in workshops so that they can make adequate use of learning outcomes in assessing qualifications from countries that rely on these descriptions. It is of course also important that European credentials evaluators make good use of learning outcomes, where possible, in assessing qualifications from other parts of the world. As Europeans, we would not be credible if we were to insist that our own qualifications are to be assessed on the basis of their learning outcomes if in assessing qualifications from other regions we were to continue to base our assessment solely on the formalities of procedure and length of study.

---

131. Information provided by the European Training Foundation to the EQF Advisory Group at its meeting on 9-10 June 2010.

The need for information and explanation is, however, not limited to qualifications frameworks and learning outcomes. It also extends to the instruments we have developed in Europe to make it easier for those not intimately familiar with our education systems to understand European qualifications. The most important instruments are the Diploma Supplement and the ECTS, which has now been developed as a credit accumulation system in addition to its long-standing function as a credit transfer system. Therefore, this is now the Europe Credit Transfer and Accumulation System, even if the Commission has quite sensibly chosen not to modify the well-established abbreviation ECTS. The explanatory notes to the Diploma Supplement were modified when the Lisbon Recognition Convention Committee met in Bucharest in June 2007 to take account of recent developments.

Attitudes to recognition

As for recognition issues within Europe, however, the main challenge at global level seems to be one of developing attitudes to recognition. This is far from a new issue, but it is a persistent one. Whereas many credentials evaluators see their role as one of helping learners get the best and fairest possible recognition of their qualifications and will look for possibilities to recognise, others tend to see themselves primarily as guardians of their own education systems. These credentials evaluators seem to see their role as protecting their own system against less than good foreign qualifications, and they will often try to find reasons not to grant recognition of foreign qualifications. This description is of course slightly exaggerated but the assertion that there are two different approaches to recognition nevertheless contains considerably more than a grain of truth (Bergan 2004).

According to the Council of Europe/UNESCO Recognition Convention, a decision not to recognise a foreign qualification must be justified in terms of substantial differences. While this is a legal obligation only on the parties to the convention, it is important to keep in mind that the convention is not only a legal instrument: it is in many ways also a guide to good practice. There is therefore nothing to prevent countries that are not a party to the convention from applying its provisions, or to keep parties from applying its provisions also to non-parties.

The term "substantial differences" implies that a difference between the qualification for which recognition is sought and the similar qualification of the host country is not in itself sufficient to justify non-recognition. Non-recognition is only warranted if the difference is substantial, which means that it must be important in relation to the purpose for which recognition is sought. No legal text can provide a complete overview of possible substantial differences, and the interpretation of this concept must be established through practice. However, there is good reason to believe that the interpretation of the concept varies considerably among the states party to the convention and that many credentials evaluators have too narrow an interpretation of what constitutes a substantial difference.

Therefore, the ENIC and NARIC networks are currently working on developing a better understanding and a more common interpretation of this key concept, and this work is also of great relevance to recognition in a global context. This work will not lead to a new legal or standard-setting text, such as a recommendation. Rather, the networks will aim to develop a better common understanding through case studies and discussion of principles and practical examples. At the joint annual meeting of the ENIC and NARIC networks in Bucharest in June 2007, network members worked extensively on a number of cases to clarify their concepts, and the discussions brought out a number of different approaches.

With the development of qualifications frameworks, arguments will increasingly need to relate to the place and function of a qualification within national qualifications frameworks. In considering whether to recognise a qualification, credentials evaluators will need to look at qualifications in relation to the five major elements that make up a qualification (Bergan 2007):

- level;
- workload;
- quality;
- profile;
- learning outcomes.

Level designates the place of a given qualification within an education system or a qualifications framework. Typical examples in national systems are bachelor's, master's and doctoral degrees; the overarching qualifications framework for the EHEA uses the generic terms first, second and third (cycle) degrees.

Workload refers to the amount of work required to successfully complete a unit of learning. The United States and Canada have long expressed workload in terms of credits, and in Europe the "common currency" is now ECTS credits. Some European countries have national credit systems where national credits can be "translated" into ECTS credits. In terms of recognition of North American qualifications in Europe and vice versa, the "translation" between US and Canadian credit systems and the ECTS is an important issue. Some countries in other parts of the world may still emphasise the length of study rather than workload.

Quality indicates that a qualification must not only be of a given level and entail a given workload; as discussed above it must also be of sufficient quality. Quality and quality assurance have become a particularly pertinent issue with the emergence of increasingly diversified provision of higher education, some of which is without established links to any national higher education system (borderless education). There is also a link to the emergence of diversified learning paths, including lifelong learning paths, whereby a given qualification may be earned through different combinations of study programmes, other kinds of learning and other experiences, such as work.

Profile can be relevant in two ways. In one meaning, profile may refer to the overall orientation of an institution or a study programme; typically in a binary system that distinguishes between university and non-university programmes. Here, the distinction would generally have to do with the role and prominence of research in the activities of the institution and as an underlying factor in its study programmes and with the extent to which a programme takes a theoretical or applied approach. The emergence of diversified learning paths is also relevant to the issue of profile.

In the second meaning, profile has to do with the individual characteristics of a qualification, for example as a first degree in physics or a second degree in linguistics. With increased flexibility in study programmes and the increased use of credits in most European countries, study programmes in most countries of the European region now allow for a measure of individual choice that can give graduates an individual profile that goes beyond the choice of a field of specialisation or, in US terms, a major. This has for quite some time been a feature of study programmes in North America and is also found in other parts of the world. Thus, students may include a number of credits in disciplines that may support their main area of specialisation or that have nothing to do with their main specialisation. Courses in a foreign language, statistics or law may, depending on the students' specialisation, be examples of both categories of courses.

One important aspect of profile, then, is the balance between specialisation and broader orientation. This is particularly relevant in the discussion of the recognition of North American qualifications in Europe and vice versa, since many European systems have traditionally emphasised specialisation over broad orientation also for first cycle qualifications, whereas the concept of liberal arts education is an important part of North American – or at least US – higher education at first degree level. Developments in many European systems, with increased possibilities for developing "personal" profiles within the framework of given study programmes, should provide for a greater measure of common ground in this respect.

Learning outcomes, as discussed, describe what a graduate knows, understands and is able to do on the basis of a qualification. Increasingly, the focus of higher education policy debates, as well as on the more specific debate on the recognition of qualifications, emphasises learning outcomes over the formal structures of study programmes.[132]

The discussion of substantial differences is complex, and it is important that recognition specialists in Europe arrive at a better common understanding of the term. It is, however, equally important that these considerations involve policy makers and recognition specialists from other areas of the world. Only through open discussion can we develop a common understanding of the main issues and a measure of agreement on how we approach the recognition of foreign qualifications.

---

132. Learning outcomes are explicitly referred to in the Recommendation on Criteria and Procedures for the Assessment of Foreign Qualifications, paragraph 37, and in the corresponding part of the explanatory memorandum to this recommendation, see www.coe.int/t/dg4/highereducation/recognition/Criteria%20 and%20procedures_EN.asp.

Conclusion

The ministerial conferences in Bergen in 2005 and London in 2007 have at least started to give the global dimension the place it deserves in the development of the European Higher Education Area. The two policy fora organised end-on with the ministerial conferences of the Bologna Process in 2009 and 2010 have further underlined the political importance of a global policy dialogue on higher education. The fair recognition of qualifications is an essential element of this global dimension, as ministers explicitly recognised in their London Communiqué. The challenges are legion, and they range from identifying appropriate partners for dialogue in a highly decentralised policy field through revising the legal framework in several regions to, most importantly, working intensively with partners on content issues like quality assurance, qualifications frameworks, learning outcomes and, crucially, attitudes to recognition. Europe has great experience in these areas but we also have much to learn from other regions. Co-operation on recognition issues requires an ability to conduct a dialogue, in which the ability to listen and to understand is as important as the ability to speak and to present one's own views clearly. Organisations like the Council of Europe and UNESCO are well placed to lead efforts in this area, but to succeed, these efforts will need the involvement of a broad range of actors at both national and institutional level. Not least, improved recognition in a global context will require an ability to look at qualifications from other regions with the same open mind with which we would like others to assess European qualifications. Achieving a better common understanding of what qualifications are about and what may be valid reasons for not granting recognition or for granting only partial recognition will not be easy and it will take time, but the potential benefits of succeeding are worth the effort this will take.

References

Adam S. (2006), "An introduction to learning outcomes: A consideration of the nature, function and position of learning outcomes in the creation of the European Higher Education Area", in Froment, E., Kohler, J., Purser, L. and Wilson, L. (eds), *EUA Bologna Handbook – Making Bologna Work*, Raabe Verlag, Berlin.

Bergan S. (2004), "A tale of two cultures in higher education policies: the rule of law or an excess of legalism?", *Journal of Studies in International Education*, Vol. 8, Issue 2, summer 2004.

Bergan S. (2007), *Qualifications: Introduction to a Concept*, Council of Europe Higher Education Series No. 6, Council of Europe Publishing, Strasbourg.

Bologna Process (2005), "Standards and Guidelines for Quality Assurance in the European Higher Education Area", available at www.ond.vlaanderen.be/hogeronderwijs/bologna/documents/Standards-and-Guidelines-for-QA.pdf, accessed on 1 July 2010.

Bologna Process (2007a), "European Higher Education in a Global Setting. A Strategy for the External Dimension of the Bologna Process", available at www.ond.vlaanderen.be/hogeronderwijs/bologna/documents/WGR2007/Strategy-for-EHEA-in-global-setting.pdf, accessed on 1 July 2010.

Bologna Process (2007b), London Communiqué, "Towards the European Higher Education Area: Responding to Challenges in a Globalised World".

Knight J. (2006), "Programmes, providers and accreditors on the move: implications for the recognition of qualifications", in Rauhvargers A. and Bergan S., (eds), *Recognition in the Bologna Process: Policy Development and the Road to Good Practice*, Council of Europe Higher Education Series No. 4, Council of Europe Publishing, Strasbourg.

Zgaga P. (2007), "Looking Out: the Bologna Process in a Global Setting", Norwegian Ministry of Education and Research, Oslo, available at www.ond.vlaanderen.be/hogeronderwijs/bologna/documents/WGR2007/Bologna_Process_in_global_setting_finalreport.pdf, accessed on 1 July 2010.

Recognition 2010: opportunities from which we cannot run away[133]

Predictions and years

Being asked to look at "Recognition 2010" is a challenge, to say the least. Republishing the article at a time when one's predictions will have been proven or disproven may be an even more difficult challenge but I will resist the temptation to recast my considerations to give them the benefit of hindsight. What readers will see in this article, therefore, is the state of affairs as they seemed in 2005 and 2006 rather than how they turned out in 2010.

One is tempted to recall the words of the Danish humorist Piet Hein, who quipped that prediction is difficult, in particular about the future.[134] If the title of this chapter indicates a certain ambiguity, this is because I sense that many of our colleagues in the recognition field see opportunities ahead, but they are not entirely comfortable with all they see. Even in a brief article like this, I hope to explore some of the opportunities and, hopefully, lay some of the apprehensions to rest. My own apprehensions have as much to do with our attitudes to change as with the change itself.

It may also be worth reminding ourselves that it is sometimes difficult to distinguish predictions – indications of what is likely to happen – from our own desires for the future – what we would like to see happen. This is not to say, however, that we should throw our hands in the air and let things happen. Predictions are useful not least because they may help us identify likely developments as well as what action we might take to help those developments go in the direction we would like. We cannot always succeed, but we can always try. The chances of success, however, are greater if we adapt them to the prevailing environment than if we only base them on wishful thinking.

In thinking about 2010, it may also be useful to remember that some years have come to symbolise predictions in a particular way. The two in most recent memory are 1984 and 2000. The first gave us the adjective Orwellian, describing the kind of society that few of us would like to live in but that some less than tender souls may well long to rule over, while the second was connected with doom and gloom. Millenarian sects believed the world would come to an end and may well have been disappointed when it did not. Computer specialists were worried about another kind of apocalypse, but they were mostly relieved when the famous "2000 bug" did not materialise after all. So 2010, then, is less dramatic and much more positive, for it

---

133. The first version of this article was published in Rauhvargers, Andrejs and Bergan, Sjur (eds) (2006): *Recognition in the Bologna Process: Policy Development and the Road to Good Practice*, Strasbourg: Council of Europe Publishing. Council of Europe Higher Education Series No 4.
134. Piet Hein's quips and aphorisms were published over a number of years as *Gruk*.

has come to signify the establishment of the European Higher Education Area and, hence, the end of the Bologna Process.

By now, 1984 is history, 2000 is the still recent past and 2010 has moved from the realm of futurology to something that is much more comfortable to policy makers and bureaucrats: medium-term planning.

Considering recognition in 2010 from a European point of view is, then, considering what, in the medium term, the recognition community may do to help make the European Higher Education Area a reality only six years from now. This chapter will make no attempt at giving a complete overview of challenges, but it will seek to address six factors that I believe will be particularly important.

The legal framework

In a way, this is not a challenge. At European level, the legal framework is largely in place, through the Council of Europe/UNESCO Recognition Convention,[135] through subsidiary texts to this convention and through the EU directives on professional recognition. At least for most purposes of recognition, I believe we by and large have the legal instruments we need.

The main challenge will therefore lie in the implementation of the existing legal framework rather than in developing a new one, and this implementation will be the main focus of this chapter. As concerns further development of the legal framework, there are three areas where this may be required.

Firstly, while increasing the number of subsidiary texts to the Council of Europe/ UNESCO Recognition Convention is no end in itself, there may still be issues that will require further texts of this kind. These issues will most likely have to do with recognition issues that were not fully covered by the convention itself, in particular issues relating to qualifications that are not entirely a part of a national system. The Recommendation on the Recognition of Joint Degrees (adopted in 2004) and the Code of Good Practice in the Provision of Transnational Education (2001) are good examples of such texts, and further texts may be needed. The relationship between recognition and quality assurance is another area in which there have been important developments since the convention was adopted, and where further standard-setting texts may be required.[136]

Secondly, while the legal framework is largely in place at European level, this is not necessarily true at national level. Many countries have updated laws and regulations on recognition, and in some countries, any international treaty ratified by

---

135. Formally, the Council of Europe/UNESCO Convention on the Recognition of Qualifications concerning Higher Education in the European Region. The full text of the convention and its explanatory report, as well as a constantly updated list of signatures and ratifications, will be found at http://conventions.coe.int; search for ETS 165.

136. A third issue, which has become much more apparent since this article was originally written, is the role of qualifications frameworks in facilitating recognition.

that country becomes part of national law. However, some countries have ratified the convention without amending their national laws. All countries party to the Bologna Process should therefore review their own legislation to ensure that it is compatible with their obligations under the convention.

Thirdly, the Council of Europe/UNESCO Recognition Convention is the first of what is often called the "new generation" of recognition conventions and, as such, it may serve as a model for other UNESCO regions of the world. While they would not copy the convention, they may find the provisions of and experience with the convention useful in updating their own legal framework. To my knowledge, the Arab region has already come far in this respect, and work is also under way in the African region. As we shall discuss later in the chapter, this is important to European countries because a common approach to recognition principles and methodology will facilitate the mutual recognition of qualifications.

Effects of laws in an internationalised environment

Laws are only effective if they are implemented and enforced. One could even question whether legal texts that are not enforced should be called laws, or whether they are rather guidelines for good practice – voluntary instruments that are certainly beneficial, but which are put into practice to the extent that people and institutions actually want to do so.

The point in our context is that, for the most part, law enforcement is linked to national authorities, national territories and national systems. There are exceptions to this, such as the legislation of the European Union and its European Court of Justice, the Council of Europe's European Convention on Human Rights and European Court of Human Rights, the UN International Court of Justice and the now defunct Central American Court of Justice (1907-18), which is the earliest example of an international court of which this author is aware (Bergan 2004). Nevertheless, laws are mostly implemented on a territorial basis, within the legal competence of national authorities.

This implies that there are limits to how effective legal regulations are in influencing behaviour outside of or between national frameworks. The international legal framework for recognition largely exists, but the mechanisms for international enforcement are weak, and there is unlikely to be political support in the foreseeable future for such mechanisms. There is no "International Court of Recognition", nor is there an "International Recognition Police", and even the very thought seems absurd.

This is not to say that the international legal framework is worthless or ineffective. It is just to say that treating it only as a traditional legal framework is missing half the point. It is a legal framework, but at least in the vast majority of cases, its legal implementation depends on national jurisdiction, which is one of the main reasons the main provisions of the Council of Europe/UNESCO Recognition Convention should be transposed into national law where this has not already been done. The exception is countries in which international treaties automatically become national law once the country has ratified them.

Attitudes to recognition

The second half of the point referred to above – the half that was missing – is that the international legal texts also serve as guides to good practice. In fact, there are countries – like Belgium – which for various reasons took a long time to ratify the Council of Europe/UNESCO Recognition Convention, but which nevertheless sought to apply the convention in practice well before they ratified it. While it is obviously desirable that all European countries ratify the Council of Europe/ UNESCO Recognition Convention, as the "Bologna ministers" committed to doing in the Berlin Communiqué[137] (Bologna Process 2003), de facto implementation of the convention in the absence of ratification is clearly preferable to ratification not followed by effective implementation.

What is at issue is the interpretation of legislation and recognition practice. Over the past two decades or so, there has been a very significant development from what is often referred to as "equivalence" to "recognition" – some would also say that we are now on our way towards an attitude of "acceptance". This development basically describes changing attitudes to how similar qualifications should be in order to be given recognition and, at a deeper level, a growing awareness of the important role recognition specialists have in providing a service to those who seek to move across borders without losing the true value of their qualifications.

This change in practice and attitudes implies leaving the very detailed comparison of curricula and structures behind in favour of a broader view. The world of recognition has its share of horror stories, and one of them is about a well-regarded professor who, as a member of the faculty senate at a European university a generation ago, made sure that any applicant who wanted to get recognition of a degree in a foreign language would be turned down unless the applicant had studied at least one work of literature dating from before 1700. This is a horror story for two reasons: firstly, that such a detailed – and presumably non-stated and thus informal – criterion would decide the fate of an application and, secondly, that a routine application would be considered by the faculty senate rather than administratively.

Recognition, however, is not about verifying that almost all elements in the foreign qualification have a counterpart in the corresponding qualification in one's own system. After all, what is the point of studying abroad if one can study the same thing at home? Studying abroad is to a large extent about getting new perspectives and being challenged in one's traditional perceptions.

Rather, recognition is about determining whether applicants' learning achievements are such that they are likely to succeed in whatever activity they want to undertake on the basis of their qualifications, whether for further study or in the labour market. Therefore, we need to assess what applicants know and can do rather than the structures and procedures through which they have obtained their qualifications.

---

137. As of 1 July 2010, all members of the European Higher Education Area except Greece and Italy had ratified the convention.

The development of qualifications frameworks is a major development in this respect because they emphasise learning outcomes and relate qualifications to an overall framework that describes not only the individual qualification but also how the different qualifications within an education system interlink and interact. A national qualifications framework describes how learners may move between qualifications within a national system, whereas an overarching framework for qualifications of the European Higher Education Area will facilitate movement between systems. A working group appointed by the Bologna Follow-up Group and chaired by Mogens Berg put forward a proposal for an overarching framework that was adopted by ministers in Bergen in 2005 as the overarching framework of qualifications of the European Higher Education Area. One important consequence for recognition is that when justifying non-recognition because of substantial differences between the home qualification and the foreign qualification for which recognition is sought, in accordance with the Council of Europe/UNESCO Recognition Convention, it will be increasingly important to do so with reference to qualifications frameworks and in particular with reference to learning outcomes and achievements.

While the development over the past couple of decades has been very positive, there is of course a caveat: it has also been very uneven. The most advanced thinking as well as practice has made great strides, but many members of the "recognition community" have not been party to this development.

Laws can be read in two ways. One can either take the view that what is not explicitly allowed cannot be done, or one can take the view that what is not explicitly forbidden is possible. In the same way, one can assess a foreign qualification by looking for differences that will justify non-recognition or one can take what Andrejs Rauhvargers in one debate referred to as a "forgiving attitude" and look for reasons to recognise the qualification. One should also keep in mind that if it is not possible to give full recognition, the first alternative should – as is clearly stated in the Recommendation on Criteria and Procedures for the Assessment of Foreign Qualifications – not be non-recognition but partial recognition. Both attitudes can be found in Europe, as shown by a survey conducted in 2001-2002 (Bergan and Ferreira 2003).

One of the main challenges for the recognition community in establishing the European Higher Education Area by 2010 will therefore be to develop the attitudes of recognition specialists from one of detailed comparison to one of broad considerations of outcomes, from one of looking at procedures to one of looking at achievements, from one of looking for problems to one of looking for solutions. Granting fair recognition does not mean that one should recognise all qualifications regardless of their merits, but it does mean that one should look at their real merits and give them due recognition for these. If we think of recognition as a bridge that allows individuals to cross the divide from one education system to another, it is important that there be no "customs station" on the other side of the bridge that, through unreasonable procedures and unreasonable attitudes to the content of qualifications, would oblige those moving across the bridge to leave much of the real value of their qualifications behind.

Ultimately, we need to work on the assumption that recognition specialists are there to help applicants get the recognition they deserve even if they do not always know how to formulate their requests. Recognition specialists are there mainly to "protect the learner", not so much to "protect the system". The recognition specialists of 2010, even more than those of today, should be knowledgeable and broad-minded experts at the service of learners and not gatekeepers trying to keep out all but the pure.

Recognition of new forms of qualifications

Traditionally, credentials evaluators assess well-documented qualifications from institutions belonging to education systems about which they have adequate information. This is, of course, an ideal situation, and it is still the most common one, but recognition specialists are increasingly faced with applications for recognition of other kinds of qualifications. Broadly speaking, these fall into two groups.

The first group is variously termed transnational education, cross-border education or borderless education (Knight 2006). Whatever their name, these are qualifications from providers that are not recognised as belonging to a national higher education system[138] or that operate outside the country in which the home institution is based. This is not a mere formality because it implies that, in most cases, the quality of the provision is not assessed and the quality of education provision is one of the main criteria in assessing a qualification. This is often true even when the home institution belongs to a national higher education system as, in many cases, there is no separate quality assessment of branch campuses or other kind of provision in foreign countries. Such provision can, however, differ significantly from that given at the home institution. It is also worth keeping in mind that the term "higher education provision" does not only cover traditional programmes given at physical institutions, but also provision through non-traditional means, such as Internet provisions.

This leads us to the second broad group, which may be termed non-traditional qualifications. This is a broad category ranging from programmes that are more or less classical in content but given through non-traditional means to informal learning and accreditation of prior learning. In this case, the common denominator is that the learning for which recognition is sought is achieved in a wide variety of ways, few of which conform to traditional conceptions of higher education, but that the results of this learning may be expressed as higher education qualifications. Expressed differently, within a coherent qualifications framework, qualifications may be obtained through different learning paths. In this context, it may be useful to keep in mind that lifelong learning may best be seen as a set of learning paths leading to qualifications that can also be obtained through more traditional learning paths.

In most cases covered by these two broad groups, we are not talking about different qualifications but about different ways of obtaining and documenting the

---

138. The term is borrowed from the Council of Europe/UNESCO Recognition Convention, where parties undertake, in Section VIII, to provide adequate information on institutions belonging to their higher education systems and on any programme operated by these institutions.

qualifications. This is a challenge to credentials evaluators because the assessment of such qualifications is more demanding. The traditional and well-tested methods are not fully applicable. However, this development is very much in line with the increased emphasis on assessment of outcomes rather than of procedures and education systems.

The global dimension

In "Bologna terminology", the global dimension – originally referred to by the unfortunate term "external dimension" – is the catchword for the relationship between the European Higher Education Area and the rest of the world.

Whatever name we choose to give it, this is a key but so far understudied aspect of the Bologna Process, with Muche (2005) an honourable exception.[139] In terms of recognition, the key questions are: how will qualifications from the European Higher Education Area be recognised elsewhere, how will we recognise qualifications from other parts of the world within the European Higher Education Area, and what changes in recognition practice will – or at least should – the establishment of the European Higher Education Area in 2010 bring about worldwide?

The three questions are interlinked, and the starting point is of considerable concern. The Bologna Process is complex, and we know that public perception of complex realities is often less than complete. In this case, one lingering perception is that the main point of the Bologna Process is reducing the first degree from four to three years – full stop. If this is indeed the dominant perception, I believe adequate recognition of degrees from institutions and systems in the European Higher Education Area might become difficult. That is at least the signals we have received from North American recognition specialists.

A first degree of 180 ECTS credits has become common within the European Higher Education Area. Saying that a first degree has to carry a workload of 240 credits is not an option, even if some countries may choose this as their prevailing model. Therefore, the discussion on recognition must focus on learning outcomes and qualifications frameworks not only within the Bologna Process, but also outside it. Also in a worldwide context, Europeans must argue that qualifications must be recognised on the basis of what learners know and can do rather than on the basis of a consideration of structures alone. The concept of qualifications frameworks must be developed also with a view to our relationships with higher education outside the EHEA, and Europeans must provide clear and comprehensible explanations of their respective national frameworks as well as of the overarching framework for the EHEA.

There is another aspect of the "global dimension". While it is important that the rest of the world be aware of and understand qualifications from Europe, we must avoid giving the impression that recognition is a one-way street. If we demand that others recognise our qualifications for their real value and not just on the basis of

---

139. Since then, studies have been added to the list, see in particular Zgaga (2007).

formal considerations of procedures and systems, we must be willing to do the same for qualifications from other parts of the world. To lay a better basis for this, it is important that the ENIC and NARIC networks initiate discussions with their counterparts in other parts of the world. The UNESCO regional committees provide an invaluable framework for this, but few if any regions have a network of functioning national information centres that would be a fully satisfactory counterpart to the ENIC and NARIC networks. In many countries, real information centres have yet to be established and European countries could play a role in this respect. In the framework of a MEDA project, UNESCO, the French CIEP (Centre International d'Etudes pédagogiques), the Council of Europe and some ENICs/NARICs engaged in establishing national information centres in four North African countries: Algeria, Egypt, Morocco and Tunisia.

Information and communication

It is not difficult to make the case that information on recognition is crucial. However, the problem is often not the lack of information per se. We live in the information society, which is characterised by an overflow of information, yet at the same time there is often a lack of reliable information of good quality, and the world of recognition is no exception. The challenge is therefore to convey appropriate and understandable information to those who need it. To try to meet this challenge, the ENIC and NARIC networks in 2004 adopted a new information strategy.[140]

This strategy takes as its starting point that information should:

- be meaningful to the users and respond to their needs;
- recognise that different users or user groups have different information needs and seek to provide information that is relevant to each group without over-burdening them with irrelevant information;
- be accessible in terms of content, language and style (*inter alia*, avoiding unnecessary complications or specialised language);
- be accurate (*inter alia*, being factually correct and also avoiding oversimplification – implying that a balance needs to be struck between accessibility and accuracy);
- originate from – and as far as possible be provided by – the competent authority closest to the source of information (the subsidiarity principle – for example, information on a given education system should be provided by the authority competent for that system);
- be up to date;
- be easily available, in printed and/or electronic form.

---

140 This part of the chapter draws heavily on the ENIC/NARIC report on information strategies, elaborated by a working group chaired by Darius Tomaščiūnas of the Lithuanian ENIC/NARIC and of which the present author was secretary. The full report bears the reference DGIV/EDU/HE(2004)6 rev.3.

Language is also an important issue in the provision of information. That information should be available in several languages is of course vital, but it is also important that, in whatever language, this information be understandable. This seems obvious and straightforward, but it can involve striking a delicate balance between being easily accessible and being accurate and complete. On the one hand, overly technical terms may not be very helpful to most target groups, but oversimplification can be equally unfortunate and may ultimately lead to misunderstanding and false hopes of recognition. Certainly, sending the complete legal texts to anyone enquiring about recognition will not be very helpful, but in some contexts it may be necessary to quote precise legal language, perhaps accompanied by an explanation of what the law actually says. Often it may also be necessary to include the necessary legal caveats to avoid having an information letter or brochure that aims to explain general rules and procedures in easily understandable terms used as evidence in a legal appeal or even a court case.

If the provision of information is to be adapted to the needs of different target groups, it is of course important that we be clear about who these groups might be, and even more important that we know who the main target groups are. The ENIC/NARIC information strategy considers the following as its main target groups:

– individual holders of qualifications;

– public authorities (typically – but not limited to – ministries responsible for higher education);

– quality assurance agencies;

– higher education institutions and bodies (typical examples of the latter would be rectors' conferences or similar structures and mobility and exchange agencies);

– employers;

– professional organisations;

– ENICs/NARICs.

It also suggests that there are two basic kinds of information. On the one hand, it refers to system information – that is, information that is relevant to a broad category of recipients and concerns the characteristics of an education system as a whole or a part of it. Typical examples would be general information on the degree structure or qualifications framework of a given country or general conditions for obtaining student support. On the other hand, the information strategy refers to information on individual qualifications or other kinds of information relevant to one specific individual. Examples corresponding to the ones listed for system information would be information on how a specific qualification relates to the degree system or qualifications framework of a given country, or the possible eligibility of a specific person for student support. It may of course be argued that, ultimately, this information will be the outcome of an assessment of an application, but potential applicants may seek this kind of information to assess their chances and see whether it would make sense for them to submit a formal application.

Schematically, the information strategy suggests that target groups and the kind of information to be provided match as follows:

Target group	Needs system information	Needs information on individual qualifications	Receives information	Provides information
Public authorities	X	(x)	X (on foreign education)	X (on own education system)
Quality assurance agencies	X	(x)	X	X
HEIs and bodies	X	X	X	X
Individual holders of qualifications	(x)	X	X	(x)
Employers and professional organisations	X	X	X	X
ENICs/NARICs	X	X	X (on foreign education)	X (on own education system)

Where X denotes that the target group in question needs or provides this type of information on a regular basis, and (x) that it does so occasionally.

Even these target groups are not necessarily uniform, however, and it may be necessary to differentiate further. For example, different public authorities may require information on:

–   higher education legislation, in particular the legal provision for recognition and quality assurance;

–   statistics;

–   qualifications framework/degree system;

–   quality assurance (methods and results);

–   what institutions or programmes are a part of any given higher education system;

–   basic concepts and instruments for recognition;

–   procedures and provision for the recognition of foreign qualifications;

–   contact details and legal status of competent authorities of other countries.

Yet, if one tries too hard to meet the specific needs of each subgroup, one ends up with no information strategy at all and goes back to treating information as a case-by-case need, each time with its own specificities.

The goal must be to identify a limited number of target groups that allow competent recognition authorities to provide standardised generic information that will answer most questions, while being open to address the individual enquiries that are not fully covered by the generic information.

Not least, a major but very difficult task is to raise the consciousness of students and employers about the need to verify the value of qualifications before they enrol in a study programme or hire someone with a given qualification. Surprisingly, many people seem to ask fewer questions about the study programme in which they plan to invest considerable effort and money than they would if they were buying a used car.

To seek to address this need for information, the ENIC/NARIC information strategy consists of four elements:

–   a code of good practice, which was formally adopted by the networks in Strasbourg in June 2004;[141]

–   a set of frequently asked questions with generic answers;

–   a list of questions prospective students and other interested parties (such as employers) should ask of education/service providers;

–   a fact sheet for national information centres, outlining information that should be readily available at national centres.

Conclusion

It is said that old soldiers never die; they just wither away. Recognition is not an old solider, and it will not wither away, nor will the need for recognition of qualifications magically disappear with the establishment of the European Higher Education Area.

The world of recognition will, however, change profoundly, or at least so I hope. Credentials evaluators should spend less time assessing clear-cut cases, and this chapter will hopefully help explain why. This means that they will have more time to devote to complicated cases; the ones that truly require the sustained attention of specialists with a good knowledge of various education systems and above all with a solid knowledge of the principles of recognition and the ability to apply those principles to individual cases. This will make the work of credentials evaluators much more interesting and also much more demanding. Above all, however, these developments should help those who seek recognition obtain a fair assessment of their foreign qualifications. This is crucial, both for reasons of individual justice and because their numbers are likely to increase and their backgrounds are likely to become much more diverse.

---

141. Available at: www.coe.int/T/DG4/HigherEducation/Recognition/ENIC%20NARIC%20Code%20 information%20provision_EN.asp, accessed on 1 July 2010.

References

Bergan S. (2004), "A tale of two cultures in higher education policies: the rule of law or an excess of legalism?", *Journal of Studies in International Education*, Vol. 8, Issue 2, summer 2004.

Bergan S. and Ferreira S. (2003), "Implementation of the Lisbon Recognition Convention and contributions to the Bologna Process", in Bergan S. (ed.), *Recognition Issues in the Bologna Process*, Council of Europe Publishing, Strasbourg, pp. 69-81.

Bologna Process (2003), Berlin Communiqué, "Realising the European Higher Education Area", adopted by European ministers of education on 19 September 2003.

Knight J. (2006), "Programmes, providers and accreditors on the move: implications for the recognition of qualifications", in Rauhvargers A. and Bergan S., (eds), *Recognition in the Bologna Process: Policy Development and the Road to Good Practice*, Council of Europe Higher Education Series No. 4, Council of Europe Publishing, Strasbourg.

Muche F. (ed.) (2005), *Opening up to the Wider World: the External Dimension of the Bologna Process*, Lemmens, Bonn. ACA Papers on International Co-operation in Education.

Zgaga P. (2007), "Looking Out: the Bologna Process in a Global Setting", Norwegian Ministry of Education and Research, Oslo, available at www.ond.vlaanderen. be/hogeronderwijs/bologna/documents/WGR2007/Bologna_Process_in_global_ setting_finalreport.pdf, accessed on 1 July 2010.

Approaches to recognition: a question of two cultures?[142]

The concept of two cultures was originally introduced by C. P. Snow in 1959 and referred to the different approaches of the humanities and natural sciences and the failure of communication between them. While a one-line summary of Snow's theory is certainly too simplistic, and while his thesis is not accepted by all,[143] the concept can, with the necessary caveats, be helpful in describing fundamental differences in people's approach to certain issues. In a different context, I have explored whether the term could meaningfully be used to describe broader differences in approaches to higher education policies (Bergan 2004). I explored different approaches to the importance of legislation in developing higher education systems and shaping higher education policies, with particular reference to the European Higher Education Area, and I made the point that while laws are absolutely necessary, like medicine, they are effective only if applied in suitable quantities and with room for professional discretion.

The purpose of the present article is to explore two basic differences in attitudes to recognition, and in particular to the concept of substantial differences, which is a key concept of the Council of Europe/UNESCO Recognition Convention.[144] The two approaches to recognition include a highly legalistic approach and one that, while also based on the provisions of relevant laws, takes a broader view of the circumstances that may lead to recognition or non-recognition. At the risk of oversimplification, one approach may be described as using the law to find reasons not to recognise a qualification – with the reasoning that if recognition is not explicitly permitted, it must be avoided – while the other may be described as using the law to find creative solutions to recognition challenges.

Some caveats are, however, in order. Neither approach can reasonably be described as reflecting an "anything goes" attitude, and neither can be characterised as seeking to obstruct all recognition. Practitioners of both approaches will agree in a good number of cases, either that recognition should be granted or that it should be refused. However, they are likely to disagree on quite a few cases in the grey area between the more clear-cut extremes of the spectrum.

142. The first version of this article was published in Hunt, E. Stephen and Bergan, Sjur (eds) (2010): *Developing Attitudes to Recognition: Substantial Differences in an Age of Globalisation*, Strasbourg: Council of Europe Publishing. Council of Europe Higher Education Series No. 13. The author would like to thank E. Stephen Hunt for valuable comments to the first draft of the article.
143. Participants in a Council of Europe project on the heritage of European universities, one of the transnational projects within the Europe, a Common Heritage campaign, were divided in their views on whether the concept was relevant to the heritage of their university, cf. Sanz and Bergan (2007)
144. Convention on the Recognition of Qualifications concerning Higher Education in the European Region, see www.coe.int/t/dg4/highereducation/Recognition/LRC_en.asp.

Attitudes to how legislation should be used may be supplemented by another set of differences in approach or culture, namely in credentials evaluators' views of what their own roles and priorities should properly be. Is their primary function to protect their own system and qualifications and to make sure that it is not devalued by the recognition of qualifications that may compare unfavourably, or is it to help individual learners by doing everything they can to have their qualifications recognised to the greatest extent possible? Again, at the risk of oversimplification, the former may be thought of as making absolutely sure the foreign qualification is precisely equivalent, whereas the latter may be content with less than full recognition and rather looks for broad comparability in level, purpose and standard.

Phrased in these terms, the alternatives may appear Manichean. On the one hand, one has the dour gatekeepers of "the system" and on the other the valiant champions of individual rights and opportunities. As is often the case, reality is somewhat more complex. Recognising sub-standard qualifications is unfortunate for individuals as well as systems. Arguably, one does individuals no favours by putting them in situations where they cannot cope, and there is a strong risk of doing that if one gives learners access to study programmes for which they are not qualified and for which a hectic catch-up session before the start of the semester, or in the course of the first academic year, will not be sufficient. Nor is it helpful, safe or socially responsible to recognise an inferior professional qualification that would permit an inadequately prepared individual to work in a technical or decision-making capacity, and such a mistake may have legal as well as other consequences. Systematically recognising sub-standard qualifications may also, in the longer run, raise doubts about the higher education system that accepts such qualifications, since this kind of recognition practice could be read as an implicit statement on the quality of one's own system. If one accepts a wide range of less than adequate qualifications, are one's own qualifications adequate? It is important to underline that the debate is not about whether to recognise sub-standard qualifications, since no serious credentials evaluator would advocate that. Rather, the debate is about what constitutes a comparable qualification and how one goes about setting recognition policy and making recognition decisions.

On the other hand, recognition is undeniably about making things possible. The individual is at the heart of recognition, because it is the individual learner and not the system who submits a qualification and whose future is affected by a recognition decision. Being granted recognition of one's qualifications can open doors to a better and more satisfying future for the individual concerned, while refusing recognition can close those doors – which in some cases may even mean making it impossible for that individual to stay in the host country. The responsibility of credentials evaluators toward individuals should not be taken lightly, and there is no indication it is. Erring on the side of generosity toward the individual, rather than toward one's own system, instinctively appears to be the decent thing to do. At the same time, however, treating some applicants more leniently could be seen as unfair to others, who fully meet all the requirements. Often, the ideal solution does not exist, and giving the individual applicant the benefit of the doubt may indeed be advisable – provided that the doubt is reasonable.

Identifying substantial differences implies deciding whether a difference between two qualifications is important enough to warrant less than full recognition of the foreign qualification. It is not just a question of identifying reasons that might make it possible to argue that the foreign qualification should be given only partial recognition, or even no recognition at all. It is a question of identifying differences that are so important that refusing full recognition is clearly the better course to take.

No legal text can possibly identify all the possible differences that may be considered "substantial", nor indeed can an article or even a book. Identifying substantial differences relies on individual judgment, which is why the question of "two cultures" is important.

As a starting point, the likelihood is that there will be differences between two different qualifications – all the more so if they were delivered by two different institutions in two different countries. Incidentally, in recognition terms it is more meaningful to refer to education systems, rather than to countries, and this is the term I will use henceforth in this article. For students considering whether to undertake all or a part of their education abroad, it would also make little sense to look for a programme exactly equivalent to one they could find at home. To speak in the language of modern management, the "added value" would be close to zero, whereas the added costs might easily be quite high.

It might be useful to keep in mind that qualifications can be seen to comprise five key elements:

– quality;

– workload;

– level;

– profile;

– learning outcomes (Bergan 2007).

To illustrate different approaches, it may be useful to consider whether and in what situations differences in quality may be considered substantial.

There is broad agreement that quality is essential to recognition. Nobody wants to recognise qualifications that are not of sufficient quality. There is, however, less agreement on how good quality is defined and identified, even though there is broad agreement that a qualification of good quality is one that makes the holder qualified – some would say "well qualified" – to pursue further studies in a given field, or exercise a given occupation. In principle, this is a reasonable enough approach, but if the purpose is defined too narrowly, the approach becomes less meaningful. A second degree in mathematics, from a well-considered higher education institution, will normally be of good quality and fit for access to a doctoral programme or for exercising a range of occupations. However, it may not be well suited for giving access to a doctoral programme in history or for employment as an airline pilot – even if pilots do need a solid understanding of mathematics and modern historians need to understand and use quantitative data. The issue here, however, is not one of quality, but concerns the profile of the qualification.

In the same vein, if the (European) qualification in question were not a second degree but a first degree in mathematics from the same well-respected higher education institution, it would normally not give direct access to a doctoral programme in any discipline, even in mathematics. That, however, does not mean that the institution does not provide first degree qualifications of good quality. It simply means that one should not confuse quality and level. The first degree in question would most likely give access to a second degree programme in mathematics, as well as qualify the holder for various occupations – albeit not at the same level as the occupations open to a holder of a second degree. Again, that does not imply a lack of quality, but rather that the first degree in question is of good quality for the purposes for which it is intended and that one should not expect it to meet purposes for which it was not intended.

Credentials evaluators would also need to be aware that a number of non-European systems do permit first degree holders to enrol in preliminary studies for the doctorate without necessarily already possessing a second degree. This is not direct entry to the doctorate itself, but rather entry into preliminary graduate studies that may lead to candidacy for the doctorate and may provide the basis for earning a master's degree, or passing special examinations and demonstrating research competence, en route to doctoral student status. Such programmes simply indicate that different higher education systems may have differing routes to the same end and that in some subjects the possession of an intermediate master's degree conveys no professional advantage and may be optional. Careful examination of these systemic differences, however, would also show that they do not permit immediate entry into doctoral research from the first degree, but only after a structured set of preparatory studies and examinations, and thus are different in format but not necessarily in purpose, quality, or even level.

If someone actually sought to use qualifications in the academic study of mathematics as the basis for seeking recognition as a pilot or a historian, we would in fact be faced with substantial differences, unless there were other evidence of relevant training or academic study, or the applicant intended to obtain the relevant education and was seeking to do so. Changing a subject is not per se a substantial difference, and even seeking to study a different subject at a higher level may be acceptable, so long as the student has studied in a closely related field, has some background in the field, or is willing to undertake the necessary preparation. University programmes already exist across Europe that encourage or recruit students who have studied in one field to undertake another, and joint degree programmes also exist.[145]

---

145. One only needs to note the students who already enter graduate business or public administration programmes from other subjects; who decide to study the history or philosophy of one of the sciences after a first degree in a science subject; who obtain post first-degree teaching qualifications in a subject area, or other examples, to realise that changing subjects and levels is no longer a rare or impossible thing even in the European Higher Education Area or elsewhere.

With relation to access to a study programme that would imply "skipping" a level, the issue is more complicated. But, even in cases such as this, it is advisable to understand the structure of programmes in other systems that permit this flexibility, under which circumstances they do so, and the obvious fact that other systems have not necessarily experienced the European transition from the former "long cycle" degrees to the post-Bologna two-cycle structure. The conclusion of a credentials evaluator who denied recognition on the basis of substantial differences might in both cases be defensible. However, the credentials evaluator would be drawing his or her conclusion on the basis of misguided arguments, if the decision were argued in terms of a substantial difference in quality rather than profile in the first case and level in the second, and if no allowance were made for programme structure or legitimate systemic differences.

Suppose, however, that a credentials evaluator were asked to assess a foreign second degree in mathematics for the purpose of access to a third degree (doctoral) programme in mathematics. There is no difference in level or profile, but the credentials evaluator argues that there is a substantial difference in quality between the two institutions and hence the two qualifications. Whether that is a defensible argument or not may depend on a number of factors.

One possibility is that the institution or programme from which the qualification was issued has undergone, but failed, a quality assurance assessment. Alternatively, it has never undergone one, or has no evidence of recognition or approval in its system. If this assessment has been carried out according to well-established criteria, such as the Standards and Guidelines for Quality Assurance in the European Higher Education Area (Bologna Process 2005), or according to United States or Canadian accreditation standards, the Australian Qualifications Framework, or similar standards, then that would be a strong indication that the qualification is in fact of insufficient quality. Few if any credentials evaluators would argue that in this case, the argument of substantial difference in terms of quality would be valid.

However, an institution might not have undergone a quality assessment either because it has not sought to do so, or because it has not had an opportunity to do so. In this case, can the lack of quality assessment be taken as an indication of lack of quality? Absence of proof is, of course, not the same as proof of absence, and it is difficult to argue that an institution that has not undergone quality assessment is automatically of insufficient quality. However, many credentials evaluators would still consider the lack of quality assessment as a substantial difference, particularly if they operate in a legalistic recognition culture that allows little or no discretion or reference to other evidence of quality besides official recognition.

It is perhaps important to underline that lack of quality assessment is not the same as lack of information about the institution. If credentials evaluators do not know whether an institution has undergone quality assessment, they should seek to find out. In our imagined example, however, the credentials evaluator has managed to establish that the institution has not undergone assessment, and it is then a question of whether it is reasonable for the credentials evaluator to leave it at that and consider the lack of assessment a substantial difference, or alternatively to try to go beyond that and find out more about the quality of the institution.

Here, credentials evaluators may well take different views. One factor is the resources at the credentials evaluator's disposal. While this may be seen as irrelevant from the applicant's point of view, in reality someone who is faced with a high number of applications and has few resources to deal with them is less likely to spend extra time tracking down supplementary information than someone who has a better balance between workload and available resources. It may also depend on why the institution has not undergone assessment. If the institution had ample opportunity to be assessed but did not wish to be, that is unfortunate for the holders of qualifications from that institution, but the onus could legitimately be put on the institution and not on a credentials evaluator. If, on the other hand, the institution had no realistic possibility to undergo quality assessment, either because the public authorities in the country where it is based offer no internationally accepted quality assurance system; because it is barred from undergoing standard quality assurance as its type is excluded (often typical of religious or governmental institutions); or because the institution does not belong to a national education system, credentials evaluators may be more inclined to seek supplementary information.

The attitude may further depend on how likely it is that credentials evaluators will be able to identify reliable supplementary information with reasonable efforts. Institutions from countries with no well-established quality assurance systems as well as cross-border providers may in fact have opportunities to undergo quality assessment, and these opportunities are likely to improve over the next few years as quality assurance agencies are less and less bound to operate solely within the territorial jurisdiction in which they are based. The European Quality Assurance Register for Higher Education (EQAR),[146] which was established in 2008, aims to provide an overview of agencies that operate in accordance with the Standards and Guidelines for Quality Assurance in the European Higher Education Area. In principle, assessments carried out by an agency in the EQAR should be accepted by other countries in the European Higher Education Area, regardless of where the agency concerned and the institution being assessed are located. Accrediting agencies in non-European systems, such as the United States and others, have established standards for quality-assuring cross-border institutions and programmes that are accepted by most, if not all, European countries, and many of these may be expected to join the EQAR in the near future.

Credentials evaluators may also have knowledge of the broader situation that might help them judge the qualification, even if precise information on the quality assessment or accreditation of a specific institution is lacking. The internationally administered University of the West Indies, or the various UN university and tertiary training establishments are not formally accredited by a national authority, but no

---

146. www.eqar.eu/index.php?id=32, accessed on 2 July 2010.

reasonable credentials evaluator would argue there is a substantial difference on that basis. On the other hand, some higher education institutions, and even some systems, may have a well-deserved reputation for lack of transparency, or a host institution may have observed over the years that students from a given country or certain institutions tend to be inadequately prepared for further study at the host institution. The point about an institution being assessed according to well-established criteria is also important. Diploma mills – providers that charge fees for delivering diplomas that require no academic work – are now being supplemented by accreditation mills, which deliver bogus accreditation statements, according to a similar scofflaw business model.

Ultimately, however, if in spite of their best efforts and their knowledge of the circumstances of an institution, credentials evaluators cannot establish that the institution is of adequate quality, most of them will probably consider the lack of quality assessment as a substantial difference.

What if an institution has been quality assessed according to well-established criteria but the credentials evaluator feels – or is obliged to insist – that these criteria do not quite meet the standards of the host country since it is not accredited nationally? And suppose that the criteria for becoming a "national university" are all but impossible for any international institution to meet, due to legal restrictions, and there is no mechanism for recognising the legitimate status of the home country accreditation, even for limited purposes, and even if the institution in question is compliant with all the expectations of guidelines such as the Code of Good Practice in the Provision of Transnational Education? In at least one European country, it seems to be quite common practice for the country to conduct its own assessment of foreign institutions. In its national action plan for recognition, this country outlines the following procedure:

> 1. A review of the foreign higher education institution by a scientific committee of university professors to determine whether it is "essentially equivalent" to that country's higher education institutions.

> 2. An assessment of the particular Department and the program the student attended is made, considering parameters such as admission requirements, number of professors who are PhD holders, teaching and examination procedures and degree titles awarded (Rauhvargers and Rusakova 2009: 45).

In this case, the host university not only disavows the quality assurance system of the home country of the applicant, but assumes it is itself a competent authority – in both the legal and the substance sense of the term – to quality assess a foreign institution. Here, it is no longer the absence of quality assurance according to well-established criteria that is seen as a substantial difference, but the absence of quality assurance by the receiving institution. It is very difficult to see how this could possibly be considered a reasonable interpretation of the concept of substantial difference.

This brief and incomplete consideration of just one of the elements that make up a qualification – quality – serves to illustrate some of the complexity of determining what may reasonably constitute a substantial difference. We examined some situations where it is either clear that there is a substantial difference, or that there is not. In the latter case, we also saw, however, that in at least one country credentials evaluators in effect define as a substantial difference something that would clearly not be considered as such by most evaluators, even if the country in question does not use the term "substantial difference".

Between the two extremes, however, we also saw that there are situations in which credentials evaluators are likely to take different actions. Some of these concern the extra effort credentials evaluators are willing to put into identifying information. It may well be argued that this does not properly speaking constitute a substantial difference, but it does give an indication of factors that may be so considered. It also points to possible differences in attitudes toward applicants: credentials evaluators who see their task as seeking to make recognition possible are likely to put more effort into identifying supplementary information that may help the applicant than are those who see their task primarily as protecting their own system.

In their overview of the NARIC survey on substantial differences, based on 10 real-life cases, Bas Wegewijs and Lucie de Bruin show that while responses to concrete cases varied, between one fifth and one third of the centres that responded to the survey seemed to base their answers more on considerations of a legal nature than on seeking to identify learning outcomes (Wegewijs and de Bruin 2010). It may be worth noting that the questionnaire at the basis of the survey provided respondents with clearly formulated alternatives, which would not be the case in real-life situations where credentials evaluators would have to reach a decision – or formulate advice to another competent authority – from scratch. It is difficult to say whether the availability of pre-formulated alternatives may have influenced the responses, either by spelling out alternatives that may have been less obvious to some respondents or by signalling that a set of answers may be acceptable.

It is also difficult to say whether the context of the survey – which could be read to imply that there was a general encouragement to justify decisions in terms of learning outcomes rather than procedures – might have influenced respondents, so that some may have justified their answers in terms of learning outcomes, whereas in their actual practice they would have emphasised formal aspects more strongly. There is little reason to believe that the survey results show too low a percentage of responses emphasising formal arguments, but on the other hand, there is also reason to believe that since most respondents were seasoned professionals, they would answer in accordance with their actual practice.

Actual practice does, of course, not always correspond to desirable practice – even in the eyes of those responsible for the practice. There may, for example, be legal or procedural restraints that oblige credentials evaluators to make decisions based on criteria that are different from those they would ideally have liked to use. Wegewijs and de Bruin's survey shows this very clearly. For example, in their first case – recognition of a South African bachelor's degree in history –

53%[147] of the respondents would have made their decision on the basis of criteria and procedures that only 46% of them characterised as best or good practice. Conversely, only some 27% of respondents would have made their decision on the basis of an assessment of learning outcomes, whereas 67% of the respondents felt this alternative represented best or good practice. In another of the cases in this survey – the one involving a Russian *kandidat nauk* – 20% of respondents would have used a criterion that none characterised as best practice and only 7% as "good".

A fictitious example described by Erwin Malfroy (Malfroy 2010), that of an applicant holding a Master of Arts in Psychological Sciences, illustrates the interplay in many assessments between formal and content aspects of the qualification. Malfroy's case in particular illustrates that legal regulations on regulated professions may, by themselves, constitute a decisive element in the recognition decision. At the same time, the discussion of this case points to factors such as possible differences between the programmes and institutions from which the qualification was earned, as well as workload, as possible substantial differences. Equally, the article points out that such differences are not necessarily substantial, and that other factors may override differences here. Not least, Malfroy's article illustrates the importance of considering learning outcomes in a discussion of possible substantial differences. Indeed, if the learning outcomes of two qualifications are broadly similar, it would seem difficult to argue that differences in forms or procedure nevertheless constitute substantial differences that would overrule the similarity in learning outcomes.

The initial considerations in this article demonstrate that there are different approaches to recognition, and that the approach which a given credentials evaluator chooses depends on a range of factors that may, taken together, justify reference to differences in culture, without falling into the trap of thinking of the world of credentials evaluation as divided into two stark camps.[148]

Nor is the difference only apparent between different credentials evaluators. Since the responses in the Wegewijs and de Bruin survey showed that many credentials evaluators would have preferred to decide differently than they have done, on the basis of different criteria and procedures, we must also draw the conclusion that there are, at least in many cases, differences in perception between those who decide on the overall legislation, regulations and policy and those who implement recognition policy.

Do the differences amount to a difference between "two cultures" in recognition, as suggested in this article? We have seen that in most cases we are not faced with a clear choice of right or wrong and that there are many shades of grey in the world of credentials evaluation. Nevertheless, there are important differences in attitude

---

147. For the sake of readability, all percentages have been rounded. This does not affect the argument.
148. With reference to societies in which all or most major societal divides coincide, so that people who vote for a given party also overwhelmingly tend to belong to the same socio-economic group, religion, ethnic background, language and so on, for which the Dutch political scientist Arend Lijphart coined the term *verzuiling* ("pillarisation").

between credentials evaluators and between the national rules and policies that different credentials evaluators work with. These are differences between individuals, but to an extent also between countries and cultures. Some individuals, as well as some cultures, seem to be more rule-bound that others, whereas other individuals and other cultures seem to be more open to considering a range of factors in their assessment.

Credentials evaluators cannot decide against the legal regulations of the country or system in which they work. However, for countries that have ratified the Council of Europe/UNESCO Recognition Convention, this convention as well as its subsidiary texts should be a key part of the legal basis on which recognition decisions are made.

The current discussions about qualifications (Bergan 2007) include consideration of subject-specific and transversal competences. Subject-specific competences relate to the specific discipline(s) in which a given qualification is obtained, such as history or chemistry, whereas transversal competences designate the knowledge, understanding and ability to do that any higher education graduate at a given level should have, regardless of his or her academic specialisation.[149] Among the transferable competences identified by the TUNING project are:

– the ability to analyse and synthesise;
– the ability to organise and plan;
– the ability to communicate orally and in writing in one's native language as well as in foreign languages;
– problem solving;
– decision making;
– critical and self-critical abilities;
– ability to communicate with experts in other fields;
– ability to work in an international context;
– ability to apply knowledge in practice;
– ability to learn;
– ability to generate new ideas (creativity);
– understanding of cultures and customs of other countries;
– initiative and entrepreneurial spirit.

Good credentials evaluators must know the subject-specific aspects of recognition, that is they must, among other things, know and understand the concept of qualifications, their own as well as the international legal framework for recognition and the education systems of foreign countries. They cannot be experts in all education systems, but they must know where they can find information on the systems of countries with which they are not well acquainted, and they must be able to assess that information.

---

149. The distinction between subject-specific and transversal competences was explored by the TUNING project, see www.relint.deusto.es/TUNINGProject/documentos/Tuning_phase1/Portada_listapart_mapa_indice%20 page 1a16.pdf, accessed on 2 July 2010.

Equally important, however, are the transversal competences that credentials evaluators should have. One cannot identify substantial differences on the basis of subject-specific competences alone. Identifying substantial differences implies an ability to ask critical questions as well as the ability to find a reasonable answer to those questions. The answer to the question "why might the difference between qualification A and qualification B be considered substantial?", or even more importantly, "why should the difference between qualification A and qualification B be considered substantial?" may be found in the legal framework, perhaps especially in the case of regulated professions, but more often it requires careful analysis of the purposes for which recognition is sought.

The essential question is "why do the learning outcomes the applicant has obtained make him or her able or unable to follow a given study programme or exercise a given employment?" Answering that question satisfactorily requires a mix of subject-specific and transversal competences. It requires that the credentials evaluator be able to assess not only a candidate's past achievement but also their future potential. It requires that the recognition decision be made on the basis of knowledge and understanding of the qualification in question and of the role and function of that qualification. It requires knowledge of the legal framework, but the decision should not be made without exercising a quality for which there can be no legal provision: common sense.

Developing the appropriate combination of subject-specific and transversal competences and not least the ability to exercise common sense is one of the main purposes of the ENIC and NARIC networks and of their consideration of the concept of substantial differences. In this author's view, there are still differences in approach that justify the idea of "two cultures" in this area, but it is also this author's hope that through continued consideration of the issue, these differences in approach will diminish. The ultimate goal must be that applicants will have the assurance that wherever they apply for recognition, their applications will be considered with the same professionalism and the same openness of mind with which the credentials evictors would like their own qualifications to be assessed.

References

Bergan S. (2004), "A tale of two cultures in higher education policies: the rule of law or a excess of legalism?", *Journal of Studies in International Education*, Volume 8, Issue 2, summer 2004.

Bergan S. (2007), *Qualifications. Introduction to a Concept*, Council of Europe Higher Education Series No. 6, Council of Europe Publishing, Strasbourg.

Bologna Process (2005), "Standards and Guidelines for Quality Assurance in the European Higher Education Area", available at www.ond.vlaanderen. be/hogeronderwijs/bologna/documents/Standards-and-Guidelines-for-QA.pdf, accessed on 2 July 2010.

Malfroy E. (2010), "Recruitment to health professions: the case of a Master of Arts in Psychological Sciences", in Hunt E. S. and Bergan S. (eds), *Developing Attitudes to Recognition: Substantial Differences in an Age of Globalisation*, Council of Europe Higher Education Series No. 13, Council of Europe Publishing, Strasbourg, pp. 51-58.

Rauhvargers A. and Rusakova A. (2009), *Improving Recognition in the European Higher Education Area: an Analysis of National Action Plans*, Council of Europe Higher Education Series No. 12, Council of Europe Publishing, Strasbourg.

Sanz N. and Bergan S. (eds) (2007), *The Cultural Heritage of European Universities*, second edition, Council of Europe Higher Education Series No. 7, Council of Europe Publishing, Strasbourg.

Wegewijs B. and de Bruin L. (2010), "Substantial differences in an EU context: conclusions from a project", in Hunt E. S. and Bergan S. (eds), *Developing Attitudes to Recognition: Substantial Differences in an Age of Globalisation*, Council of Europe Higher Education Series No. 13, Council of Europe Publishing, Strasbourg, pp. 79-96.

Qualifications frameworks: an instrument to resolve substantial differences?[150]

Introduction

Qualifications frameworks have become a key element of the European Higher Education Area (EHEA),[151] where ministers adopted an overarching framework of qualifications of the EHEA (QF-EHEA) in 2005 and committed to developing national frameworks compatible with the QF-EHEA. The deadline for developing national frameworks was originally set for 2010, but was extended by ministers at their 2009 meeting so that all 47 countries of the EHEA are now committed to developing their national frameworks and preparing them for self-certification by 2012.

While higher education is more internationalised and has come further in the development of qualifications frameworks than other parts of the education system, the concept of qualifications frameworks is by no means limited to higher education. Several of the pioneers in this area developed comprehensive frameworks, covering all parts of their education system. As one example, the Scottish framework – which is distinct from the framework for England, Wales and Northern Ireland – encompasses 12 levels ranging from educational achievements by learners with severe learning disabilities to doctoral qualifications. The European Qualifications Framework for lifelong learning (EQF-LLL)[152] was developed by the European Commission and formally adopted in 2008. It encompasses eight levels from primary school to doctoral qualifications and the 32 countries[153] to which it applies will reference their own qualifications against the EQF-LLL.

Even if qualifications frameworks now play a key role in European higher education and education policies, they are not a European invention. Australia, New Zealand and South Africa were pioneers in developing qualifications frameworks, for somewhat different reasons. In the case of Australia and New Zealand, the main motivations were to make their qualifications more transparent and hence to make them more attractive. In the case of Australia in particular, this was linked to the

---

150. The first version of this article was published in Hunt, E. Stephen and Bergan, Sjur (eds) (2010): *Developing Attitudes to Recognition: Substantial Differences in an Age of Globalisation*, Strasbourg: Council of Europe Publishing. Council of Europe Higher Education Series No. 13. The author would like to thank E. Stephen Hunt for valuable comments to the first version of the article.

151. See the Bologna website on qualifications frameworks: www.ond.vlaanderen.be/hogeronderwijs/bologna/qf/qf.asp.

152. Often also referred to simply as EQF. However, EQF-LLL is preferred here in order to emphasise the lifelong learning aspect of this framework and to avoid possible confusion with the QF-EHEA. See http://ec.europa.eu/education/lifelong-learning-policy/doc44_en.htm.

153. All members of the European Union and the European Economic Area, as well as some other countries that participate in relevant EU programmes.

fact that this country hosts a large number of foreign students who need recognition of their qualifications when they return home or move on to third countries. In the case of South Africa, the main motivation was one of social cohesion. The apartheid era left many South Africans with qualifications that could not be documented and/ or had been earned through non-traditional learning paths. A national qualifications framework afforded better opportunities for recognition of qualifications like these. Both of the primary reasons that led to the development of the three pioneering frameworks – improved transparency and greater social cohesion through education – are relevant to the discussion of qualifications frameworks as possible instruments to resolve substantial differences and improve fair recognition of qualifications.

Before moving on to a more detailed consideration of qualifications frameworks, however, the author would like to recognise that Ireland and the United Kingdom – with separate frameworks for Scotland, on the one hand, and England, Wales and Northern Ireland on the other – were pioneers in developing national qualifications frameworks in Europe and that Denmark played a crucial role in putting qualifications frameworks on the European higher education agenda through two important Bologna conferences in 2003[154] and 2005[155] as well as through Mogens Berg's chairmanship of the Bologna working group on qualifications frameworks from 2003 until 2007.

Additionally, it is important to emphasise that the development and implementation of a qualifications framework is a prerogative of the national education system. Within the EHEA, decisions have been taken by the co-operating countries to develop and self-certify qualifications frameworks and to tie these to overarching regional frameworks. This has been a voluntary process specific to the EHEA. Even if many countries around the world are in the process of developing qualifications frameworks, or are discussing whether to do so, countries outside Europe often use quite different approaches to qualifications frameworks, or have no national framework in a formal sense. What follows pertains primarily to the European context. In no way should it be implied that having a national qualifications framework is expected or required of countries outside of the EHEA even if some 120 countries and territories are now developing frameworks,[156] that it should follow the European model, or that not having a qualifications framework is a substantial difference for non-European countries with respect to European recognition of their qualifications.

The concept of qualifications frameworks

Qualifications may be seen as consisting of five major components (Bergan 2007):

– quality;
– workload;

---

154. www.bologna-bergen2005.no/EN/Bol_sem/Old/030327-28Copenhagen/030327-28Report_ General_Rapporteur.pdf.
155. www.bologna-bergen2005.no/EN/Bol_sem/Seminars/050113-14Copenhagen/050113-14_General_ report.pdf.
156. Information provided by the European Training Foundation.

– level;
– profile;
– learning outcomes.

Qualifications specify or certify educational achievements. In the former sense, they describe typical degrees, such as a bachelor's, master's or doctoral degree. In the latter sense, they describe the achievement of a specific learner. In both cases, qualifications describe something specific: a given typical achievement or a given achievement of a given learner. Qualifications frameworks, on the other hand, are more general or systemic. They describe a set of qualifications – a system – and how they fit together. Qualifications relate to individual awards, while qualifications frameworks relate to education systems.

The concept of qualifications frameworks is at the same time both old and new. At one level, it can be argued that any country that has an education system – and that includes all countries of the world except, perhaps, a very few countries where public authority has broken down due to internal strife – has a qualifications framework. In this sense of the term, a qualifications framework is the same as a degree system, and any formalised system of education has a number of degrees at different levels, some – even most – of which can only be obtained if a learner has first obtained one or more degrees at lower levels in the education system.

That, however, is not the sense in which the term is most commonly used. In this second sense – referred to in earlier days as "new style qualifications frameworks" – the term refers not just to the individual qualifications that make up the framework, but in particular to how these qualifications interlink and how learners can move between the different qualifications that make up the framework. This is most often thought of as moving to a higher qualification on the basis of a lower one, and that is perhaps the most common form of movement within a system. However, movement can also be sideways and even downwards. To take only two examples from higher education, someone with a legal qualification, which would normally be at second degree level, may wish to take a second (master's) level degree in economics or a first (bachelor's) degree in public administration.

Qualifications frameworks should also emphasise learning outcomes, and they should describe the generic learning outcomes one can expect learners to obtain for a certain qualification. Learning outcomes describe what learners should know, understand and be able to do on the basis of a given qualification. All three elements are important. Knowledge is of course important but the very traditional view of education that emphasises facts alone – often in the form of rote learning – as the purpose of learning is no longer tenable. Knowledge without understanding can even be dangerous, and higher education is sometimes accused of providing learners with knowledge, but not with the ability to apply that knowledge. This may not be a fair accusation, and those who make it sometimes have a view of higher education that reduces it to an advanced form of preparation for the labour market, but it does emphasise that knowledge must be understood and put to use.

Think of how we learn a foreign language. We must know vocabulary and grammar as well as the rules of pronunciation and usage, but we must also understand them in order to be able to express ourselves in our newly acquired language – to put the language to use. Knowing the different declensions of Russian nouns, adjectives and verbs is a formidable challenge for those who learn Russian as a foreign language, particularly if Russian is their first Slavic language, but understanding how the rules work in practice is a requirement for being able to speak and write Russian, which is the likely goal of most of those who take up the language.

While describing what a learner knows, understands and is able to do is the traditional definition of learning outcomes, this author has increasingly come to believe that a description of a learner's attitudes should be added to the definition. This is rooted in the view that higher education serves a variety of purposes. In addition to preparing learners for the labour market – the purpose that is most prominent in public debate, at least in Europe – higher education should also prepare learners for life as active citizens in democratic societies, an area in which many US higher education institutions have better enunciated policies than do their European counterparts (AAC&U 2007). Higher education should contribute to learners' personal development and it should provide society with a broad and advanced knowledge base (Bergan 2005, Council of Europe 2007). Developing attitudes of societal engagement and commitment to democracy and intercultural dialogue are, in this author's view, essential generic learning outcomes for higher education.

Qualifications frameworks thus combine a description of learning paths – the different ways in which learners may move within the system and earn qualifications – and learning outcomes. Formal aspects are not absent from the description of qualifications frameworks, but they play a less prominent role than in the description of traditional education or degree systems. The intention is that the emphasis shift from institutions to learners, from provision to learning, and from formal procedures to content.

Qualifications frameworks, then, describe qualifications in terms of level and learning outcomes. They will often give an indication of the workload typically required to reach the qualification, but they will recognise that this is an indication only and that there are several learning paths to the same qualification. Workload will also depend on previous learning outcomes: a learner who is already proficient in a Slavic language will obtain a given level in Russian more rapidly than a learner for whom Russian is the first foreign language. Quality is an important component of qualifications frameworks because, at least within the EHEA, quality assurance agencies will assess the quality of institutions with a view to the qualifications framework within which a given institution provides its qualifications, and conversely, qualifications will not be included in the framework if the institution providing them has not successfully undergone a quality assurance process.

Learning outcomes may be generic or subject specific. Generic learning outcomes, such as communication skills, the ability to reason in abstract terms, or aptitude for working both as part of a team and individually, are those that may be expected from any higher education graduate at a given level, irrespective of his or her field of study. Subject-specific learning outcomes, on the other hand, are, as the name indicates, specific to a given discipline: what a historian knows, understands and is able to do in relation to history or a chemist in relation to chemistry. Generic learning outcomes are included in the description of qualifications frameworks, whereas subject-specific learning outcomes are normally not. There may, however, be descriptions of subject-specific learning outcomes agreed by institutions or by the discipline community[157] that are not a part of the national qualifications framework, but that may nevertheless be valuable guides to what, say, the holder of a second degree in linguistics will know, understand and be able to do in relation to this discipline.

National and overarching frameworks

As we have already hinted at, qualifications frameworks may be one of two kinds: national or overarching.

National qualifications frameworks should perhaps more accurately be called system-specific frameworks, since they describe the qualifications in a given education or higher education system and since, as in the case of Belgium or the United Kingdom, one country may have more than one education system. Most often, however, one country has one education system, and we will stick to the term "national" with the caveat that the term also covers cases where a country has more than one education system.

National qualifications frameworks, then, describe all the qualifications in an education system, if the framework is comprehensive, or in a higher education system, if we are faced with a higher education qualifications framework. Whereas Australia, New Zealand and South Africa developed comprehensive frameworks, developments in Europe have been more mixed: some countries are seeking to develop comprehensive frameworks while others opt to develop higher education frameworks, which may be supplemented by a more comprehensive framework later. It would even be possible for a country to comply with the QF-EHEA and the EQF-LLL by developing a higher education framework only. Within the EHEA, ministers have committed to developing frameworks for higher education, whereas the requirement with regard to the EQF-LLL is that countries reference their qualifications against the overarching framework. Even if this does not require a national qualifications framework, it seems reasonable to assume that the vast majority of countries will indeed develop national frameworks for other parts of their education system too. One reason for the latter option may be that even if higher education qualifications may seem complex, they are considerably less complex that vocational qualifications, and there are also stronger international precedents in higher education.

---

157. The TUNING project (Tuning Educational Structures in Europe) provides a series of examples of subject-specific learning outcomes agreed by representatives of disciplines from several European countries, see http://tuning.unideusto.org/tuningeu.

As noted, all members of the Bologna Process have committed to developing national qualifications frameworks by 2012. Developing a national framework is a relatively complicated process that takes time. The Bologna Co-ordination Group[158] on Qualifications Frameworks has outlined 11 steps, which are not to be taken as mandatory, nor are they necessarily to be accomplished in the order outlined by the group, but they give an indication of what is involved:

1. Decision to start: taken by the national body responsible for higher education.

2. Setting the agenda: the purpose of our national qualifications framework.

3. Organising the process: identifying stakeholders; setting up a committee/ working group.

4. Design profile: level structure, level descriptors (learning outcomes) and credit ranges.

5. Consultation: national discussion and acceptance of design by stakeholders.

6. Approval according to national tradition by minister/government/legislation.

7. Administrative set-up: division of tasks of implementation between higher education institutions, the quality assurance agency and other bodies.

8. Implementation at institutional/programme level; reformulation of individual study programmes to learning outcome-based approach.

9. Inclusion of qualifications in the national qualifications framework; accreditation or similar.

10. Self-certification of compatibility with the EHEA framework (alignment to Bologna cycles, etc.).

11. Establishing a dedicated website aimed at national stakeholders, as well as international partners (this step, in particular, should be accomplished as early as possible in the process and the site should be updated and developed as work on the national framework progresses).

As of July 2010, eight national frameworks for higher education had been self-certified against the QF-EHEA: those of Belgium (Flemish Community), Denmark, Germany, Ireland, Malta, the Netherlands, the United Kingdom (England, Wales and Northern Ireland) and the United Kingdom (Scotland). The case of Malta is particularly noteworthy because in autumn 2009, Malta became the first country to self-certify its national framework against the QF-EHEA and reference it against the EQF-LLL in the same operation. The other members of the EHEA are at various stages in the development of their national frameworks, and a survey carried out by the Bologna Co-ordination Group in early 2009 showed that while more than 30 countries had completed the first three steps and, some 25 had completed steps four and five, around 15 countries had already completed steps six and seven (Bologna Co-ordination Group on Qualifications Frameworks 2009a and 2009b). However, developments are now relatively rapid and a similar survey undertaken

---

158. This group was called a "co-ordination group" between 2007 and 2010 and a "working group" before the ministerial meeting of the Bologna Process in May 2007 and after that in March 2010.

in early 2010 showed that a larger number of countries are well advanced in the process. This survey also showed that countries' estimates of when they will complete the various steps of the process of developing a national framework are now more realistic than they were even a year earlier.

In addition to the three pioneering countries – Australia, New Zealand and South Africa – many countries outside the EHEA have developed or are developing qualifications frameworks. Malaysia has an established framework overseen by a qualifications authority, Thailand is well under way, some Canadian provinces have established provincial frameworks, and in the United States discussions on developing a framework have been cautiously launched. These are only select examples, since developments now seem to be so rapid that even if anything like a complete overview were established, it would most likely be outdated before publication. Qualifications frameworks have very much become part of the global discourse, and increasingly also part of the global practice, of higher education reform.[159] As we saw previously, as of June 2010, the European Training Foundation estimated that some 120 countries and territories were in the process of developing their frameworks or, in some cases, had already done so.

It is important to note that there may well be several qualifications located at the same level within a national framework. If level one denotes a first cycle qualification, there may be different kinds of such qualifications that are all at the same level in the national qualifications frameworks, but that may have slightly different characteristics. As an example, level six in the Irish qualifications framework comprises two distinct qualifications that the Irish framework describes as follows:

Level 6 Advanced Certificate

What is this?

An Advanced Certificate award enables development of a variety of skills which may be vocationally specific and/or of a general supervisory nature. The majority of Level 6 holders take up positions of employment. A Certificate holder at this level may also transfer to a programme leading to the next level of the framework.

Example An example of awards at Level 6 includes Advanced Certificate Craft-Electrical.

Awarding Body The awarding body for this award is the Further Education and Training Awards Council (FETAC).

Level 6 Higher Certificate

What is this?

The Higher Certificate is normally awarded after completion of a programme of two years' duration in a recognised higher education institution. A Certificate holder at this level may transfer to a programme on the next level of the framework.

---

159. This was demonstrated by a conference on the global dimension of qualifications frameworks organised by the European Training Foundation in January 2009, see www.etf.europa.eu/web.nsf/opennews/AA73545A989E34FAC12575520053DFA5_EN?OpenDocument.

Example: An example of awards at Level 6 Higher Certificate is a Certificate in Business Studies.

Awarding Body The awarding bodies for this award are the Higher Education and Training Awards Council (HETAC), the Dublin Institute of Technology (DIT) and the Institutes of Technology (IOT) with delegated authority.[160]

In terms of the QF-EHEA, both would be short cycle qualifications within the first cycle.

Where Europe has been truly innovative is with regard to overarching frameworks. These are more general than national frameworks, and they set the parameters within which the relevant national frameworks will be developed. One way of seeing overarching qualifications frameworks is that they describe the outer limits within which national frameworks will be developed. Within these limits, there is scope for considerable variation that allows countries to take account of their own specific needs, strengths and traditions, but at the same time the overarching framework ensures that this variation between national frameworks is kept manageable. There is nothing to prevent a country from developing a national framework where the learning outcomes for a first degree are such that a typical student would need 10 years or more after completion of secondary school to obtain the qualification, but this would not be a national framework compatible with the QF-EHEA, nor would it be in accordance with the overall trends of higher education reform in other parts of the world. For the same reasons, the example is of course entirely fictitious.

As we have seen, the QF-EHEA was adopted by the ministers of the Bologna Process in 2005, and it applies to the 47 countries of the European Higher Education Area. As will be seen from the overview below, the QF-EHEA does not include a description of what have come to be described as "short cycle" qualifications. Typically, short cycle qualifications have a workload of approximately 120 ECTS[161] credits – although some have more or less – and are a feature of professional higher education. In the United States, the Associate Degree would be an example of the kind of qualification that in Europe is often referred to as "short cycle". Short cycle qualifications are to be found in many countries, and the decision by the 2005 ministerial conference of the Bologna Process gave education systems the possibility of including intermediate qualifications within each of the three cycles of their national qualifications frameworks. It seems safe to assume that these will most often be short cycle qualifications within the first cycle.

---

160. www.nfq.ie/nfq/en/about_NFQ/framework_levels_award_types.html.
161. European Credit Transfer and Accumulation System. "Accumulation" was added to the name after the ECTS had been in operation for some time and the original abbreviation was kept.

QF-EHEA

	Outcomes	ECTS credits
First cycle qualification	Qualifications that signify completion of the first cycle are awarded to students who: – have demonstrated knowledge and understanding in a field of study that builds upon their general secondary education, and is typically at a level that, whilst supported by advanced textbooks, includes some aspects that will be informed by knowledge of the forefront of their field of study; – can apply their knowledge and understanding in a manner that indicates a professional approach to their work or vocation, and have competences typically demonstrated through devising and sustaining arguments and solving problems within their field of study; – have the ability to gather and interpret relevant data (usually within their field of study) to inform judgments that include reflection on relevant social, scientific or ethical issues; – can communicate information, ideas, problems and solutions to both specialist and non-specialist audiences; – have developed those learning skills that are necessary for them to continue to undertake further study with a high degree of autonomy.	Typically include 180-240 ECTS credits
Second cycle qualification	Qualifications that signify completion of the second cycle are awarded to students who: – have demonstrated knowledge and understanding that is founded upon and extends and/or enhances that typically associated with the first cycle, and that provides a basis or opportunity for originality in developing and/or applying ideas, often within a research context; – can apply their knowledge and understanding, and problem-solving abilities in new or unfamiliar environments within broader (or multidisciplinary) contexts related to their field of study; – have the ability to integrate knowledge and handle complexity, and formulate judgments with incomplete or limited information, but that include reflecting on social and ethical responsibilities linked to the application of their knowledge and judgments; – can communicate their conclusions, and the knowledge and rationale underpinning these, to specialist and non-specialist audiences clearly and unambiguously; – have the learning skills to allow them to continue to study in a manner that may be largely self-directed or autonomous.	Typically include 90-120 ECTS credits, with a minimum of 60 credits at the level of the second cycle

Third cycle qualification	Qualifications that signify completion of the third cycle are awarded to students who:	Not specified
	– have demonstrated a systematic understanding of a field of study and mastery of the skills and methods of research associated with that field;	
	– have demonstrated the ability to conceive, design, implement and adapt a substantial process of research with scholarly integrity;	
	– have made a contribution through original research that extends the frontier of knowledge by developing a substantial body of work, some of which merits national or international refereed publication;	
	– are capable of critical analysis, evaluation and synthesis of new and complex ideas;	
	– can communicate with their peers, the larger scholarly community and with society in general about their areas of expertise;	
	– can be expected to be able to promote, within academic and professional contexts, technological, social or cultural advancement in a knowledge-based society.	

As we have also seen, at approximately the same time that the QF-EHEA was adopted, the European Commission launched work on the European Qualifications Framework for lifelong learning (EQF-LLL), which was formally established in spring 2008.

The QF-EHEA and the EQF-LLL are the most prominent examples of overarching qualifications frameworks. There are, however, frameworks in existence or under discussion in some other parts of the world, such as the discussions within the Co-operation Council for the Arab States of the Gulf about a possible overarching framework for this region, which encompasses Bahrain, Kuwait, Oman, Qatar, Saudi Arabia and the United Arab Emirates. As the Bologna Process is considered with interest as a possible inspiration (much more than a model to be copied) for higher education in other areas of the world, one might imagine that overarching frameworks may in time be developed for, or within, some other regions. In addition, one might imagine that some federal states might opt for national frameworks with characteristics close to those of overarching frameworks, which would serve to ensure that provincial or state frameworks develop coherently.

Even if much of the European debate has focused on the overarching frameworks, it is the national qualifications frameworks that are closest to the daily lives of learners. The relationship between national and overarching frameworks may be summarised as follows:

National frameworks	Overarching frameworks
– closest to the operational reality – owned by national system – ultimately determine what qualifications learners will earn – describe the qualifications within a given education system and how they interlink	– facilitate movement between systems – are the face of qualifications from the region (for example, EHEA) to the rest of the world – provide the broad structure within which national qualifications frameworks will be developed ("outer limits" for diversity)

As we have seen, the QF-EHEA is specific to higher education, while the EQF-LLL is comprehensive. This implies that they share a set of qualifications, namely those pertaining to higher education. It may therefore be argued that Europe has two distinct overarching frameworks for higher education, at least as concerns the 32 countries of the EQF-LLL, all of which are also party to the QF-EHEA. In a formal sense, this is true and the two frameworks do not describe the higher education qualifications in exactly the same terms. However, the descriptions are similar, and, most importantly, it is entirely possible to develop national qualifications frameworks for higher education that are compatible with both overarching frameworks. This was demonstrated very clearly through the Maltese self-certification referred to above.

Self-certification

Self-certification has been developed as a concept within the EHEA and the discussion here will therefore be confined to national frameworks compatible with the QF-EHEA. Within the EQF-LLL, referencing is a similar process with criteria largely modelled on those for self-certification within the QF-EHEA.

Self-certification is the final step in the development of national qualifications frameworks and it is the means through which the competent public authorities convince their international partners that their national framework is compatible with the QF-EHEA. Countries are sovereign with full authority over their education systems, and no international body can certify a national framework in lieu of the competent national authority. However, self-certification is not a question only of formal authority but also of legitimacy, acceptance and the creation of trust. A country that published a statement simply saying its national framework is certified as compatible with the QF-EHEA could not be obliged to change its statement in formal terms, but it is unlikely such a statement would convince partners inside or outside the EHEA, and it would therefore be of little benefit to the country concerned. In such a case, which is likely to remain fictitious, peer pressure would probably be applied in very considerable doses.

The self-certification report may be considered as the "visiting card" of the national qualifications framework concerned; it is the one document through which the competent authorities will demonstrate, through reasoned arguments according to agreed criteria, that their framework is compatible. This has strong implications for recognition, because if a national framework is convincingly self-certified as "QF-EHEA compatible", it will be much less likely that there are substantial differences between this framework and other similar frameworks.

While the scope of this article does not allow us to explore the criteria and procedure for self-certification in detail,[162] it is worth underlining that one of the requirements agreed to by ministers is that there be involvement by foreign experts in the self-certification process. This adds credibility and improves transparency, and it is also useful because foreigners may question elements of a framework that may be self-explanatory to those intimately familiar with it, but may require explanation to outsiders. Self-certification reports are normally developed by a group composed of national and foreign experts and then adopted by the competent national authorities. It is then published on the Bologna website[163] as well as on the ENIC/NARIC website,[164] so that all completed reports are easily accessible.

Qualifications frameworks and recognition

The answer to the question asked in the title of this article – are qualifications frameworks a useful instrument to resolve substantial differences? – is a "yes, but …". Seen from a recognition point of view, a qualifications framework is above all a transparency instrument. A qualifications framework should make it easier to determine whether a foreign qualification ought to be recognised, or whether there are substantial differences between this qualification and similar qualifications in the country in which recognition is sought. In particular, a qualifications framework should help answer any questions pertaining to level, quality assurance, workload (to the extent that this is a relevant question for recognition) and generic learning outcomes, as well as the functions of a given qualification in terms of access to further studies and possibly to the labour market in its country of origin. Qualifications frameworks are, as we have seen, less likely to answer questions pertaining to profile or subject-specific learning outcomes. In answering this set of questions, qualifications frameworks have the potential both to reduce the workload of credentials evaluators and to reduce the elements of a qualification on which substantial differences might possibly exist. While it may be possible to consider that the profile of two qualifications at a similar level in two different qualifications frameworks may constitute a substantial difference for certain purposes of recognition, it would be much more difficult to argue that there are similar differences in terms of level, quality, workload or generic learning outcomes if both frameworks have been self-certified against the QF-EHEA. In this case, the argument would in fact need to be that the self-certification report as published is unconvincing, which

---

162. For further details, see www.ond.vlaanderen.be/hogeronderwijs/bologna/qf/documents/Bologna_Framework_and_Certification_revised_29_02_08.pdf.
163. See www.ond.vlaanderen.be/hogeronderwijs/bologna/qf/national.asp#C.
164. See www.enic-naric.net/index.aspx?s=n&r=ena&d=qf.

would be a strong indictment of the competent public authorities as well as of the foreign experts who have participated in the self-certification.

Qualifications frameworks should therefore be of considerable help in furthering fair recognition, as required by the Council of Europe/UNESCO Recognition Convention, but it is important to underline that they are not some kind of magic formula to solve all recognition problems. They should facilitate the assessment of individual qualifications, but they will not make such an assessment superfluous, nor will they lead to "automatic recognition". While it may be assumed that first degrees from two different national frameworks self-certified against the QF-EHEA will be of similar level, quality, workload and generic learning outcomes, an assessment will still need to be undertaken, and for some purposes of recognition, it will most likely also include profile and subject-specific learning outcomes.

At the same time, as underlined in the introduction to this article, the absence of a national or overarching qualifications framework cannot be construed as a substantial difference in itself. In the present state of affairs, this would imply that only qualifications from six higher education systems within the EHEA should be recognised, and these would be supplemented by qualifications from a limited number of countries outside the EHEA. A national qualifications framework is an instrument that furthers recognition but it is not a requirement. Many countries inside and outside the EHEA are in the process of developing their frameworks, or are discussing whether to do so, but a number of countries may ultimately decide not to do so, or even debate whether this is the right direction to take. This does not render their qualifications any less valuable. Qualifications frameworks will help recognition, but the absence of qualifications frameworks should not make recognition any more difficult in the future than it has been in the past, before qualifications frameworks came into existence. Qualifications frameworks or not, credentials evaluators will need to use the transparency instruments they have at their disposal, gather the required information and make their decisions, with due regard to international and national regulations and guidelines, but without leaving aside the element of decision making that is impossible to describe in legal terms: common sense.

References

AAC&U (2007), *College Learning for the New Global Century*, Association of American Colleges and Universities, Washington DC.

Bergan S. (2005), "Public responsibility for higher education and research: what does it mean?", in Weber L. and Bergan S. (eds), *Public Responsibility for Higher Education and Research*, Council of Europe Higher Education Series No. 2, Council of Europe Publishing, Strasbourg.

Bergan S. (2007), *Qualifications. Introduction to a Concept*, Council of Europe Higher Education Series No. 6, Council of Europe Publishing, Strasbourg.

Bologna Co-ordination Group on Qualifications Frameworks (2009a), "Report on Qualifications Frameworks", Strasbourg/Brussels: Bologna Process and Council of Europe. Available at: www.ond.vlaanderen.be/hogeronderwijs/bologna/conference/documents/2009_QF_CG_report.pdf.

Bologna Co-ordination Group on Qualifications Frameworks (2009b), "Synthesis of the Replies Received from National QF Correspondents", Strasbourg/Brussels: Bologna Process and Council of Europe. Available at: www.ond.vlaanderen.be/hogeronderwijs/bologna/conference/documents/Synthesis_NQF_Reports_March2009.pdf.

Council of Europe (2007), Recommendation CM/Rec(2007)6 of the Committee of Ministers to member states on the public responsibility for higher education and research.

IV. Speeches

Ministerial conference of the Bologna Process, Bergen, 2005

Bergen, 18 May 2005

It is a great pleasure for me to reiterate the Council of Europe's strong and continuing support for the European Higher Education Area. This has just been confirmed by the Action Plan adopted by our Third Summit of Heads of State and Government, held in Warsaw earlier this week. This effort is very much within the logic of our work as a pan-European organisation working for democracy, human rights, the rule of law and social cohesion – in other words, for a Europe of values. I would also like to take this opportunity to pay tribute to the good co-operation we have developed with the representatives of the European Commission, UNESCO, the EUA, ESIB[165] and EURASHE in the Bologna Follow-up Group.

Today, I would like to focus on five factors that will, in the Council of Europe's view, to a large extent decide whether the European Higher Education Area will be a success. Firstly, it must be a truly European area. This has been achieved with the admission today of Armenia, Azerbaijan, Georgia, Moldova and Ukraine, along with the admission of seven countries two years ago in Berlin. We hope that one day political conditions in Belarus will make it possible also for the academic community of that country to take its rightful place in the Bologna Process. The challenge is now to make all countries equal partners, and the Council of Europe will continue to play a key role in this respect.

Secondly, the European Higher Education Area must be open towards the rest of the world. There are very real problems with the perception of "Bologna" in other parts of the world, and we must address them now to reach our goal of being attractive.

Thirdly, the European Higher Education Area must be an area of substance, and the stocktaking report shows that we are well on our way. The Bologna Process must build the bridge that enables learners to cross the divide between different education systems without leaving the real value of their luggage behind at the customs station. It must also make the divide between systems smaller, and it must encompass all learners, including the 2 million in short cycle higher education.

Fourthly, the European Higher Education Area must be one of social cohesion. A European Higher Education Area cannot aim at less than equal opportunities for all its members. It cannot aim at less than enabling all individuals to fully develop their abilities and their potential. It cannot afford to do less than give all Europeans the opportunity to put their abilities, skills and knowledge at the service of others.

---

165. The ESIB has since changed its name to the ESU – the European Students Union.

Fifth, we must have the courage to make difficult decisions. Public responsibility must remain a key feature of the European Higher Education Area, and this will require a hard look at how the public responsibility can be exercised in modern, complex societies. In other words, we must follow up the debate launched by the Council of Europe in 2004 and manifested in the very recent publication you have before you.[166]

We must also have the courage and the political will to address issues where other parts of public policies interact with higher education policies. Mobility of students, staff and graduates throughout Europe cannot be achieved if we do not have the courage to address the difficult issues of visas, work permits and the portability of social security rights. We cannot complete the European Higher Education Area if we do not rise to this challenge.

The ultimate measure of the success of the European Higher Education Area will be that it enables students, staff and graduates to move freely throughout Europe, that it engages constructively with the rest of the world and that its policies enable higher education and research to fulfil its major purposes:

- preparation for life as active citizens in democratic society;
- preparation for sustainable employment;
- personal development;
- the development and maintenance of a broad, advanced knowledge base.

Ladies and gentlemen, there is a Norwegian saying to the effect that after sun, there will be rain. Let us disprove this. Let us make sure that after Bergen, there will always be sun in European higher education – even midnight sun.

---

166. The reference is to Weber, Luc and Bergan, Sjur (eds) (2005): *The Public Responsibility for Higher Education and Research*, Strasbourg: Council of Europe Publishing. Council of Europe Higher Education Series No. 2.

Ministerial conference of the Bologna Process, London, 2007

London, 17 May 2007

It gives me great pleasure to address you today on behalf of the Council of Europe. Our role here demonstrates that the Bologna Process is leading to a European Higher Education Area in the true sense of the term, encompassing all parts of our continent. Examples of good practice are found in every part of Europe, including in our newer members. We are pleased that Montenegro has become the 46th member of the Bologna Process, a week after it became the 47th member state of the Council of Europe. I would also like to take this opportunity to underline the vital contribution of the consultative members.

The Council of Europe is fully committed to the Bologna Process:

– through the Follow-up Group and Board;

– by assisting the newer members of the process;

– by providing, with UNESCO, the only binding text of the process: the Lisbon Recognition Convention;

– and by addressing a range of key policy issues.

Yet, my purpose here is not to talk about what the Council of Europe has done, but rather to suggest some actions we should all undertake together to make the European Higher Education Area a reality by 2010.

The reforms of the Bologna Process are far reaching, and they are important. Carrying them out has not been easy, it has sometimes required political courage and it has taken an effort to build agreement around key policies and goals in each country. Goals reached give cause for satisfaction, but they are also the stuff of which new challenges are made.

As we look towards 2010, we must also look beyond 2010.

The attractiveness of Europe will increasingly depend on the quality and relevance of our teaching, learning and research. These are conditions *sine qua non*: we cannot build a successful higher education area on anything less than top quality education and research. Quality development is and should be a key concern of every teacher, student, administrator and policy maker. Quality development is the prerequisite for quality assurance, and it is not a spectator sport.

Nevertheless, our greatest challenge is perhaps to articulate a clearer vision of why higher education is crucial to our future. Preparation for the labour market is important, but let us also talk about higher education in preparation for democratic citizenship, personal development and the development of a broad, advanced knowledge base.

Not least, let us consider these four major purposes of higher education as comple-mentary rather than as contradictory. Our graduates must be able to tackle the big issues as well as the bottom line. European higher education will be admired not only for its value added but also for the values embedded in it and transmitted through it. Our higher education will be admired for the subject-specific skills it provides as well as for the generic competences that enable higher education graduates to solve problems and put issues into context. Our graduates, whatever their field, must be able to challenge preconceived assumptions with a critical mind – critical and constructive. They must be able to communicate with people from other back-grounds, linguistically and culturally. Higher education is successful only where knowledge is accompanied by understanding, creativity and the ability to act. It is a paradox that while we have more highly trained specialists than ever before, we seem to have fewer intellectuals.

We would like the European Higher Education Area to inspire our students and staff to do their best, yet we find it easier to speak about our structures than about our values. It was only in 2006 that the values on which we build were explicitly addressed at a Bologna conference organised by the Holy See in co-operation with UNESCO/CEPES and the Council of Europe.[167] Our values as well as our cultural heritage are an important part of what makes us attractive. They are at the core of higher education as well as of the European construction. Can we imagine the European Higher Education Area without these basic values? Institutional autonomy, academic freedom and public responsibility are basic concepts of the Bologna Process and we should adhere to a common understanding and practice of them. Can we claim that we have already achieved this? Can we claim that institutional autonomy and academic freedom have now been adequately established, once and for all?

We want to be attractive to others, yet our voices sometimes bear the noise of cacophony rather than the music of symphony. Since we are likely to have two similar but not identical qualifications frameworks, it is important that we minimise discrepancies between them. The framework adopted by ministers in Bergen should be the basis for explaining European higher education qualifications to the rest of the world. The Council of Europe is pleased to take responsibility for co-ordinating the sharing of experience in the development of national qualifications frameworks compatible with this truly European framework and we will seek to work with the European Commission so that experience with implementing the European higher education framework will also be of help in implementing the European Qualifications Framework for lifelong learning.

We would like the European Higher Education Area to inspire not only our own students and staff but also those of other continents. We have an opportunity here in London, as ministers will be able to adopt a strategy for the Bologna Process in a global

---

167. See Sadlak, Jan, Miller, Michael and Bergan, Sjur (eds): *The Cultural Heritage and Academic Values of the European University and the Attractiveness of the European Higher Education Area*, special issue of *Higher Education in Europe*, Volume XXXI, Number 4, 2006.

context. We would like others to understand our reforms and to be inspired by them. This also means we need an agreed description of the European Higher Education Area – its principles and structures – for an articulate dialogue with our partners.

We would like to be attractive to others, yet we do not seem to wish to be so attractive that others will want to live with us and not just visit. This paradox points to the interaction between higher education policies and other areas of public policy. We cannot proclaim academic mobility to be one of our priorities if we do not at the same time look at current obstacles to mobility. Governments must make it easier for students and scholars to obtain visas, work permits and social security for the European Higher Education Area to become a reality. The initiative taken by the European Commission to ease visa regulations for academic exchanges is an important step in the right direction.

It has been said that money is not everything except to those who have none. Higher education is certainly not in that unfortunate situation. Many higher education institutions are making very substantial efforts to implement the reforms of the Bologna Process within their current budgets, or as the euphemism would have it, "with zero growth". Yet, ambitious goals do require great financial resources. This is a triple challenge to governments: firstly, in finding the means to increase public funding for higher education and thus demonstrate its importance; secondly, in establishing frameworks that will encourage funding of higher education from other sources; thirdly, in resisting the temptation to use funding from other sources as an excuse to cut public funding. Public authorities set public priorities, and there is no more potent instrument to set public priorities than public budgets. Our responsibility to taxpayers cannot be reduced to turning SOS – save our souls – into SOM – save our money.

The public responsibility for higher education is – as ministers have underlined twice – a cornerstone of the European Higher Education Area. For this to be a reality, we must look at how this is exercised in modern societies. We must look at the public responsibility for laying down the framework within which all higher education, public and private, will be provided. We must look at the public responsibility for ensuring equal opportunity to higher education. We must look at the public responsibility for financing higher education as well as for actual provision. The Council of Europe has undertaken important work in this field and our Committee of Ministers adopted a recommendation on the public responsibility for higher education and research.[168] This is a significant recommendation, but the public responsibility for higher education must remain a key topic of the European Higher Education Area beyond 2010.

Higher education and research should play a key role in developing the kind of society we would like to leave to future generations – societies that are sustainable environmentally and politically, socially and ethically, economically and culturally. The European Higher Education Area must meet the test of workable structures, as it must meet the test of a workable and inspiring vision of the contribution of

---

168. Recommendation CM/Rec(2007)6 of the Committee of Ministers to member states on the public responsibility for higher education and research.

higher education to a society based on democracy, human rights and the rule of law and proficient in intercultural dialogue; a Europe coherent enough to be strong and diverse enough to be interesting; a Europe unafraid to engage with the broader world.

Ultimately, higher education must inspire and prepare us to do well, but also to do good.

Ministerial conference of the Bologna Process, Leuven/Louvain-la-Neuve, 2009

Leuven, 28 April 2009

In the classical French tragedy, the best of all fates was to be loved but it was far better to be hated than to be ignored. As we prepare to proclaim the European Higher Education Area in a year's time, I believe we can agree that – at least by the measures of Racine and Corneille – the Bologna Process has been a success. Many in the education community are enthusiastic about the reforms, some are dead set against them but few are indifferent. The Bologna Process has also received the most genuine form of praise – interest and emulation from other parts of the world.

The interest in the Bologna Process transcends the higher education community. The Council of Europe's Parliamentary Assembly will consider a report, prepared by Lord McIntosh, on the Council's contribution to the Bologna Process. Among other things, the report will raise the question of whether the current structures of the Bologna Process are sufficient to ensure its viability in the long run.

The Assembly report underscores the Council of Europe's long-standing support for and contribution to the Bologna Process. In 2007, ministers entrusted us with a particular responsibility for co-ordinating the sharing of experience in the development of national qualifications frameworks, and we are particularly pleased that we have been able, with the European Commission, to build very close co-operation between the "Bologna framework" and the European Qualifications Framework (EQF) for lifelong learning. In my view, one of the most important achievements since the London ministerial conference in 2007 is that we can now say with confidence: it is perfectly possible to develop a national framework compatible with both the EHEA framework and the EQF. I would like to pay tribute to my colleagues in the Commission who have made this co-operation possible.

The Council of Europe is also strongly engaged in the Bologna Follow-up Group; in working with the most recent Bologna members; as a contributor to the reflections on "Bologna beyond 2010" and the global dimension of the Bologna Process; and not least in the area of recognition. Here, it may be worth pointing out that the recent analysis of the national action plans submitted in 2007 makes it abundantly clear that much remains to be done to make the legal texts a reality. That is a challenge, not least in each individual "Bologna country".

* * *

In 10 years, students, staff, higher education institutions and public authorities have changed the face of European higher education. That is no small feat but it does not dispense us from the need not only to look back but also to look forward.

The Bologna Process has changed degree structures and instituted guidelines for quality assurance, and it is developing qualifications frameworks. It has changed structures and it has changed laws.

That is important. It is also the relatively easy part. What we face now, on the threshold of the European Higher Education Area, is the challenge of making structures come alive, of making legal regulation actual practice and of making things like learning outcomes a description of reality and not virtuous fiction. Great ideas can move mankind but great ideas can also be perverted and reduced to details of bureaucratic regulation. Reforms that start with enthusiasm can peter out in indifference unless a vision can be sustained above and beyond measures and regulations.

The first decade of the Bologna Process has rightly focused on structural reform. Like our medieval fortresses, however, structures only make sense if they fulfil a purpose. As our societies change, so must higher education. Qualifications frameworks make sense not because they are attractive theoretical structures but because they help learners find diverse pathways to the kind of competences our societies need.

I believe four elements are particularly important to how the European Higher Education Area will develop over the next decade.

Firstly, from our public debate, we could easily be led to believe that the competences we need are those that help the economy in the short term. That is not wrong – but it is also not exactly right.

We need that, but we need so much more. We need the competences that make our societies sustainable economically but also those that make societies sustainable politically, culturally, socially and environmentally. That society is unlikely to be devoid of material well-being, but it is equally unlikely to be devoid of engaged citizens and of people who care about each other, devoid of intellectual curiosity and the pleasure of discovery or devoid of the ability to conduct intercultural dialogue.

Our societies are increasingly complex, and they cannot function unless as citizens we have broad and advanced competences. We cannot fulfil our roles as citizens unless we are able to put our specialist knowledge into a broader context, unless we are able to think across the boundaries of disciplines as well as of countries, unless as citizens we are able to analyse complex phenomena, often on the basis of incomplete information, and unless we get our values right. Knowledge is crucial but we cannot be good citizens unless we complement knowledge by understanding and an ability to act. These are learning outcomes in the true sense of the word. We need specialists and we need intellectuals – people who can see the broader context, weigh short-term and long-term benefits and dangers and do not only what is technically feasible but also what is ethically defensible.

Secondly, our societies are increasingly complex also in terms of actors. Public authorities cannot act in the same way today as they did a generation ago and obtain the same results. If we believe there is a public responsibility for higher education, we must examine the role and responsibilities of public authorities. The Council of Europe made an important contribution through its 2007 recommendation on the public responsibility for higher education and research,[169] and we are about to examine the role of public authorities in ensuring university autonomy, in close co-operation with the Magna Charta Observatory. The role of public authorities is a key issue that must be high on the agenda of "Bologna beyond 2010".

Thirdly, the complexity of our societies also implies that our policies must address the full range of missions of higher education. We need first class research institutions, but we also need institutions that excel in teaching and learning, in community service and in applying knowledge and understanding. At individual level, we need excellent teachers as well as researchers and academics who work with their communities. Sometimes these institutions and persons are one and the same, but not always. Our policies and reward systems, at institutional as well as individual level, must encourage all the missions of higher education. In all of these, we need excellence.

Fourthly, membership of the Bologna Process is conditioned on a state being party to the European Cultural Convention as well as commitment to reforms, and it is difficult to see a workable alternative framework for the European Higher Education Area. We welcome the interest in the Bologna Process from other parts of the world and we fully support the organisation of Bologna policy fora both end-on with ministerial conferences as here in Leuven/Louvain-la-Neuve and separately on specific topics, such as the conference the Council of Europe co-organised in Kazakhstan in February 2009. The strong interest in the Bologna Process in other parts of the world must be met through concrete co-operation on substance: on structural reform as well as on issues like university autonomy and student participation and through practical measures like the appointment of "Bologna contacts" in interested countries.

* * *

As it heads towards its second decade, the European Higher Education Area will not only continue to live in interesting times. It will make the times in which we live interesting.

Since I started by referring to the literary heritage of the country that hosted the Sorbonne meeting in 1998, let me end by a quotation that originates on the shores of the Pacific. In his book *El sueño chileno*[170] – the Chilean dream – the sociologist Eugenio Tironi says: the answer to the question "what kind of education do we need?" lies in the answer to another question, "what kind of society do we want?"

That, ladies and gentlemen, summarises the challenge of the Bologna Process in the years to come. It is a challenge that will keep us busy, and it is also one to which we will rise only if we continue to work together as Europeans and as citizens of the world.

---

169. Recommendation CM/Rec(2007)6 of the Committee of Ministers to member states on the public responsibility for higher education and research.
170. Tironi, Eugenio (2005): *El sueño chileno: comunidad, familia y nación en el bicentenario* [The Chilean Dream: Community, Family and Nation at the Bicentennial], Santiago de Chile: Taurus.

Ministerial conference of the Bologna Process, Budapest and Vienna, 2010 – On qualifications frameworks[171]

Budapest, 11 March 2010

Reforming Europe's degree structure has undoubtedly been one of the major achievements of the Bologna Process. The European Higher Education Area will be characterised by a three tier degree structure. While this pattern has deep roots in European culture – think only of the three estates of bygone days – the three levels of higher education qualifications represent something of a revolution. In many countries the prevailing patterns had been one long, so called "university degree" followed by a doctorate, and in the minds of many students as well as academics, speed was not of the essence in obtaining either.

The European Higher Education Area is united around this three tier structure and committed to developing it into national qualifications frameworks focusing on learning outcomes and on how learners can move within and between education systems. Many paths may lead to one and the same qualification, and there may be several qualifications at the same level. The link between quality and qualifications is crucial: if you cannot ascertain that a given qualification is "good enough", the discussion stops then and there.

The difficult part is putting the concept to practice. Qualifications frameworks will help learners only if we make structures a reality, only if we self-certify what really deserves to be self-certified as compatible with the overarching "Bologna framework" and only if we manage to make the focus on learning outcomes a living reality and not a mere policy statement or formal description divorced from the daily lives of students and teachers. That challenge includes finding a proper place for short cycle qualifications. The co-operation with the European Qualifications Framework for lifelong learning and hence with the European Commission must continue.

I am optimistic that Europe will succeed, but to succeed we must recognise the difficulty of the challenge. We must recognise that none of us has succeeded perfectly, we must be relatively open about where we need further improvement and we must be willing to learn from each other. As the Bologna Process turns into the European Higher Education Area, this spirit of constructive humility and co-operation that has characterised it must continue.

---

171. At the ministerial conference in Budapest and Vienna, the consultative members were invited to speak on a specific topic; in the case of the Council of Europe on qualifications frameworks and on the recognition of qualifications. Both speeches are reproduced in the present volume.

We must also dare address an issue that we have not been eager to attack. Qualifications do not exist in a vacuum. They build on our academic heritage and they must meet the needs of society. One of our main challenges in Europe is that we define the needs of society far too narrowly. Economic development is important, but so are personal development and the development of the kind of societies in which we want to live. Whether we talk about subject-specific or generic competences, we cannot afford to limit these to what is immediately useful. A few years ago, the Bologna Follow-up Group had a chance to admire a correspondence course in the Morse Code, complete with cassettes for independent practice. That course was certainly immediately useful at the time but the mastery of dots and strokes had limited lasting value, which is why the course is now in the Technical Museum in Berlin.

Qualifications frameworks, then, have an important formal and structural aspect and I believe we are reasonably close to meeting our goals, even if a few problems remain. National plans for the development of national frameworks now seem more realistic that they did a year ago.

Secondly, qualifications frameworks must exist not only as structures but as living practice. This is a steeper challenge since it involves changing attitudes and habits. This will take longer but we will succeed if we recognise both the difficulty of the challenge and the importance of succeeding.

Thirdly, qualifications frameworks are an instrument not only to further a knowledge economy, however important that is, but to develop a society based on knowledge, understanding and the ability to act; one based on democratic culture, European values and the ability to dialogue with those who come from different backgrounds; one built through joint efforts by students, staff, higher education institutions, social partners and political decision makers. Here, in particular, we would be wise to echo the words of Robert Frost: "we have promises to keep and miles to go before we sleep".

Ministerial conference of the Bologna Process, Budapest and Vienna, 2010 – On recognition

Budapest, 11 March 2010

Later today, we will board a train that will take us from Budapest to Vienna in about the time it will take to enjoy a good central European dinner. We will enjoy the dinner but we will not be nostalgic for the time when elaborate border controls and identity checks made the journey long and cumbersome.

Would our qualifications be able to travel as easily and speedily as we will do tonight? This, to me, is one of the essential questions for the European Higher Education Area. Are we able to carry our intellectual luggage across borders and put all of our qualifications to good use in our new country – or do mobile learners still run into procedures and practices unencumbered by developments in European co-operation over the past two decades?

The basic rules and regulations to make life easier for mobile learners are in place. The Council of Europe/UNESCO Recognition Convention has now been ratified by all Bologna countries except two, and the country that joined us today, Kazakhstan,[172] was among the early signatories. The ECTS is widely used; the Diploma Supplement a little less so but it is still issued in a majority of the Bologna countries.

Practice, however, is less promising. A key principle of the Council of Europe/UNESCO Recognition Convention is that foreign qualifications should be recognised unless you can demonstrate that there is a substantial difference between the qualification for which recognition is sought and the corresponding qualification of the home country. To say that this requires more attention is an understatement. Too often, even minor differences are considered to be a reason for non-recognition and too often recognition practice is not put into the broader context of promoting co-operation and mobility.

Fair recognition requires good policies. The independent assessment of the Bologna Process[173] is silent about the national action plans submitted by ministers in 2007, but these plans give reason for concern because many are reports on an unsatisfactory state of affairs rather than road maps to better practice in the future.[174] If national policies are too intent on "protecting" their own qualifications system and too little

---

172. Kazakhstan joined the European Higher Education Area on 11 March 2010.
173. Available at: www.ond.vlaanderen.be/hogeronderwijs/bologna/2010_conference/documents/ IndependentAssessment_1_DetailedRept.pdf, accessed on 7 July 2010.
174. See Rauhvargers, Andrejs and Rusakova, Agnese (2009): *Improving Recognition in the European Higher Education Area: An Analysis of National Action Plans*, Strasbourg: Council of Europe Publishing. Council of Europe Higher Education Series No. 12.

aware of their role in helping learners, fair recognition will not follow. If national policies seek to compare procedures and structures rather than assess students' real knowledge, understanding and ability to act expressed through learning outcomes, fair recognition will not follow. If national policies do not seize upon qualifications frameworks as instruments that make qualifications easier to understand, fair recognition will not follow. And if fair recognition does not follow, the fact that 45 of the now 47 Bologna countries have ratified the only legal text of the European Higher Education Area will not ensure mobility.

Fair recognition alone is of course not enough to ensure mobility. Scholarships, improved visa regulations, work permits and other elements that cannot be detailed in three minutes are also required. But unless all Bologna countries improve their efforts to put the European legal framework for recognition into practice nationally, the European Higher Education Area will not reach its goal of 20% mobile students by 2020. The Council of Europe, UNESCO and the European Commission will continue our work to improve recognition but it is worth underlining that the subsidiary principle is as important to ensuring good practice as it is to making good decisions.

To make the European Higher Education Area an area of academic mobility for students and staff, we must develop institutional and national recognition practices that catch up with the international legal regulations, we must look more for reasons that make it possible to recognise foreign qualifications and less for those that may give us a reason to refuse recognition, and we must approach foreign qualifications with the same openness of mind with which we would like our own qualifications to be considered abroad. To meet our mobility goals, we must take not the nostalgia train but the train to the future; the train that crosses borders with a maximum of speed; the one that uses the legal framework to make recognition possible rather than to prevent it from happening – the train that aims at making the European Higher Education Area a living reality that makes a difference in the lives of students and teachers.

The 70th Anniversary of International Students' Day, Brussels, 2009

Brussels, 17 November 2009 at a conference co-organised by the European Students' Union (ESU) and the Organising Bureau of European School Student Unions (OBESSU)

It is a great honour for the Council of Europe to be associated with the celebration of the 70th anniversary of the International Students' Day. We gather here in the same year that the Council of Europe celebrates its 60th anniversary and in the same month that we celebrate the 20th anniversary of the fall of the Berlin Wall.

Some would see irony in the fact that of these three events, which are all significant in their own way, it is the International Students' Day that is the oldest. Let this coincidence be a starting point for two reflections.

Firstly, maybe the image of the "eternal student" is not so bad after all. Students are learners – as the T-shirts of one of the participants says: "experts in going to school" – as well as social actors. In our policies, we emphasise lifelong learning. Even if it is true that many higher education institutions have been slow to see their responsibility as centres of lifelong learning, and even if it is true that the public image of students as 20-25 year olds has been slow to adapt to the reality of a much more diversified student population, would we actually want to stop learning – would we want to stop being students?

To continue being students helps keep our minds young even as our bodies show the signs of years passing by. The quest for eternal youth is as old as humankind, and now we have found the "cure": always be a student at heart and in mind. There are many definitions of lifelong learning but I prefer my own: lifelong learning is the kind of learning that, by definition, nobody can speak about from the point of view of a fully accomplished learner.

Nevertheless, the second reflection is perhaps the more important one. The fact that 17 November has been celebrated as the International Students' Day for 70 years shows the continuous importance of students to our societies, not only because of the potential they represent for the future but also for the roles they play today, as members of the academic community and as citizens.

On three occasions, 17 November has taken on a very special significance: in 1939 in the fight against Nazism, in 1973 in the fight against a right-wing military regime and in 1989 in the fight against communism. On these three occasions, the date we are celebrating today became a very concrete symbol of the role of students in fighting dictatorship and promoting democracy. On many other occasions also, students have stood up for democracy. Sometimes students have undertaken spectacular actions that are easy to locate in time and space, such as Jan Palach setting himself on fire in Prague, students standing up against tanks in Tiananmen Square or standing trial for fighting against inhumane regimes like the members of the White Rose. Often, students working for democracy in difficult conditions have done so away from the limelight and with a perseverance that makes it impossible to link them to a specific date. We are celebrating today, on 17 November, but students work for democracy every day of the year.

Our academic values are intimately linked with the ideals of democracy: the search for truth, freedom of expression and critical thinking. However, we should not let ideals make us blind to reality. Students have often stood on the side of democracy and justice – but not always. For every academic hero, it is not too difficult to think of an academic villain. Students were involved in the attacks of 11 September. The Sendero Luminoso was created by a philosophy professor and many of its members were students. Courts dispensing injustice in political trials under regimes of all political colours are run by judges who, for the most part, have solid academic credentials – in other words, by former students who either learned nothing about ethics or otherwise conveniently forgot what they learned. Students were a vital part of the Civil Rights Movement in the United States but they were also among those who sought to keep universities in the Deep South all-white.

Our academic values are essential to keeping democracy alive. We were reminded of this in the past decade or two. When the Berlin Wall fell, many were naive in their belief that democracy would come overnight, that once we had elections and democratic institutions, we would have democracy. Our education system probably did its share: how many civics courses and textbooks have not been long on institutions and procedures and short on values and content?

Democratic institutions are essential but not sufficient. They cannot work unless they are built on democratic culture. For democracy to be real, citizens must be convinced that they have a stake in the well-being of their societies and that their contribution to democracy should be more than a vote every two or four years. Citizens must commit to the idea that public space is our common good and that it is more than the sum of our individual private spaces. Democracy means, among other things, that decisions are made by deliberation and that conflicts are solved by peaceful means.

Democracy is not like riding a bike or skiing: once you have learned it you know how to do it even if you practise it only sporadically. Rather, democracy is like a language: if you do not practise it regularly, you forget how to use it and eventually you may no longer understand it. Democratic culture must be reconstructed in each successive generation and it must be kept alive in each of them.

Facing stark examples of injustice requires a strong dose of courage, and the difficulty of mustering courage should not be underestimated by those of us who have never had to face extremes. There are people in the student movement, such as Tatsiana Khoma who was expelled from her university in Belarus because of her activities in ESU and who is present here today, who could tell us more about courage than most of us would ever be able to understand. But in these stark situations, the alternatives are also clear. In the everyday life of societies, heroic courage is less of a requirement but the alternatives and the importance of each individual's participation are less clear cut. In our busy daily lives, it is easy to believe that democratic participation can safely be left to others. However, what everyone leaves for others to do will never get done.

There are societies in which students working for democracy need exemplary courage. In many societies, however, one of the main challenges of the student movement is to overcome political and societal apathy.

We live in societies in which contacts with people from other backgrounds and cultures are a reality and not an option. I firmly believe our societies are much the richer for it, but many of our citizens take the opposite view: foreigners represent a problem because they are different. Students and other academics have an important role in developing society's attitudes to foreigners at a time when many political parties play on people's fears of what is different, and they should do so on the basis of academic values. To be sure, some foreigners represent problems, as do some people that are native born. It is a fundamental tenet of academic work not to jump to general conclusions on the basis of individual examples without seriously assessing whether individual examples are just that or whether they are representative. Surely, it is not difficult to find examples of foreigners who play very important roles in their adopted societies.

The Council of Europe is an organisation dedicated to intercultural dialogue, as shown through the adoption of a White Paper called "Living Together as Equals in Dignity" in 2008. Intercultural dialogue is developed through education, and students and other academics should be an important part of the movement.

Some would prefer to talk about clients rather than students, since clients who pay for a service presumably have stronger rights to complain about a service paid for and not quite delivered.

Firstly, it is difficult to accept that clients have stronger rights to express criticism than members of a community.

Secondly, however, what seems like an innocent semantic shift betrays fundamentally different realities. Clients are interested only in the end product that they buy, and one could argue of course that this is entirely consistent with an "outcomes orientation" or "results based budgeting". Clients have no interest in the internal workings of providers. If a provider delivers what clients want at a reasonable price, they will stay. If not, they will move elsewhere. If students are clients, why should they care about our higher education systems and institutions?

If students are students, however, things are very different. If students are students, they are members of the academic community, and members of a community have an inherent stake in the well-being of their community. This does not mean they will always be happy with their community – blind patriotism is as dangerous within the academic community as it is in other communities. But it does mean that when students see things that need to be improved they will work to improve them and not simply walk away. Clients move on easily, but members of a community stay to build their community and emigrate only when there seems to be little hope of repair and much reason to despair.

Do we want our higher education institutions to be populated by clients who shop around or by students who care enough about our higher education to help improve it? Which of the two are the better guarantee for the quality that all governments and all serious institutions want to assure and improve?

The ESU and OBESSU face a formidable challenge in making students better aware of the stakes of their citizenship in the academic community, but the ESU and OBESSU are also excellent examples of why students should engage in the public space.

The Bologna Process has greatly benefited from the contribution of excellent student representatives who have certainly stood up for student rights but who have not seen their mission only as engaging on a limited range of issues. ESU is influential within the Bologna Process precisely because student representatives engage on all education issues – because it considers higher education policy making as a coherent whole and not as a turf to be defended. The ESU believes that defending student interests implies thinking about all aspects of education, and its work in the Bologna Process proves it is right. Even those who may not agree with the ESU position on a specific issue know that the ESU arrives at its positions on the basis of due consideration and that the student voice must be taken seriously by those who agree as well as by those who disagree.

The ESU shows the meaning of citizenship also by thinking about the broader purposes of higher education. The Bologna Process has achieved important structural reforms but we have been less good at outlining the purposes that the reformed structures should serve. As shown by our medieval fortresses, a structure that loses its purpose will either need to find new purposes or face withering decay.

Looking at European debate today, one can easily believe that education has one purpose only: preparation for employment. That is an important purpose, and we do not need to look far to understand that. The Council of Europe argument is not that preparation for the labour market is not an important purpose of higher education, but rather that it is not the only important purpose of higher education. In making this argument, the ESU is one of our most valuable partners and supports.

The ESU joins the Council of Europe in arguing that higher education is about preparation for the labour market but equally for democratic citizenship, for personal development and for the development and maintenance of a broad, advanced knowledge base. The ESU joins the Council of Europe in arguing that these are not conflicting purposes, that we need not choose between them but that we must do all of this at the same time. An education that prepares for citizenship also furthers personal development, and it provides competences that are highly relevant for employment.

The ESU joins the Council of Europe in arguing that providing the higher education that enables us to develop the kind of societies in which we would like our children and grandchildren to live is a public responsibility, and the ESU joins us in underlining the need to think deeply about what this public responsibility implies in a complex society with many actors.

We agree that public responsibility extends to ensuring equal opportunities to quality higher education – to access, for sure, but also equal opportunities to complete one's education. The social dimension of the Bologna Process is less easy to measure than structural reform, and the Bologna Process needs the ESU to remind us that this does not make it less important. All that can be measured is not important, and all that is important cannot be measured.

Celebrating International Students' Day is important. It is also relatively easy. Once the sounds and lights of celebration have dimmed down to the clamour of everyday life, the ESU will continue not only to fight for the rights of students but to make a student contribution to the development of European higher education. The ESU will continue to remind us that professionalism is less a question of being well paid than of being well educated, well prepared and well articulated. In educational terms, the ESU will continue to remind us that subject-specific as well as generic competences are essential in developing higher education policies, and the ESU will help us navigate between the Scylla of *Fachidioten* and the Charybdis of management consultants.

Europe – in the true sense of the term, encompassing all countries of our continent – has achieved a lot in higher education over the past decade. The European Higher Education Area is not an area of perfection but it is an area of success – so much so in fact that it is being looked at with great interest from most other parts of the world. It is not always easy to identify what is specifically European about reforms that have incorporated many elements from other parts of the world – qualifications frameworks come to mind – and that are now being imitated and adapted elsewhere.

There is, however, at least one aspect that is very distinctly European, and that is the way in which student representatives participate in shaping higher education policy. The role that the ESU plays in the Bologna Process is unlike that played by any other student organisation elsewhere. This kind of student involvement in policy-making access is a truly European dimension of the Bologna Process – and it is a dimension I strongly hope will not forever remain European alone.

International Students' Day celebrates its 70th anniversary, but students are of course both much older than that as a group and at the same time a force of youth and innovation. May the International Students' Day remind us of the importance of being young in mind and never to stop learning and thinking.

And may the ESU and OBESSU continue to bring fresh breaths of innovation and constructive criticism into European higher education policy. May the ESU and OBESSU continue to challenge us on our social conscience, including toward other areas of the world. May the ESU and OBESSU continue to challenge us to see the full range of purposes of higher education and what these mean for the reform of our structures.

Not least, may the ESU and OBESSU continue to represent students as active citizens and as members of the academic community. May they always be the student unions – and may they never become European associations of education consumers.

Sales agents for publications of the Council of Europe
Agents de vente des publications du Conseil de l'Europe

BELGIUM/BELGIQUE
La Librairie Européenne -
The European Bookshop
Rue de l'Orme, 1
BE-1040 BRUXELLES
Tel.: +32 (0)2 231 04 35
Fax: +32 (0)2 735 08 60
E-mail: order@libeurop.be
http://www.libeurop.be

Jean De Lannoy/DL Services
Avenue du Roi 202 Koningslaan
BE-1190 BRUXELLES
Tel.: +32 (0)2 538 43 08
Fax: +32 (0)2 538 08 41
E-mail: jean.de.lannoy@dl-servi.com
http://www.jean-de-lannoy.be

BOSNIA AND HERZEGOVINA/
BOSNIE-HERZÉGOVINE
Robert's Plus d.o.o.
Marka Maruliça 2/V
BA-71000, SARAJEVO
Tel.: + 387 33 640 818
Fax: + 387 33 640 818
E-mail: robertsplus@bih.net.ba

CANADA
Renouf Publishing Co. Ltd.
1-5369 Canotek Road
CA-OTTAWA, Ontario K1J 9J3
Tel.: +1 613 745 2665
Fax: +1 613 745 7660
Toll-Free Tel.: (866) 767-6766
E-mail: order.dept@renoufbooks.com
http://www.renoufbooks.com

CROATIA/CROATIE
Robert's Plus d.o.o.
Marasoviçeva 67
HR-21000, SPLIT
Tel.: + 385 21 315 800, 801, 802, 803
Fax: + 385 21 315 804
E-mail: robertsplus@robertsplus.hr

CZECH REPUBLIC/
RÉPUBLIQUE TCHÈQUE
Suweco CZ, s.r.o.
Klecakova 347
CZ-180 21 PRAHA 9
Tel.: +420 2 424 59 204
Fax: +420 2 848 21 646
E-mail: import@suweco.cz
http://www.suweco.cz

DENMARK/DANEMARK
GAD
Vimmelskaftet 32
DK-1161 KØBENHAVN K
Tel.: +45 77 66 60 00
Fax: +45 77 66 60 01
E-mail: gad@gad.dk
http://www.gad.dk

FINLAND/FINLANDE
Akateeminen Kirjakauppa
PO Box 128
Keskuskatu 1
FI-00100 HELSINKI
Tel.: +358 (0)9 121 4430
Fax: +358 (0)9 121 4242
E-mail: akatilaus@akateeminen.com
http://www.akateeminen.com

FRANCE
La Documentation française
(diffusion/distribution France entière)
124, rue Henri Barbusse
FR-93308 AUBERVILLIERS CEDEX
Tél.: +33 (0)1 40 15 70 00
Fax: +33 (0)1 40 15 68 00
E-mail: commande@ladocumentationfrancaise.fr
http://www.ladocumentationfrancaise.fr

Librairie Kléber
1 rue des Francs Bourgeois
FR-67000 STRASBOURG
Tel.: +33 (0)3 88 15 78 88
Fax: +33 (0)3 88 15 78 80
E-mail: librairie-kleber@coe.int
http://www.librairie-kleber.com

GERMANY/ALLEMAGNE
AUSTRIA/AUTRICHE
UNO Verlag GmbH
August-Bebel-Allee 6
DE-53175 BONN
Tel.: +49 (0)228 94 90 20
Fax: +49 (0)228 94 90 222
E-mail: bestellung@uno-verlag.de
http://www.uno-verlag.de

GREECE/GRÈCE
Librairie Kauffmann s.a.
Stadiou 28
GR-105 64 ATHINAI
Tel.: +30 210 32 55 321
Fax.: +30 210 32 30 320
E-mail: ord@otenet.gr
http://www.kauffmann.gr

HUNGARY/HONGRIE
Euro Info Service
Pannónia u. 58.
PF. 1039
HU-1136 BUDAPEST
Tel.: +36 1 329 2170
Fax: +36 1 349 2053
E-mail: euroinfo@euroinfo.hu
http://www.euroinfo.hu

ITALY/ITALIE
Licosa SpA
Via Duca di Calabria, 1/1
IT-50125 FIRENZE
Tel.: +39 0556 483215
Fax: +39 0556 41257
E-mail: licosa@licosa.com
http://www.licosa.com

MEXICO/MEXIQUE
Mundi-Prensa México, S.A. De C.V.
Río Pánuco, 141 Delegacíon Cuauhtémoc
MX-06500 MÉXICO, D.F.
Tel.: +52 (01)55 55 33 56 58
Fax: +52 (01)55 55 14 67 99
E-mail: mundiprensa@mundiprensa.com.mx
http://www.mundiprensa.com.mx

NETHERLANDS/PAYS-BAS
Roodveldt Import BV
Nieuwe Hemweg 50
NE-1013 CX AMSTERDAM
Tel.: + 31 20 622 8035
Fax.: + 31 20 625 5493
Website: www.publidis.org
Email: orders@publidis.org

NORWAY/NORVÈGE
Akademika
Postboks 84 Blindern
NO-0314 OSLO
Tel.: +47 2 218 8100
Fax: +47 2 218 8103
E-mail: support@akademika.no
http://www.akademika.no

POLAND/POLOGNE
Ars Polona JSC
25 Obroncow Street
PL-03-933 WARSZAWA
Tel.: +48 (0)22 509 86 00
Fax: +48 (0)22 509 86 10
E-mail: arspolona@arspolona.com.pl
http://www.arspolona.com.pl

PORTUGAL
Livraria Portugal
(Dias & Andrade, Lda.)
Rua do Carmo, 70
PT-1200-094 LISBOA
Tel.: +351 21 347 42 82 / 85
Fax: +351 21 347 02 64
E-mail: info@livrariaportugal.pt
http://www.livrariaportugal.pt

RUSSIAN FEDERATION/
FÉDÉRATION DE RUSSIE
Ves Mir
17b, Butlerova ul.
RU-101000 MOSCOW
Tel.: +7 495 739 0971
Fax: +7 495 739 0971
E-mail: orders@vesmirbooks.ru
http://www.vesmirbooks.ru

SPAIN/ESPAGNE
Mundi-Prensa Libros, s.a.
Castelló, 37
ES-28001 MADRID
Tel.: +34 914 36 37 00
Fax: +34 915 75 39 98
E-mail: libreria@mundiprensa.es
http://www.mundiprensa.com

SWITZERLAND/SUISSE
Planetis Sàrl
16 chemin des pins
CH-1273 ARZIER
Tel.: +41 22 366 51 77
Fax: +41 22 366 51 78
E-mail: info@planetis.ch

UNITED KINGDOM/ROYAUME-UNI
The Stationery Office Ltd
PO Box 29
GB-NORWICH NR3 1GN
Tel.: +44 (0)870 600 5522
Fax: +44 (0)870 600 5533
E-mail: book.enquiries@tso.co.uk
http://www.tsoshop.co.uk

UNITED STATES and CANADA/
ÉTATS-UNIS et CANADA
Manhattan Publishing Company
468 Albany Post Road
US-CROTON-ON-HUDSON, NY 10520
Tel.: +1 914 271 5194
Fax: +1 914 271 5856
E-mail: Info@manhattanpublishing.com
http://www.manhattanpublishing.com

Council of Europe Publishing/Editions du Conseil de l'Europe
FR-67075 STRASBOURG Cedex
Tel.: +33 (0)3 88 41 25 81 – Fax: +33 (0)3 88 41 39 10 – E-mail: publishing@coe.int – Website: http://book.coe.int